Fontana Introduction to Modern Economics
General Editor: C. D. Harbury

Economics of the Market

Gordon Hewitt

formerly Lecturer in Economics
at the Civil Service College

Economics of
the Market

Fontana/Collins

First published in Fontana 1976
Second Impression October 1978
Third Impression September 1980
Copyright © Gordon Hewitt 1976

Made and printed in Great Britain by
William Collins Sons & Co. Ltd, Glasgow

Contents

Preface

Most subjects are divided into major branches, and economics is no exception. Readers studying for 'A' level, or first year university examinations and professional courses, find their time divided between one or other of the two main areas, known as microeconomics and macroeconomics.

This book is intended as a companion for the microeconomics section of these courses, and is concerned with an analysis of the component parts of the economic system – individuals, firms, even complete industries, and with problems of resource allocation. By contrast, macroeconomics analyses the operation of the economic system as a whole.

An outline of the subject matter of both microeconomics and macroeconomics can be found in the introductory volume to the series, *An Introduction to Economic Behaviour*, by C. D. Harbury, while in the volume, *Income, Spending and the Price Level*, A. G. Ford develops the principles of macroeconomics in more detail. Examples of how the theory presented in this book can be applied to the world of finance are found in G. H. Peters, *Private and Public Finance*.

I am grateful to the Department of Political Economy at Glasgow University for the opportunity of lecturing on microeconomics to a wide range of students, and to the Civil Service College for encouraging me to write this book. Many stimulating discussions about the problems of presenting microeconomic concepts to students were held with J. N. Robinson of the University of Reading, D. R. Croome of the Polytechnic of Central London, K. G. D. Smith of the University of Glasgow, and W. Vause, formerly of the Civil Service College. I am deeply indebted to Professor C. D. Harbury of the City University, without whose help none of this would have been possible.

Chapter 1

Introduction

The subject of microeconomics is basically about choice – the making of decisions between alternatives. The purpose of this opening chapter is to illustrate the types of choice which economics seeks to explain.

Human Wants are Unlimited

People have certain needs and desires. They need somewhere to live, some food to stay alive, some clothes to wear. In addition to these basic necessities, people have a desire for a whole range of goods and services – cars, washing machines, soap powders, television sets, insurance, banks, books, carpets, furniture, heat, golf clubs – the list is virtually endless.

To state that human wants are unlimited is really to state the obvious. After all, every reader of this book will almost certainly desire a greater quantity or higher quality of goods and services than he or she already has. Why, then, can't everybody, particularly in today's so-called 'Affluent Society', have more goods and services or better goods and services than at present?

Resources are Limited

The answer is that those elements which are necessary to produce this unlimited range of goods and services are limited in supply. These 'elements' are known as factors of production or resources. Indeed we can think of economic activity as a process by which society's resources are combined to produce a range of goods and services which people desire. However, because at one end of the process there are unlimited wants, and at the other end limited resources, people plainly cannot have everything they desire.

The term 'resources' usually includes the following major categories of input which are used in the activity of producing goods and services:

(*i*) **Labour** This category refers to the contribution made by human beings to the production process. The contribution may be mainly physical effort, as for example in the case of workers whose job involves much manual work; or, in the case of top executives in business, the effort may be mainly mental, as in thinking out ways of producing goods, or devising new methods of selling goods and so on.

In measurable terms, an economy's labour resources can be defined as the total number of people in the population who are willing to work and seeking to be employed. The size of an economy's available labour force is obviously limited by the size of its population. However, it also depends on the age distribution of its population – the number of people in the economy, for example, who are below the school leaving age and past retirement age.

In 1971 the total population in the United Kingdom was just over 53 million. About 21 million, however, fell into the age categories of below 16 and over 65, so the total potential labour force was reduced to 32 millions. In addition, 9 million women could be classified as full-time housewives, so that the number of people actually willing to work was about 23 million. In 1971, however, the average level of unemployment was about 700,000, so the United Kingdom's total employed labour resources amounted to roughly 22,300,000.

(*ii*) **Capital** This resource is made up of all those physical goods which are produced for the purpose of helping to provide a range of goods and services. Capital resources, therefore, are not items which directly satisfy human wants. Rather they are part of the means by which goods and services in an economy can ultimately be produced.

Capital, as a factor of production, is a physical phenomenon. It includes physical items which may be combined with labour and other resources in the production process. Factories and buildings in which production takes place are examples of capital. So, too, is machinery used in all types of production – tractors, machine tools, combustion engines, textile machines, mining equipment, turbines used for generating electricity, computers, and so on.

Also included in an economy's capital resources are physical items which contribute specifically to the provision of services, rather than the production of goods. Examples of this are railway rolling stock, ships, aircraft and buses. Similarly educational buildings – such as universities, schools and polytechnics – hospitals, houses and roads are also classified as capital, since they contribute to the provision of services which people want.

In 1971, the total stock of capital resources in the United Kingdom was valued at about £140,000 million, of which plant and machinery accounted for approximately thirty-one per cent. Of course, *additions* to the stock of capital are being made every year. In other words, some resources in the economy are being used to produce items such as machine tools and computers, rather than goods and services which flow directly into the hands of the economy's citizens. For example, an extra £7,000 million of capital equipment was produced in the United Kingdom in 1971 but only fifty per cent of this really added to the economy's capacity to produce *extra* goods and services. The other fifty per cent was produced to replace existing capital which had worn out.

The act of building a factory or a school or the making of a piece of machinery is referred to as 'investment'. In the language of economics, investment is the act of creating capital. For example, if a firm decided to set up a new factory in the Midlands and install several machines to help manufacture a range of soap powders, then the value of the factory and the machines would be defined as investment. The firm would have created capital to produce a commodity which would contribute to the satisfaction of people's wants.

(*iii*) **Natural Resources** This factor is often referred to simply as 'land' thereby highlighting the most obvious natural resource which any country possesses. In the widest sense, natural resources are really the physical attributes, e.g. fertile land, water, minerals etc., as well as all other natural attributes which a country enjoys, including climate.

Of course, many natural resources may need the application of labour and capital before they can be used to produce goods and services. For example, coal has been an endowment of nature for thousands of years, but only with the application of mining equipment and human effort has it become a source of energy. In addition, some endowments of nature can lie undetected. For example, the discoveries of gas and oil under the North Sea transformed previously unknown natural features into economic resources.

Although this classification of factors of production into labour, capital and natural resources is very general, it is useful for focusing attention on what are essentially the **inputs** to the process of producing goods and services. By categorising resources in this way, it is possible to spotlight and comprehend the fundamental problem with which economics is concerned. Basically there is a confrontation between unlimited human wants on the one hand, and limited resources (in the sense of a limited amount of labour, capital and natural resources) on the other. The outcome of this confrontation is that it is not possible to satisfy all human wants in our economy at the same time.[1] There are simply not enough resources to produce all those goods and services which people desire.

Choices and Alternatives

Since resources in our economy are limited in supply, while human wants are unlimited, clearly there must be *alternative* ways of employing the resources available. For example, we could use a piece of land for building a school. The site, however, might also be used to erect a factory which would produce a range of electrical equipment. In other words, the site has alternative uses. If it was decided to use the land for the school, then the decision would preclude the possibility of creating a factory in that specific location. We can say, therefore, that building a school would involve the *sacrifice* of a factory.

Similarly, a stretch of agricultural countryside could be used as farming land to grow food. However, it might also be a suitable area on which to build an airport. Again we have an example of alternative uses for a limited resource. A decision to use the land for an airport would involve a sacrifice of the food which might have been produced if the land had been used in an alternative way.

The notion that resources are limited, have alternative uses and therefore involve a sacrifice when they are used in some particular way is a feature common to all the factors of production outlined previously. Let us imagine, for example, that the government of the day so manages the economic system that all available labour resources in the economy are fully employed at a certain point in time.[2] A decision to employ an extra 1,000 men in the motor car industry in Britain means that alternative forms of employment for these men have been sacrificed. By assisting in the business of

---

[1] Indeed this is true of *any* economic system where there are limited resources.
[2] In fact achieving 'full employment' of labour has been a major concern of governments for some time (*see* A. G. Ford, *Income, Spending and the Price Level*, in this series).

manufacturing cars, they are thereby precluded from helping to manufacture chemicals or some other products.

Sewing machines in the clothing industry could be used to make men's clothes or women's clothes; in a food processing factory, a canning machine could be used to can strawberries or peas – but not both at the same time. Printing presses can be used by publishers to print books of paperback quality, or very expensive glossy productions. Capital equipment, therefore, is also a resource capable of alternative uses.

Opportunity Cost

There is one common theme underlying all the examples in the previous section. Whenever limited resources with alternative uses are employed in a particular way, some 'sacrifice' is involved. The 'sacrifice' can be thought of as a *'cost'* and is defined in economics as an **opportunity cost,** which is a measurement of the value of the resource in an alternative use. This concept is central to microeconomics and is worth illustrating in a little more detail so that the reader will confidently understand its meaning and implications.

Consider a hypothetical (and obviously very unrealistic) economy, where only two types of goods are produced – cigarettes and books. All this economy's resources – its land, materials, labour force and capital equipment – will be occupied in the manufacture of these commodities. One very convenient method of representing the relevant alternatives is by means of a graph depicting a production possibility curve, as illustrated in Diagram 1.1.

This curve represents the various combinations of cigarettes and books which the economy is capable of producing in a certain time period (say monthly) when all resources are being used as efficiently as possible. In other words, one assumes that there is no unemployment; also, since resources are used in the most technically efficient way, the curve shows the *maximum* combinations of cigarettes and books that could be made.

Quantities of cigarettes are measured on the vertical axis, and quantities of books on the horizontal axis. If the economy's resources were used purely to produce cigarettes, then 5,000 (shown by the point T) could be produced. Alternatively, if the whole labour force, all capital equipment, materials and land were used to make books, then the economy could produce 4,000 books (as shown by the point H).

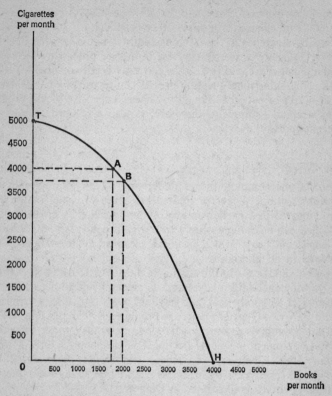

Figure 1.1 Production possibility curve

The curve TH is the production possibility curve for this economy, because it shows the maximum combinations of the two goods which are capable of being produced. Assume that resources are allocated between the two industries so that the pattern of economic activity can be represented by the point A. At this point, the economy is producing 4,000 cigarettes and 1,750 books. Now consider what would happen if an extra 250 books were produced. In terms of the graph this would imply a move down the production possibility curve from point A to point B.

Since the economy has limited resources, and they are already fully and efficiently employed in the production of cigarettes or books, there will have to be a shift of resources from the cigarette industry to the books industry to enable these extra 250 books to be made. It can be seen from the production possibility curve what the effect would be on cigarette production. At point B, only 3,750 cigarettes would be produced, compared with 4,000 at point A. In other words, producing an extra 250 books has forced this economy to sacrifice 250 cigarettes.

The **opportunity cost,** therefore, of these additional 250 books is 250 cigarettes because that is the output lost by not using these resources in an alternative way. Point A and point B thus illustrate two possible combinations of these goods which can be produced when the economy's resources are allocated in different ways.[3]

Consider now two further situations. First, suppose the economy is at point Y in Diagram 1.2, where 2,000 books and 2,000 cigarettes are being produced. Since Y lies inside the boundary of the curve, this means *either* that some resources are not being used efficiently *or* that some resources are not being employed at all.

It is possible, for example, to increase the economy's production of books by an extra 1,200 (to the point P). Such a move, however, would not mean a drop in cigarette output because, at point P, 2,000 cigarettes are still capable of being produced.

The extra books have not involved any sacrifice of cigarettes because no resources have needed to be transferred. It is possible for this economy to acquire the extra books either by using existing resources in the book industry more efficiently, or bringing formerly unemployed resources back into use. The important implication, then, is that there is no opportunity cost in moving from U to P – nothing has been foregone.

After the winter of 1971 when over one million people in Britain were unemployed, production of goods and services in many industries began to expand. In some cases, this expansion was brought about by bringing unemployed people back into the labour force, rather than by a shift of efficiently employed resources from one industry to another. In other words, when some resources in the economy were unemployed, getting more of one good did not automatically mean having to do with less of some other good. In such cases, no opportunity cost was involved.

Secondly, a point such as X in Diagram 1.2, which denotes a

[3] For a fuller discussion of production possibility curves, *see* C. D. Harbury, *An Introduction to Economic Behaviour*, Ch. 3, in this series.

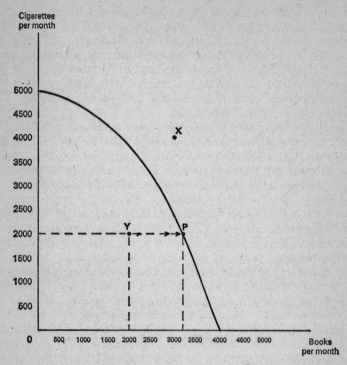

Figure 1.2 A move from Y to P involves no opportunity cost; but X is unattainable

combination of 4,000 cigarettes and 3,000 books, is clearly unattainable given the economy's existing amount of resources and the state of technical knowledge. If, of course, the economy acquired more resources, then the production possibility curve would move outwards to the right so that the point X might, in due course, be attained.

Opportunity Cost and Economic Analysis

Although we have illustrated the notion of opportunity cost in a very unrealistic economy where only two goods are produced, the reader should not get the impression that the concept's usefulness is limited to such unreal situations. Indeed the concept of opportunity cost is one of the basic tools used by professional economists when analysing any problem involving the use of resources.

Consider an example such as the decision to raise the school leaving age to sixteen. What is the 'cost' of this decision? First, we would certainly include the cost of extra teachers. If they could potentially have been employed elsewhere in the economy then there is an opportunity cost in employing them in teaching. Similarly, extra books and teaching materials, perhaps extra school buildings, will represent opportunity costs if they were produced by resources with alternative uses.

There is, however, another element to be included in the opportunity cost of this decision. If the school leaving age was not raised, many people aged between fifteen and sixteen would be part of the working population and be contributing to the production of goods and services in the economy. By raising the school leaving age to sixteen, however, the *potential* output of these people is sacrificed since they are withdrawn from the labour force. Here is an example in practice of a resource where the alternatives are, very broadly, to employ them or keep them at school. If they are kept at school, then an opportunity cost is involved because the economy is sacrificing their potential contribution to the immediate production of goods and services. Thus we would want to add the cost of potential output sacrificed to the other opportunity costs – salaries, materials and building costs, etc. – to find the full opportunity costs involved.

Allocation Decisions

The production possibility curve showed what combinations of goods and services were available in a very simplified economy. It also implied that underlying these combinations were a number of critical decisions about the allocation of resources in the economy. For example:

(*i*) **What kinds of goods and services will be produced?** If it is not possible to produce every conceivable item that people want, then a decision has to be made about what goods and services the limited resources are going to be used to produce. In our previous example, if only two goods were to be produced, then why cigarettes and books, rather than some other goods?

(*ii*) **What quantities of goods and services will be produced?** Next comes the problem of deciding the relative quantities of each good and service that should be produced. In Diagram 1.1, for example, what determines whether the economy will be in position A or position B?

(*iii*) **By what methods are goods and services produced?** A choice has also to be made about the relative quantities of labour, capital and raw materials to be used in the production of each type of good. What determines how much of each limited resource will be used in the cigarette industry and books industry respectively?

(*iv*) **For whom?** The fourth decision concerns the question of who gets the goods and services produced, and, consequently, to what extent any individual's wants are satisfied. What determines who will receive the cigarettes and books actually made? All of these choices relate to the fundamental decision about how to allocate limited resources between a range of alternatives. Explaining how these allocation decisions are made is the primary purpose of this book.

We know, for example, that in recent years the United Kingdom economy produced annually, amongst other things, about 2 million tons of meat, 36 million barrels of beer, 147 million tons of coal, 7,000 million therms of gas, 24 million tons of crude steel, 61,000 tons of soap, 2,400,000 television sets, 523,000 record players, 1,055,000 washing machines, and 1,742,000 cars.

Of the total labour force of 24 million, about 58,000 people were employed making food, drink and tobacco; 900,000 were employed in the electrical engineering industry; 202,000 people worked in the shipbuilding industry; the textile industry employed 650,000 people, and 500,000 people helped produce clothes and footwear.

Of the total value of plant and machinery created annually, the agricultural industry was responsible for using about £100 million; the coal mining industry invested £52 million in plant and machinery; the food, drink and tobacco industry accounted for £183 million; the chemicals industry £307 million; and the railways £10 million.

Even such a partial glimpse of economic activity in the United Kingdom shows that decisions regarding the allocation of resources were obviously taken. The interesting question is – by what mechanism were the decisions taken?

How Allocation Decisions are Made

One method by which these allocation decisions can be made is a system of **markets** for goods, services, and resources. In markets, people can express a preference for what they want by the **price** they are prepared to pay. An economy made up of a vast interconnected system of markets can thereby set up *relative* prices for goods, services and resources, and it is through the mechanism of prices that resources can be allocated between alternative uses, and goods and services between people.

The major part of this book is concerned with explaining and analysing the processes of markets and the mechanism of prices in order to illustrate how decisions about the allocation of resources in an economy are made, and what the outcomes of these decisions are.

Economists are also interested in using this knowledge of the price mechanism to make predictions about how certain kinds of changes will affect the allocation of resources. What will happen in the economy if people's preferences for certain goods or services change? What will happen if people become more keen to buy coal? What will happen if production conditions (e.g. a rise in costs) in an industry change?

Increasing emphasis has recently been placed on this *predictive* power of economic analysis. One indication of this has been the increasing number of economists working in government departments, who use their understanding of economic analysis to predict how various economic trends might affect the pattern of resource allocation in the economy.

Indeed, we might extend our interest in the predictive power of analysis to cover the implications of policies designed to intervene in some way with the price mechanism. Can we say what would happen if the government decided to control legally the price of a particular good? Or limit the quantity of a particular good to be produced? What would happen if the government decided that the number of people working in a particular industry (as happened in the case of shipbuilding) would have to be maintained, despite pressures via the market mechanism to make many of them redundant and perhaps reallocate them eventually in other industries?

Economic Welfare

Later in the book, we focus attention on another aspect of the operation of markets and the price mechanism. How well does the system perform its job of allocating resources? Consider the gigantic task faced by an economic system like that of the United Kingdom. A working population of 24 million people has to be combined with a capital stock worth £140,000 million in order to produce a range of goods and services which will only partially satisfy the wants of 55 million people. How can we judge whether the price mechanism will ensure that the *best* decisions about the allocation of resources are taken?

After we have examined how the price mechanism works, we shall attempt to establish some criteria by which we can judge its performance. In simple terms, does the price mechanism do its job well or badly? It all depends, of course, on what we define its job to be, and on how we define 'well' or 'badly'. But if the satisfaction of human wants is the reason for economic activity, then is it possible to judge the system by the extent to which it does satisfy human wants?

A considerable body of economic theory called Welfare Economics (surrounded by equally considerable controversy) has attempted to provide some answers to these questions. Using the production possibility curve in Diagram 1.1, the essence of the argument can be summarised as follows:

(*i*) Of all the possible combinations of the products in the economy, which *particular* combination would most satisfy human wants, i.e. create maximum economic welfare? Is it denoted by point A, point B, or some other point?

(*ii*) To what extent does the allocation of resources by means of the **price mechanism** provide that particular combination of goods and services which would maximise the satisfaction of human wants? And to what extent, and for what reasons, does it fail?

The reader will already know from experience that in an economy like that of the United Kingdom all markets are not left to make allocation decisions without intervention by the government. Apart from what are known as **macroeconomic** functions[4] such as managing the general direction of the economy to avoid unemployment and inflation, governments in Britain have also taken some responsibility

---

[4] These macroeconomic functions are discussed in detail in A. G. Ford, *Income, Spending and the Price Level*.

for more detailed intervention in the working of some particular markets.

Sometimes the intervention is direct. In the markets for some agricultural products direct controls on prices, or on the quantities produced, are maintained. Similarly, local authorities control the level of rents charged for the housing which they provide. Also, a range of industrial activity including the provision of coal, gas, electricity, railways and postal services is controlled by the government rather than by private enterprise. These 'nationalised industries', as they are called, give the government the opportunity to influence directly the amount of the good or service to be produced, the price at which it is to be sold, the amount of capital investment to be undertaken and the volume of employment in the industries.

Sometimes the intervention in markets is more indirect. The government has the power to influence some markets which are dominated by large firms, and to prevent two large firms joining together under a common bond of ownership (a process known as a **merger**). Also, firms are not entirely at liberty to locate themselves in any area of Britain. For over forty years, successive governments have operated restraints and inducements to encourage industry to move out of the South-East of England and into the less developed regions.

Some goods and services are not bought and sold in markets at all, but provided by the government at no direct charge to the people who use them or benefit from them. The classic examples are the national system of defence and virtually all roads. Also, although some educational and medical services (e.g. private fee-paying schools and private consultants who charge fees) do operate on a market basis, on the whole people do not buy education and medical care in the way that they buy a car, a shirt, or a book. Expenditure on schools, colleges, universities and hospitals is largely undertaken by the government, financed through receipts from general taxation, and provided to users without charge.

The receipts from taxation mentioned in the previous paragraph come from two major sources – taxation on people's incomes and firms' profits, and taxation levied on a range of goods and services. These two sources are often called direct and indirect taxation respectively. One interesting aspect of income tax in Britain is that it operates progressively, i.e. the higher the level of income earned, the greater is the proportion of it due in tax. A progressive system such as this raises considerations of equity and fairness, and enables governments to affect the distribution of income between people.

Government activity on such a scale has led economists to say that Britain has a 'mixed economy', in comparison to a purely private enterprise economy where the state has an extremely limited role to play, or to a collectivist economy (as in the Soviet Union) where the key allocation decisions referred to earlier are made almost entirely by state officials. One important consequence of analysing the workings and judging the performance of markets is that we may understand more clearly the rationale behind government intervention and the system within which we live.

Chapter 2

Markets, Demand and Supply (Part One)

This chapter gives a general outline of what is meant by the concept of a **market**, as well as explaining how a market functions.

Markets

The term **market** has a special meaning in economics. It implies a coming together of buyers and sellers of a good or service for the purpose of agreeing the terms on which the good or service will be bought and sold. The best-known type of market which fits easily into our definition is the kind that could be found until recently in Covent Garden in London where a large number of people met to buy and sell fruit, or is still found in the Billingsgate fish market. In Glasgow there is a well-known market called Barrowland which opens only on Saturdays and Sundays and where buyers and sellers come together to trade in all sorts of articles from second-hand magazines to washing machines.

Now these are markets in the traditional sense – relatively well-defined geographical areas where there is an equally well-defined product (or group of products) on sale. These are also areas where easily identifiable groups of buyers and sellers come into personal contact in order to agree about the terms of exchange of the product concerned.

In relation to the total quantity of goods and services bought and sold in our economy the kind of markets mentioned in the last paragraph now play an extremely minor role. Most goods and services are bought and sold in all areas of the country, and when we talk about the market for a certain product we normally imply the activities of buying and selling wherever they might occur.

For example, it is customary to talk in terms of the United Kingdom market for potatoes. Potato producers, over 45,000 in number, are widely dispersed throughout the country and potatoes are bought by families everywhere as part of their daily food diet.

Looking at the market for potatoes in these terms, we know that the average price varied considerably over a number of years in the 1960s. In 1965, for example, the average market price of potatoes was £14.20 per ton, but this rose dramatically to £19.35 per ton in 1966. It then dropped again to £14.65 per ton in 1967 and rose to £15.50 per ton in 1968.

The markets for some goods such as wool, wheat, copper and cocoa are often thought of in world-wide terms because these articles are bought and sold in so many countries throughout the world. Discussions about such products often quote **world prices.** In early 1973, for example, there was a very steep rise in the world prices of many raw materials and foodstuffs. The price of cocoa in the world market reached a peak of £980 per ton and then, in the space of one month, the price fell back to £730 per ton. Similarly, the world price of copper had been climbing steadily, eventually reaching £837 per ton. Only one week after this price had been reached, it fell to £786 per ton.

The point about the above examples is not that the prices of some goods can be highly volatile (others are much less so), but that we can identify markets of various geographical dimensions – from Covent Garden to the world. Essentially, however, all markets have as a common characteristic two sides engaged in the activities of buying and producing some definable good or service. For analytic purposes we will describe the transactors in the market as **consumers** (who demand goods and services) and **producers** (who supply them).

Before beginning the analysis, it is worth stressing one initial assumption which we are going to make. Markets are assumed to be **competitive,** which broadly means that they consist of large numbers of both buyers and sellers. No single buyer or seller is assumed to be large enough to exert any form of control over the terms of sale of the good or service. Later on in the book we shall see what happens when this assumption is relaxed.

Demand

The concept of **demand,** in economic analysis, denotes a situation in which consumers wish to possess some good or service, have the financial ability to pay for it, and are prepared to use their financial resources to acquire it. For example, there may be many people who desire a larger house. But this desire is not equivalent to demand as the term is used by economists. Some people may wish extra space and have the necessary financial resources to purchase, but demand only becomes effective if they are willing to use their purchasing power in order to obtain it.

What factors determine consumer demand for a product, for example eggs, during a specific time-period, say per week, month or year? In practice, of course, there may be many influences. It may be that the level of consumers' incomes is an important determinant of demand. As people become richer they may wish to increase their purchases of eggs. Another determinant might be consumers' tastes. For example, a very famous advertising campaign which preached the slogan 'Go to work on an egg' had a considerable impact on consumer demand.

Yet another determinant of consumer demand – the price of the product – is conventionally regarded by economists as so important that it forms the starting-point of our analysis. We are going to simplify matters for the moment by focusing our attention solely on price as a determinant of demand. To do this, we assume that all other possible determinants of demand such as incomes and tastes do not change.[1] Our approach is therefore to see how the price of a good might affect the quantity which people would be willing to buy during a specific time-period when all other determinants of demand are constant.

Let us imagine the task of a market researcher who wishes to explore the characteristics of demand. In particular, the researcher is interested in discovering how many eggs would be purchased per week at a series of possible prices, assuming that all other influences affecting consumer buying habits remain constant. What sort of picture is the researcher likely to obtain?

Table 2.1   **Market Demand Schedule for Eggs**

Price (p)	Quantity Demanded per week
6	3,000
5	6,000
4	9,000
3	12,000
2	15,000

[1] Such an assumption is given a Latin term called *ceteris paribus* which means 'assuming other things remain equal'. For a fuller discussion of the place of this type of assumption in economic analysis, *see* C. D. Harbury, Ch. 9.

The reaction of consumers might be described by the figures shown in Table 2.1. If eggs were to be priced at 6p each, it is estimated that consumers would be prepared to buy 3,000 per week. If the price fell to 5p each, the quantity demanded would rise to 6,000 eggs per week. Notice that if the price continued to fall consumers would wish to buy more and more eggs until at a price of 2p the quantity demanded would be 15,000 per week. This table, linking prices with the quantities consumers would be willing to buy, is called a **demand schedule.**

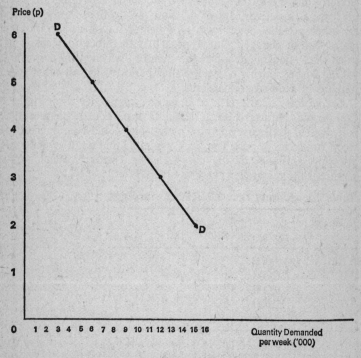

Figure 2.1 Market demand curve for eggs

The schedule can, of course, easily be illustrated by a graph, as in Diagram 2.1. Prices are measured on the vertical axis, and quantities demanded on the horizontal axis. By joining up all these points representing particular price-quantity combinations, we derive a line[2] which is called a **demand curve.** We now have an insight into consumers' potential buying habits in the market for eggs at a range of possible prices. The demand curve gives us no information about what price is actually being charged for eggs. It simply tells us how many eggs consumers would buy if the price of eggs was in the range from 6p to 2p each.

In general, demand curves when plotted in this way slope downwards from left to right, implying that the lower the price of a product the higher will be the quantity demanded by consumers. This inverse relationship between prices and quantities demanded is believed by economists to represent a general tendency in consumers' buying behaviour for virtually all goods and services. Though there are theories explaining why economists expect such a pattern to exist in practice (these will be explained in detail in Chapter 4) it does, for the moment, seem to be an intuitively reasonable proposition that as the price of most goods falls consumers will buy more. There are certainly many examples in practice which lend weight to the acceptance of this relationship.

When colour television sets were first sold in Britain, their price was extremely high and the quantity demanded was, not surprisingly, extremely low. But as the price of colour television sets began to fall the quantity demanded increased. Now it may be the case that over a period of two to three years some of those other determinants mentioned above, such as incomes, were changing and that it is unfair to attribute the whole of the increased quantity demanded to a fall in price. But there is little doubt that to some extent the fall in price did contribute to the increased quantity demanded.

It must be mentioned here, however, that there are some exceptions to the assumption that demand curves are downward sloping. These occur in the case of goods and services where lower prices tend to lead to less being demanded and not more; conversely higher prices would be associated with a higher quantity demanded.

One example of such an exception is a good or service which has some status appeal, such as expensive jewellery or perfumes. If a good has a certain 'snob appeal', there can be an association in the minds of consumers between the price of the good and its quality.

[2] A demand 'curve' does not need to be in the form of a straight line.

Consumers might therefore consider that the higher the price of the good the better the good is in a quality sense; and so the quantity demanded might be higher at higher prices. Strangely enough, a good with characteristics diametrically opposite to those of **status goods** tends to provide another exception to the normal demand curve shape. The term **inferior goods** is given to commodities which consumers tend to buy in lower quantities. Examples of inferior goods are found in the diets of the populations of underdeveloped countries. In such cases commodities such as rice tend to form a very large proportion of the staple diet. A fall in price can then result in people being able to afford to spend more of their incomes on alternative and more attractive goods such as meat. The predictable result is a fall in purchases of rice.

Where people's expectations about the future price level of a good are important, higher prices can sometimes be associated with an increase in the quantity demanded of the good. One notable example occurred in the market for owner-occupier houses during the years 1971 and 1972 when the price of many houses actually doubled, and the average price rise throughout the country was about forty per cent. When prices at first began to rise rapidly there was no decrease in the quantity of houses demanded. Instead many people expected house prices to rise even faster in the future and so demand was actually boosted by the prevalent wish of many consumers to buy before they were priced out of the market.

Other Determinants of Demand

We can now begin to remove the assumption that all other determinants of demand remain constant. As these other determinants are allowed to change, we shall see what effect they have on the demand curve for a product.

(*i*) **Consumers' Incomes** It may be the case that the demand for some goods and services is fundamentally affected by consumers' incomes. As an example, let us suppose that the demand curve for long-playing gramophone records is represented by DD in Diagram 2.2.

This demand curve shows that if the price of L.P. records was £5 each, then consumers would be prepared to buy 100,000 records per week. If consumers in this market experienced a rise in their incomes it would be reasonable to expect that they would be willing to buy more L.P. records, say, 150,000 per week, even if the price remained

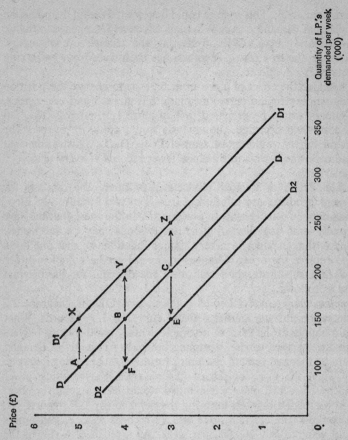

Figure 2.2 Shift in demand curve when determinants (other than price) change

at £5. Such a change would be shown by a movement from point A on the demand curve DD to point X.

Similarly, if the price of L.P. records had been £4 each and the quantity demanded 150,000, a rise in incomes would lead to more being demanded. Such a change might be shown by a movement from point B on the original curve DD to point Y, i.e. 200,000 L.P.

records per week. This process could be repeated for all the points on the original demand curve. What has effectively happened is that a new demand curve, D_1D_1, reflecting the change in consumers' behaviour due to a rise in incomes, has been traced out by linking points X, Y, Z, and so on.

Therefore the effect of a rise in incomes is to change the position of the whole demand curve, meaning that at each and every price, consumers would be prepared to buy more L.P. records. If a fall in income had occurred, the analysis would apply in reverse. The demand curve would move from DD to D_2D_2, illustrating that consumers would wish to purchase fewer records at every price.[3]

(*ii*) **The Prices of Related Products** Very often, the markets for different products are interlinked in one of two broad ways. First, goods may be **complements** to one another in the snese that they are normally used together. Alternatively, goods may be **substitutes**, meaning that they perform very similar functions so that one good could replace the other. Changes in the price of a complementary good or a substitute good will affect the demand for the original good as follows:

Complementary Goods: Let us suppose that DD in Diagram 2.2 again represents the market demand curve for L.P. records. What would happen if the price of a complementary good (record players in this case) were to rise, assuming other determinants of demand including incomes remain constant? Intuitively, the feeling might be that when the price of record players rises, the resulting lower quantity of record players demanded would have a spillover effect on to its related market, lowering the demand for L.P. records. If, for example, the original price of L.P. records was £3, consumers would want to buy 200,000 per week. As a result of a rise in the price of record players, we might expect that fewer L.P. records would be demanded, say 150,000, even if the price remained at £3. This change is shown by a movement from point C to point E.

Indeed whatever the original price of L.P. records, we might expect that a rise in the price of record players would lead to fewer L.P. records being demanded, e.g. a move from point B to point F if the price was £4. By linking points such as F and E, it can be seen that a rise in the price of a complementary good has shifted the whole demand curve for the original good back to the left (D_2D_2), indicating that at each and every price, consumers would be prepared

[3] It is not necessary for shifts in the curves to involve parallel movements.

to buy less of the original good. If the price of record players were to fall, then this would imply an increased demand for L.P. records at all prices, indicated by a movement of the original demand curve DD to the right (to a curve such as D_1D_1 in Diagram 2.2).

Substitute Goods: Forty-five rpm records and L.P. records can be regarded as very close substitutes since they perform almost exactly the same function.

Consider now what would happen to the demand for L.P. records if the price of forty-five rpm records were to fall. The latter would become *relatively* less expensive compared to L.P. records, and this would mean a decrease in demand for L.P. records as some people began to substitute forty-five rpm records. The resulting effect would be to move the whole demand curve for L.P. records to the left, indicating that consumers wished to buy fewer L.P. records at each and every price. Such a change would be shown by a shift of the demand curve in Diagram 2.2 from DD to D_2D_2.

Alternatively, if the price of forty-five rpm records were to rise, this would make L.P. records relatively less expensive. Consumers would be willing to purchase more L.P.s at all prices, and this would be shown by a shift in the demand curve from DD to D_1D_1 in Diagram 2.2.

(*iii*) **Consumers' Tastes** Tastes form another influence which might affect consumer demand and thus the position of the demand curve, in the same way as incomes and the prices of related goods. Imagine, for example, what would happen to the demand for L.P. records if an advertising campaign was launched. If, as a consequence, consumers' tastes moved in favour of L.P. records, we might expect consumers to be willing to purchase more of them. In terms of Diagram 2.2, for example, consumers might be prepared to purchase 200,000 L.P. records per week at a price of £4, instead of 150,000 per week, as a result of the change in tastes; or 250,000 per week at a price of £3, instead of 200,000.

In other words, a change in tastes in favour of a product moves the demand curve out to the right – in Diagram 2.2 we would interpret this move as a shift of the demand curve from DD to D_1D_1, illustrating consumers' willingness to buy more L.P. records at each and every price. Conversely, a change in tastes away from L.P. records would move the whole demand curve back to the left – as indicated by the move from DD to D_2D_2 in Diagram 2.2.

There is no doubt that in the markets for many products, fashion and taste play a vital role in determining demand. This is true not only of goods which are naturally subject to swings in fashion, such as clothes and footwear, but also products such as cosmetics and soap powders, where advertising can play an important role in shaping consumer demand. According to the American economist, J. K. Galbraith, 'In consequence, their (i.e. consumer) economic behaviour becomes in some measure malleable. No hungry man who is also sober can be persuaded to use his last dollar for anything but food. But a well-fed, well-clad, well-sheltered and otherwise well-tended person can be persuaded as between an electric razor and an electric toothbrush.'[4]

(*iv*) **Summary of Factors Affecting Demand** What has been done so far, then, is to postulate two sets of relationships. First there was the initial relationship between the quantities demanded of a product at a series of possible prices, assuming all other factors remain constant. This relationship was shown in the form of a demand curve.[5] Secondly a relationship was shown between the quantity demanded of a product and various other factors – income, prices of complements and substitutes, and tastes – and it was shown how a change in each affected the position of the basic demand curve.

Readers will almost certainly have cause to use demand curves during their studies, and the following point cannot be stressed too much. The effect of a change in price of a product with other conditions constant is represented by a *movement along the demand curve*, whereas the effect of a change in any of the other determinants is shown by a *shift of the whole demand curve*.

Suppose we wanted to know what happens in the market for eggs following a change in their price. We can obtain this information purely from the initial demand curve DD in Diagram 2.1. If the price changed from 4p each to 3p each, the quantity demanded would increase from 10,000 to 15,000 per week. The effect is seen as a movement along the same demand curve.

Suppose we now wanted to know what would happen in the market for eggs if any of the other factors affecting demand were to change. Diagram 2.2 summarised the idea that changes in these other determinants involve a shift of the whole demand curve, as distinct from a movement along the same curve. When a change in price

[4] J. K. Galbraith, *The New Industrial State*, p. 5.
[5] The relationship can also be expressed as an equation: *see* C. D. Harbury, pp. 190–92.

takes place, we speak of the resulting *change in the quantity demanded of a good* (as represented by a movement along the demand curve). When a change in any of the other determinants takes place, we speak instead of a *change in demand* (as shown by a shift of the demand curve).

Supply Curves

Now we turn to the other activity carried on in a market, that of supply. We must try to list those factors which determine the quantity of a product which will be offered for sale to a market by all the producers engaged in its production. As was the case with demand, there may be many influences at work though initially we shall single out the market price of the product and assume that other factors affecting supply remain unchanged.

The relationship which we wish to establish is between different prices of a product and the quantities of that product which firms in the market would offer for sale at those prices. To revert to our example of the market for eggs – how many eggs would be supplied at various prices? Such a relationship is set out in Table 2.2, which is known as a **supply schedule.**

Table 2.2 **Market Supply Schedule for Eggs**

Price (p)	Quantity Supplied per week
6	15,000
5	12,000
4	9,000
3	6,000
2	3,000

If the price of eggs was 2p each, then egg producers would be willing to supply 3,000 eggs per week. At a price of 3p, the quantity of eggs offered for sale would be 6,000. Notice that as the price of eggs increases, we assume that the quantity which would be supplied expands until 15,000 eggs per week are offered for sale at a price of 6p. Using this information about the potential response of firms to a series of prices, we can present the relationship in graphical form, as in Diagram 2.3.

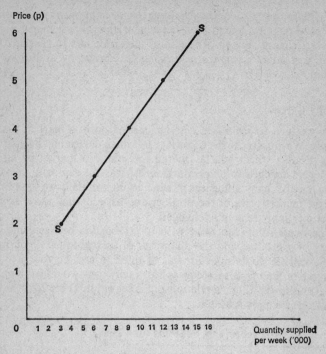

Figure 2.3 Market supply curve for eggs

This graphical representation is called a **supply curve.** The curve SS slopes upwards from left to right implying that the higher the price of the product, the greater will be the quantity offered for sale to the market. We shall have to defer until later chapters a detailed consideration of why we should expect such a positive association between prices and the quantities of a good offered by producers. But for the moment let us assume that, in the market as a whole, the higher the price of a product the greater the level of profits that can be earned from it, and that consequently there is an incentive for a greater quantity to be supplied.

Other Determinants of Supply

In drawing this supply curve, it has been assumed that other factors affecting supply remain constant. The most important of these factors would include the following:

(*i*) **Cost of Factors of Production** A change in the cost of the factors (labour, land or capital) used in the production of goods may change the quantity of the product which firms are willing to supply.

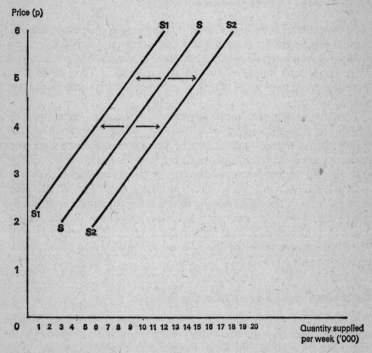

Figure 2.4 Shift in supply curve when determinants (other than price) change

As shown in Diagram 2.4, for example, a rise in the costs of the factors used to produce eggs would move the whole supply curve to the left (from SS to S_1S_1). This indicates that at each price producers would offer fewer eggs for sale. For example, at a price of

4p, 6,000 eggs per week would be supplied, compared with 9,000 eggs per week before the rise in costs took place. If the price was 5p, then producers would be willing to supply only 9,000 eggs per week instead of 12,000 before the rise in costs.

Conversely, a fall in the cost of factors of production would tend to shift the supply curve down to the right, implying that producers would be willing to offer greater quantities to the market at all prices. Such a move would be indicated by a shift of the supply curve from SS to S_2S_2 in Diagram 2.4.

(*ii*) **Production Technology** Conditions of supply in many markets depend largely on the state of production technology. Indeed, many producers now spend considerable sums of money on the activities of research and development, by which methods are devised to manufacture goods more cheaply, more efficiently and in greater quantities.

The application of a more advanced and cheaper technology to the production of a good will obviously affect the conditions of supply in the market. At all prices, producers would be able and prepared to offer greater quantities for sale – a change denoted, for example, by the movement of the supply curve from SS to S_1S_1.

Occasionally, completely new products are discovered. For example, one of the direct results of the American space programme in the 1960s was the discovery and development of an extremely heat-resistant material used in the space-craft. This material provided the ideal surface for the commercial production of non-stick pots and pans.

Conclusions about Factors Affecting Supply

Just as we did for consumer demand, we have now set up a basic relationship, shown in the supply curve, which links prices with quantities of a good which its producers are prepared to sell. The supply curve illustrates the fact that if the price of the product changes (assuming other determinants remain constant), we can predict what will happen to the quantity supplied by observing a *movement along the same supply curve*.

We also noted other factors influencing supply conditions. Should any of these change, there will be a *shift of the whole supply curve* to a new set of quantities of the good which firms would supply at all prices.

Again, it is extremely important to distinguish between the influences which cause a movement along the curve (changes in price) and those which cause a shift in the position of the curve itself (a change in any one of the other factors mentioned). When a change in the price of a product takes place we speak of the resulting *change in quantity supplied*. We refer to a *change in supply* when one of the other determinants changes.

Demand and Supply Together – the Basic Market Model

Each side of a market has now been analysed separately. One relationship has been established between prices and quantities demanded, and another between prices and quantities supplied. However, it must be stressed that neither demand curves nor supply curves by themselves can determine the market price of the product, or the quantity of the product actually bought and sold. This is because demand and supply curves are really schedules of intentions. They give an insight into consumers' and producers' potential behaviour and show what consumers would be prepared to purchase and producers prepared to supply if certain prices were to prevail.

In order to determine how a market operates to determine both the price of a product and the quantity bought and sold, the demand and supply conditions need to be considered simultaneously. This can be done by superimposing a demand curve and a supply curve on to the same graph as in Diagram 2.5.

The curves in Diagram 2.5 illustrate the demand and supply conditions in the market for eggs, referred to earlier in the chapter. What can be inferred from this diagram about the operation of the market for eggs? Consider what would happen if the price of eggs was 5p. At this price consumers would be willing to buy 6,000 eggs per week, but producers would wish to supply 12,000 eggs per week. There would, therefore, be a situation of excess supply, with 6,000 eggs per week being left unsold.

The situation of excess supply, however, would not normally last. Producers would obviously find stocks of eggs piling up which they would be unable to sell at a price of 5p. In an attempt to get rid of unsold stocks and prevent over-production, their reaction would be to reduce prices and to supply fewer eggs. Graphically, this is shown by a movement down the supply curve from A to E.

As prices began to fall, consumers would increase purchases.

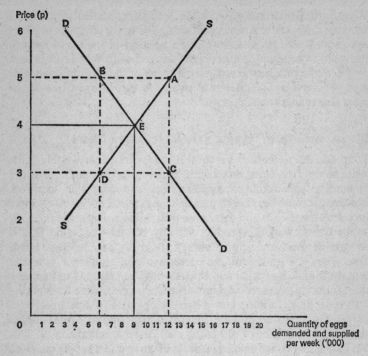

Figure 2.5 The basic market model

This would be seen in a movement down the demand curve from B to E. Thus if the market price of eggs was at a level which caused excess supply, forces on both sides of the market would tend to move the price to a level (E) at which the quantity demanded was exactly equal to the quantity supplied.

Conversely, suppose the market price of eggs was 3p. In this situation, the quantity demanded would be 12,000 eggs per week, but producers would be prepared to supply only 6,000 eggs per week. The result would be an excess demand for eggs at a price of 3p. This situation, however, would not normally last because some consumers who could not obtain eggs would offer more than 3p. This would tend to raise the market price of eggs. In Diagram 2.5

there would be a movement up the demand curve from C to E.

As the price rose, and as producers realised the shortage of supply in relation to demand, they would respond by increasing production, i.e. there would be a movement up the supply curve from D to E. Economic forces again would tend to act on both the demand and supply sides of the market to set up a price of 4p, at which the quantity of eggs consumers wished to buy would be exactly equal to the quantity which producers would be willing to supply.

The price of 4p, at which the intentions of buyers and sellers are exactly matched, is given the special name of **equilibrium price.** The notion of equilibrium is usually seen in the natural sciences as a point of rest, where opposing forces are equally balanced. Once this point of equilibrium is reached there is no tendency for any further change to occur, unless the system is affected by some external force.

Translating this notion into economic language, it can be seen from Diagram 2.5 that 4p is the equilibrium price in the market for eggs. It is the only price at which the quantity demanded equals the quantity supplied. We have also seen that if, for any reason, a price other than 4p were to exist, forces would be set up to push the market towards the equilibrium level. Once reached, this equilibrium price would tend to persist. A price change would only occur if the market were to be disturbed by some change in the basic conditions of supply and demand responsible for determining the position of the curves.

Changes in Equilibrium Price

The equilibrium price and quantity once established in a market will last for as long as market conditions are represented by the initial demand and supply curves. In reality, of course, demand and supply conditions – incomes, tastes, technology, etc. – change very frequently in many markets.

A change in any of these conditions would, as shown earlier, shift the position of the demand curve or supply curve. The effect of this would be to alter the level of equilibrium price and quantity in the market. Let us assume for simplicity that the conditions on one side of the market remain constant. Within this overall framework it is possible to make some general, though important, predictions about what will happen when changes occur on the other side of the market.

(*i*) **Changes in Demand with Supply Constant** Let us consider first of all what might happen as a result of a change in one of the determinants of demand (apart from price) assuming that no change takes place in the determinants of supply. For example, by using the tools so far developed in this chapter we can analyse the effects of advertising promotions (such as the 'Go to work on an egg' campaign) on the market for eggs. The demand and supply curves for eggs, DD and SS respectively, are illustrated in Diagram 2.6.

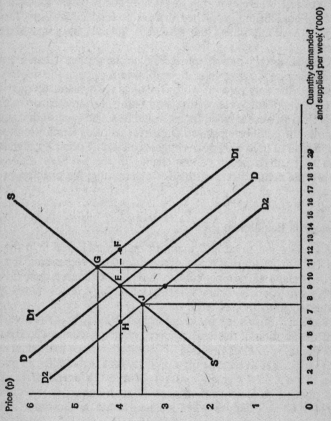

Figure 2.6 Changes in demand conditions with supply constant

A successful advertising campaign would change consumers' tastes in favour of eggs. Its results could be represented graphically by a shift of the demand curve to the right, e.g. from DD to D_1D_1. Consequently at the initial equilibrium price of 4p, there would be excess demand measured by the quantity EF. This shortage would eventually result in consumers offering more for eggs and producers supplying more until a new equilibrium price was reached at point G, where the new demand curve intersects the supply curve.

The overall effect, then, of an increase in demand (via a change in tastes in favour of the product) would be to raise the equilibrium price of eggs from 4p to $4\frac{1}{2}$p; and there would be an increase in the quantity of eggs bought and sold from 9,000 per week to 10,500 per week. As long as the demand curve for a product slopes downwards from left to right and the supply curve slopes upwards from left to right, an increase in demand will result in an increase in price and an increase in the quantity bought and sold.

Let us now suppose that a change in demand takes place in the opposite direction. What would be the effect on the market for eggs if, for example, consumers' incomes were to fall? We have already established that the result would be a shift in the demand curve to the left, meaning that at each price consumers would wish to buy fewer eggs. The shift in the demand curve due to a fall in incomes can be represented by the change from DD to D_2D_2 in Diagram 2.6.

At the original equilibrium price of 4p there would now be excess supply, shown by the quantity EH, of 3,000 eggs per week. Egg producers would have a surplus of eggs on their hands and so, in an attempt to reduce the surplus, prices would be lowered, and production decreased. The market would achieve equilibrium again at the intersection of the demand curve D_2D_2 and the supply curve, i.e. at point J.

The result of the fall in demand is seen as a reduction in the price of eggs from 4p to $3\frac{1}{2}$p, and a decrease in the quantity of eggs bought and sold from 9,000 per week to 7,500 per week. Assuming that the demand and supply curves for a good are normally shaped we can predict that a fall in demand for a good will lead to a fall in the price of the good and a reduction in the quantity bought and sold.

(*ii*) **Changes in Supply with Demand Constant** Let us now turn our attention to changes on the supply side of a market and assume that demand conditions remain constant. First we will see what happens in the egg market if costs of production rise throughout the egg-producing industry. If we again let the market for eggs be represented initially by the demand curve DD and the supply curve SS as in Diagram 2.7, the effect of a rise in costs would be to shift the position of the supply curve for eggs from SS to S_1S_1.

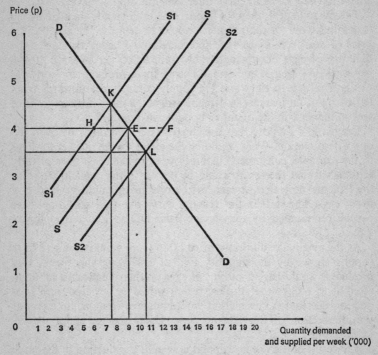

Figure 2.7 Changes in supply with demand constant

At an initial equilibrium price of 4p, this shift in the supply curve would cause excess demand of 3,000 eggs per week (EH in the diagram). Faced with a shortage of eggs, consumers would begin to bid up price to re-establish equilibrium in the market at point K, where the new supply curve S_1S_1 intersects the demand curve DD.

The overall effect of the fall in supply would be a new equilibrium price of eggs, 4½p instead of 4p, and a fall in the quantity of eggs bought and sold from 9,000 per week to 7,500 per week. In general, whenever the demand and supply curves for a product have the assumed shape, a fall in supply with demand held constant will lead to a rise in the price of the product and a fall in the quantity bought and sold.

If a change in supply occurred in the other direction the effects are now easily predicted. Let us suppose, for example, that farmers introduced more efficient production techniques throughout the industry, thus shifting the supply curve for eggs from SS to S_2S_2 as shown in Diagram 2.7. At the original equilibrium price of 4p, there would now be an excess supply of eggs shown by the distance EF, since at a price of 4p producers would offer 12,000 eggs for sale but consumers would wish to buy only 9,000 eggs per week. Producers would lower price until equilibrium was reached at point L, i.e. where the price was 3½p and quantity 10,500 per week.

The effect of an increase in supply in this market, then, has been to lower the price of the product and increase the quantity bought and sold. Such an effect always follows an increase in supply whenever the demand and supply curves for a product are normally shaped.

Simultaneous Changes in Demand and Supply

Finally in this chapter we shall consider perhaps the most realistic situations of all, namely those involving simultaneous changes in demand and supply. In many markets it is often found that incomes, tastes, costs of production, technology, etc., are constantly changing. The analysis which we have developed in this chapter can at least help to bring some order into the chaos that often appears to surround a market situation where so many changes are taking place, and point out the general direction of the effects which are likely to be seen.

There are four possible sets of simultaneous changes which we can consider: (*i*) An increase in both demand and supply; (*ii*) An increase in demand accompanied by a decrease in supply; (*iii*) An increase in supply accompanied by a decrease in demand; (*iv*) A decrease in both demand and supply. Let us consider each in turn in relation to the market for eggs which we have been analysing so far.

(*i*) **An Increase in Demand and Supply** The market for eggs can again be represented by the demand and supply curves DD and SS respectively, and is initially in equilibrium where the price is 4p and the quantity of eggs bought and sold is 9,000 per week. Now let us suppose that two changes take place in the market. Consumers' incomes increase and, at the same time, costs of production fall throughout the industry. These changes are shown by a shift in the demand curve from DD to D_1D_1 and the supply curve from SS to S_1S_1, as shown in Diagram 2.8.

The overall effect of an increase in demand and supply in this market is first an increase in quantity bought and sold from 9,000 eggs per week to 13,500 eggs per week, and secondly a slight increase in price from 4p to $4\frac{1}{2}$p. This price increase, however, results purely from the magnitude of the shifts in the curves. Had the demand curve been shifted to the intermediate position D_2D_2, then, although the quantity of eggs bought and sold would still have increased, the equilibrium price would have fallen from 4p to 3.8p. (Indeed, it is possible to shift the demand and supply curves and maintain the price of eggs at 4p.)

It is possible to conclude that when an increase in demand and supply occur in a market, the quantity of the product bought and sold will always increase, provided that the curves are normally shaped. The direction of the price change, however, depends on the extent of the shifts of both curves and it is possible that the price of the product will rise, fall or remain at the same level.

(*ii*) **An Increase in Demand and a Decrease in Supply** Let us now imagine that the market for eggs is affected by the following two changes – a change in tastes in favour of eggs and a rise in costs affecting all producers. If the demand curves DD and SS are again taken as our starting point, the change in tastes might shift the demand curve to D_1D_1 and the rise in costs might shift the supply curve to S_3S_3 as shown in Diagram 2.9.

The effect of the demand and supply curves shifting to these positions is first that the price of eggs rises from 4p to $5\frac{1}{2}$p, and secondly the quantity of eggs bought and sold increases from 9,000 per week to 10,300 per week. While it is certainly the case that an increase in demand and a decrease in supply will always cause the price to rise by some amount (again assuming the curves to be normally shaped), the increase in the quantity of the product bought and sold illustrated above has come about purely by the magnitude

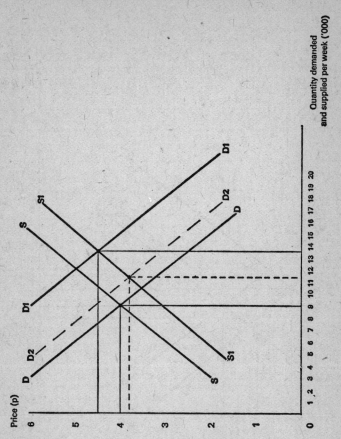

Figure 2.8 Effects of an increase in demand and supply

of the shifts of the curves. If the demand curve had been shifted to position D_2D_2 as illustrated in Diagram 2.9, it can be seen that the quantity of eggs bought and sold would decrease from 9,000 per week to 8,000 per week.

We can therefore say that if a market for a good is affected by both an increase in demand and a decrease in supply, the price of the good will certainly rise. But the quantity of the good could

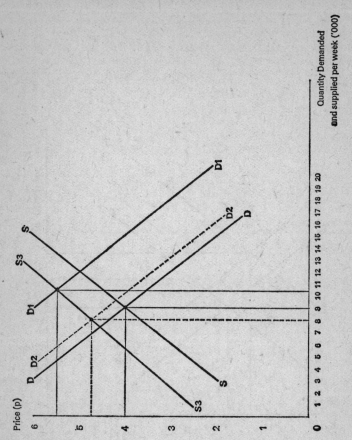

Figure 2.9 Effects of an increase in demand and a decrease in supply

either rise, fall or even remain the same as at the initial equilibrium level depending on the extent of the shift in the supply and demand curve.

(*iii*) **An Increase in Supply and a Decrease in Demand** Let us reverse the order of the changes in the previous example. If the market for eggs was simultaneously affected by a change in consumers' tastes away from eggs and a fall in costs of production among all egg suppliers, what effects would such changes have on the price of eggs and the quantity bought and sold? The initial market curves are represented by DD and SS in Diagram 2.10, and as a result of the two changes mentioned, the demand and supply curves shift to D_3D_3 and S_1S_1 respectively.

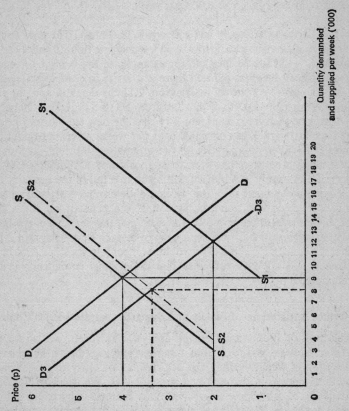

Figure 2.10 Effects of an increase in supply and a decrease in demand

The new equilibrium price and quantity established by these changes are 2p and 12,000 eggs per week respectively. Now while an increase in supply and a decrease in demand will always bring about a fall in the price of a product (as shown in the present example), the direction of the quantity change again depends entirely on the magnitude of the shifts of the curves. In other words, the combination of an increase in supply and a decrease in demand results in a fall in price but the quantity bought and sold could either rise, fall or remain at the original equilibrium level. For example, if the supply curve had shifted to S_2S_2, the quantity of eggs bought and sold would have fallen to 8,000 per week.

(*iv*) **A Decrease in Supply and a Decrease in Demand** The final combination of changes to be considered is a decrease in both supply and demand. What would happen, for example, in the market for eggs if consumers' incomes fell and there was a rise in costs affecting all egg producers? As shown in Diagram 2.11 the demand and supply curves shift from DD to D_3D_3 and from SS to S_3S_3 respectively.

It can be seen from Diagram 2.11 that the new equilibrium price and quantity are 3.7p and 5,000 eggs per week; price and quantity have both fallen compared with the original equilibrium positions. It is always the case that a decrease in demand accompanied by a decrease in supply in a market will result in a fall in the quantity of the good bought and sold. But we cannot determine exactly in which direction price will move because this is dependent on the scale of the shifts in the curves. If, for example, the demand curve had shifted instead to position D_4D_4, it can be seen from Diagram 2.11 that the market price of eggs would rise from 4p to 4.2p. And it is possible to shift both curves so that the original equilibrium price remained at 4p.

Further Applications of Supply and Demand Analysis – Price Control

The tools of supply and demand analysis have been used so far to explain how price is formed in a market, and to indicate the general direction in which we may expect price and quantity to move when certain changes in demand and supply occur. We can also use our analysis to provide some insight into markets where, for some reason, price is controlled at a specific maximum or minimum level.

(*i*) **Maximum Price Control** Let us suppose that the market for local authority rented houses in the hypothetical city of Westbury is represented by the demand and supply curves DD and SS in Diagram 2.12. If houses were to be allocated by the price mechanism, it can

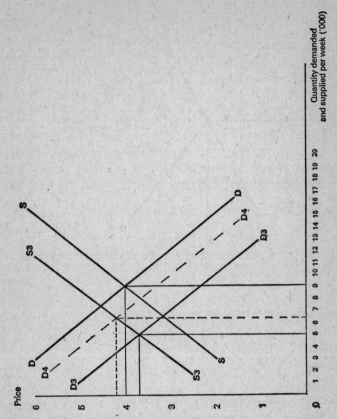

Figure 2.11 Effects of a decrease in demand and supply

be seen that the level of rents would be OR, and the quantity of houses demanded and supplied OQ.

Let us suppose that the city of Westbury Council decides that a rent level of OR is too high (perhaps because the citizens of Westbury have relatively low incomes), and decides to fix a maximum rent level of OR_1. The effects of such a policy are easy to predict. At a rent level of OR_1, the quantity of houses supplied would be OQ_2, whereas the quantity of houses demanded at OR_1 would be OQ_3.

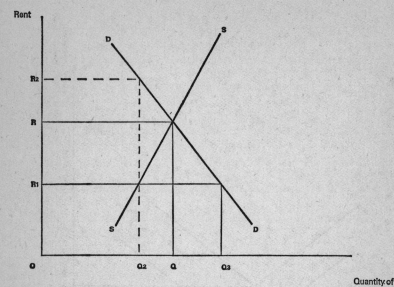

Figure 2.12 Maximum price control

Since OQ_3 is greater than OQ_2, the first prediction we can make is that fixing the level of rents below the equilibrium level would lead to a situation of excess demand for council houses – represented by Q_2Q_3.

It should be remembered that if the price in a market is below the equilibrium level, and the price mechanism is free to work, the price in the market would be forced upwards, eventually rationing out the available supply among potential consumers. In the city of Westbury, however, the price mechanism for council houses is controlled and therefore cannot perform its function of allocating the supply of houses. Some other method, then, must be found of allocating the supply of houses, OQ_2, among the potential consumers.

One very obvious method is to adopt a policy of 'first come – first served', whereby the available supply of OQ_2 is simply taken up by the people who are at the top of the waiting list for houses. Of course this does not solve the problem of the amount of unsatisfied demand Q_2Q_3 – which would be shown in the fact that Westbury, like most local authorities, would have a waiting list for council houses the length of which was precisely Q_2Q_3.

Another method of allocating resources (which could be used in conjunction with a policy of 'first come – first served') might be the establishment of some priority system by which the Westbury Council chose to allocate houses to certain types of citizen on the basis of some criteria – e.g. the elderly, large families, people with physical handicaps, people who have lived in Westbury for at least five years, etc.

When a maximum price is set below equilibrium in the market for a product a very common method of allocating the limited supply (often used during World War II to allocate food) has been through some system of rationing. The available supply of the product, for example, might be allocated on the basis of a limited quantity for each consumer (perhaps by issuing coupons entitling consumers to a limited quantity of the good). Rationing also applies to a limited extent in the case of the city of Westbury, which would almost certainly make it impossible for any family to have more than one council house in any case.

Whenever excess demand occurs in a market because of some system of price control it is often found that the price mechanism works to a limited extent through the phenomenon of a **black market.** Generally, a black market occurs if some consumers are willing to pay a higher price for the product than the controlled price, and if it is possible for them to obtain more of the available supply than they could normally get through a system of 'first come', priorities or rationing.

As an example of black market prices, let us consider the case of a luxury car, the XJ12, produced by a leading British manufacturer. As soon as it began to be supplied to the market this particular model acquired an international reputation for quality and speed. But at the price set by the manufacturers the quantity demanded greatly exceeded the quantity supplied. The manufacturers, however, felt it was not in their long-term interests to raise the price in response to market conditions. As market analysis would predict, long waiting lists for the XJ12 developed. In this situation, some customers were prepared to pay more than the list price for a scarce model, and a black market did indeed develop to some extent since a few dealers advertised for 'offers' for the XJ12s which they had in stock.

In a diagram similar to 2.12, for example, the supply curve for XJ12s might be represented by SS, and the demand curve by DD. At the fixed price of OR_1 (below the level OR where DD and SS intersect) there is excess demand – represented by Q_2Q_3. Now let us suppose that a black market develops, whereby the available supply OQ_2 could be allocated to consumers at whatever price they were prepared to pay. What would such a price be? Obviously OR_2, which is the price consumers would be willing to pay for quantity OQ_2 according to the demand curve DD.

(*ii*) **Minimum Price Control** Examples can also be found of prices being fixed above the equilibrium level. There has been much competition in recent years amongst holiday companies to attract people to go abroad for a few days during the winter. The government, however, laid down a minimum price for holidays of a certain duration (mainly three or four days) below which companies were not allowed to charge. The effects of this policy can be shown in Diagram 2.13.

If DD and SS are the demand and supply curves for foreign holidays in winter, the price would normally be OP. But what would happen if a minimum price of OP_1, which lies above OP, was established? The quantity of holidays demanded at a price of OP_1 is OH_1, whereas the quantity offered for sale would be OH_2.

The first prediction we can make, therefore, is that setting a minimum price above the equilibrium level in a market would lead to a situation of excess supply – represented in Diagram 2.13 by H_1H_2. Looking at the situation from the sellers' point of view, a legal minimum price means a shortage of demand at that price, and the most likely result would be an attempt by some holiday companies to indulge in price cutting, either by direct or indirect means.

The most common indirect method of price cutting in order to attract more customers was the offer of gift vouchers wherever people booked up for a holiday. Indeed many holiday companies stated quite explicitly in their advertising brochures that the vouchers were intended to make up for the lower price they would really have liked to have charged.[6]

---

[6] For further examples, *see* C. D. Harbury, *An Introduction to Economic Behaviour.*

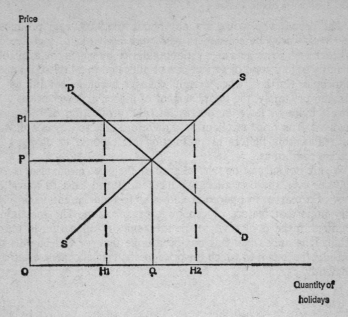

Figure 2.13 Minimum price control

Conclusions

In this chapter we have set out some general methods of analysing market operations, price formation, and the causes of price changes. One of the most popular clichés in economics is that 'You can explain anything by supply and demand'. This statement exaggerates the explanatory powers of the tools of analysis which we have developed so far. But there is little doubt that a sound understanding of economics depends on the student having mastered the elements of supply and demand analysis.

We have shown how the price mechanism performs an important allocative function. For example, in the market for eggs which we have discussed in this chapter, the price mechanism reconciled buyers' and sellers' intentions so that 9,000 eggs per week would be produced and sold; not 8,000, 10,000 or some other figure.

The people who would actually obtain the 9,000 eggs produced per week would be consumers who were prepared to sacrifice 4p for each egg. Price acts as a rationing device by which the available quantity of any good or service can be allocated to a limited number of people. Further, when certain changes occur in conditions of demand or supply, the establishment of higher or lower prices will attract more or fewer resources into the production of the good involved. The price mechanism is therefore able to act as a device for reallocating factors of production in response to changes in market conditions.

We are not suggesting that reliance on the price mechanism is the only, or even the best allocative method. But at least this general view of a market in operation allows us to focus attention on one very important feature of economic organisation. The remaining chapters in the book analyse the mechanics of allocation in more detail. It is only when this has been done that we will be able to consider the extent to which the price mechanism allocates resources efficiently.

Chapter 3

Markets, Demand and Supply (Part Two)

We shall now analyse the nature of demand and supply in a little more detail. These concepts are powerful instruments for providing insight into the general forces at work in a market. However, economists often wish to know more about market tendencies than the rather bold facts that the quantity demanded of a product will normally rise as price falls (and vice versa), and that the quantity supplied generally rises with price (and vice versa).

One particular piece of vital information concerns the responsiveness of the quantity demanded or supplied to a price change. Part of our interest here stems from our knowledge that quite large price changes in some goods such as salt and bread bring about relatively little response in quantity demanded or supplied, whereas even a small price change in other products, such as cars, has a much greater effect on the quantity demanded. Partly, our interest stems from many decisions which have to be made on the basis of an estimate of such responsiveness.

For example, let us consider a proposal by London Transport Executive in 1970 to the Greater London Council to increase the level of flat-rate fares (i.e. constant charges irrespective of the length of journey) on the Red Arrow buses, which provide a fast, limited-stop service in the Central London area. In this case it was possible to organise an experiment in which the effects of two levels of fare (6d and 9d, in pre-decimal terms) were surveyed during two separate weeks (within one month of each other). By comparing the information derived from each week's investigations, it was hoped to gain some evidence about precisely how the demand for Red Arrow bus services responded to such a fare change. The results of the surveys are shown in Table 3.1.

The total amount of revenue collected from the buses during each of the weeks was calculated.

From Table 3.1 it can be seen that in every service an increase in revenue was recorded. Now we know from the analysis of the previous chapter that a rise in price will lead to a decrease in the quantity

Table 3.1   **Revenue from Red Arrow Bus Services**

Route Number	Revenue from 6d Fare (Week 1) £	Revenue from 9d Fare (Week 1) £
500	723	807
501	1124	1241
502	960	1093
503	456	609
505	471	533
506	519	626
507	1247	1432
509	372	458
513	872	880

of a good demanded. If we can therefore assume that, in the case of Red Arrow bus services, other determinants of demand remained constant over the time which elapsed between the two 'test' weeks, the effect of the increased fare would be to decrease the number of journeys undertaken. However, the evidence in Table 3.1 suggests that the number of weekly journeys undertaken after the fare increase must have changed relatively little from the number of journeys per week before the fare change since more revenue was received at the *higher* fare level.

The concept used by economists to describe the responsiveness of the quantity demanded of a product to a price change is called **price elasticity of demand.** We shall now turn our attention to the way in which price elasticity of demand is measured by economists and the economic forces which determine whether the response of quantity demanded of some products to a price change is relatively great or relatively small.

Measurement of Price Elasticity of Demand

Because the concept of price elasticity of demand is so often used to estimate how the quantity demanded will respond to a price change, and to compare the results for different goods, it is convenient to have some method of precise measurement. The formula used for calculating the price elasticity of demand (E) is:

$$E = \frac{\text{Proportionate Change in Quantity Demanded}}{\text{Proportionate Change in Price}}$$

or

$\frac{\varDelta Q}{Q} \div \frac{\varDelta P}{P}$, where the Greek symbol $\varDelta$ (the letter Delta) stands for 'change in', and Q and P represent the original quantity and price.[1]

The reader may initially wonder why we should measure E in percentage or proportionate terms. To explain this, it is only necessary to refer to the need for a value of price elasticity of demand to act as a comparative measure. If we measured responsiveness of demand in absolute terms, some nonsensical results would follow. Let us suppose, for example, that the price of tomatoes changed by 1p per pound from 25p to 24p, with the quantity demanded rising from 50,000 lbs to 60,000 lbs per week; and that the price of newspapers fell from 4p to 3p, with the quantity sold rising from 1,000,000 per week to 1,010,000 per week. In both cases price has fallen by 1p and the quantity demanded has risen by 10,000 units. But we could not therefore infer that both products exhibit a similar demand response induced by a price change. Everything here depends on how large a change in price of 1p is relative to the original price – a 1p fall in the price of tomatoes represents a 4 per cent change from the original level whereas a 1p fall in the price of newspapers represents a 25 per cent decrease on the original level. Furthermore, the change in quantity demanded of 10,000 units is relatively large compared with the original figure for tomatoes (a 20 per cent change) but relatively small (a 1 per cent change) for newspapers. Clearly the demand response is basically very much more pronounced in the case of tomatoes where the *percentage* change in quantity is five times as large as the *percentage* change in price. By comparison the large percentage fall in newspaper prices has only changed demand by 1 per cent, or by one twenty-fifth of the percentage change in price.

A value for price elasticity of demand can be calculated from a demand curve as shown in Diagram 3.1. Let us imagine a fall in price of L.P. records from £5 to £4. The resulting effect would be an increase in demand from 100,000 to 200,000 per week. According

[1] To be formally correct, the value of price elasticity of demand is normally negative, since an increase in price (i.e. a positive $\varDelta P$) leads to a decrease in quantity demanded (i.e. a negative $\varDelta Q$), and vice versa. Hence the values of symbols $\varDelta Q$ and $\varDelta P$ in the formula above normally move in opposite directions. The value of E, therefore, should normally be preceded by a negative sign. Conventionally, however, we ignore this algebraic nicety.

to the formula stated above, we could therefore say that the price elasticity of demand for L.P. records was given by

$$E = \frac{\text{Proportionate Change in Quantity Demanded}}{\text{Proportionate Change in Price}}$$
$$= \frac{100\%}{20\%} = 5$$

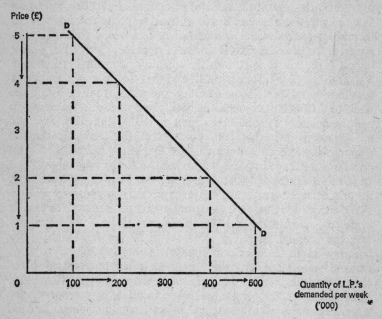

Figure 3.1 Price elasticity of demand for L.P. records

When the price of L.P. records falls from £5 to £4, it can be seen that there is a greater proportionate change in the quantity demanded than in price.[2] A word of warning about calculating the value of price elasticity of demand is needed before the analysis goes any further. It might seem intuitively reasonable to believe that had we

[2] The reader will observe immediately that the demand elasticity for tomatoes, in the example at the head of the page, is also 5, whereas that for newspapers is one twenty-fifth. Demand elasticities of less than unity are further considered below.

used a price of £4 as our starting point and calculated the value of price elasticity when the price of L.P. records rises from £4 to £5 we should get the same answer as before, i.e. five. But this belief would be misplaced, because using £4 as a base:

$$E = \frac{50\% \text{ (i.e. a fall from 200,000 per week to 100,000 per week)}}{25\% \text{ (i.e. a rise from £4 to £5)}}$$
$$= 2$$

Now again there has been a greater proportionate increase in quantity demanded than in price, but the value of price elasticity of demand is undoubtedly different. The reason for the conflict, which occurs even though we have taken measurements over the same range of the demand curve, is explained by the way we have used the formula for calculating price elasticity of demand. Strictly interpreted, the formula should be applied to very small movements along the demand curve, whereas we have used it to calculate price elasticity over a relatively wide portion of the demand curve.[3] In cases where it is not convenient to measure very small changes in price, we can avoid the ambiguities shown above by calculating price elasticity of demand on the basis of the average values of price and quantity demanded over the relevant portion of the demand curve.

If, for example, we analysed that portion of the demand curve from £5 to £4 and took the average price of £4.5 and the average quantity of 150,000 as our base figures, then measuring the elasticity of demand for a price change in either direction would give us the same result. That is, considering either a fall in price from £5 to £4 or a rise in price from £4 to £5,

$$E = \frac{100,000}{150,000} \div \frac{1.0^{4}}{4.5} \quad \text{where} \quad \begin{array}{l} 100,000 = \Delta Q \\ 150,000 = Q \\ 1.0 = \Delta P \\ 4.5 = P \end{array}$$
$$= 3$$

Again there is no doubt that over this range of the demand curve the proportionate change in quantity demanded is greater than the proportionate change in price whatever the direction of the price change. However, by using average values of price and quantity

---

[3] This is often referred to as *arc elasticity*, whereas the formula is really intended to measure elasticity at a particular *point* on the demand curve.

[4] The correct formula would now be $E = \dfrac{\Delta Q}{\dfrac{Q_1 + Q_2}{2}} \div \dfrac{\Delta P}{\dfrac{P_1 + P_2}{2}}$

to calculate price elasticity of demand, we have now removed the ambiguity shown up by our initial calculations.

We have so far calculated the price elasticity of demand for L.P. records when the price of L.P.s falls from £5 to £4. This does not mean to say, however, that the price elasticity of demand for L.P.s will always have the value of 3. In fact elasticity of demand will normally depend on the portion of the demand curve being analysed, and the result can be expected to change at different parts of the demand curve.[5]

If, as shown in Diagram 3.1, the price of L.P.s changed from £2 to £1, the resulting effect on the quantity demanded would be an increase from 400,000 per week to 500,000 per week. Again taking the average value of price and quantity as our base figures, the value of price elasticity of demand would be:

$$E = \frac{100,000}{450,000} \div \frac{1.0}{1.5} \qquad \text{where} \qquad \begin{aligned} 100,000 &= \Delta Q \\ 450,000 &= Q \\ 1.0 &= \Delta P \\ 1.5 &= P \end{aligned}$$
$$= \tfrac{1}{3}$$

On the portion of the demand curve between £2 and £1, the value of price elasticity of demand is one-third, which means that the proportionate increase in quantity demanded is less than the proportionate fall in price. We should therefore expect that a demand curve will exhibit different values of price elasticity depending on which part of the curve the market is actually operating. Indeed, on a linear demand curve price elasticity will take on a range of values from infinity (where it cuts the price axis) through one (at the mid-point along the curve) to zero (where it cuts the quantity axis). To prove this proposition consider the demand curve in Diagram 3.2.

Let us first compute price elasticity at point A which is exactly midway on the curve DD_1. For a very small price change from OP to OP_1,

$$E = \frac{QQ_1}{OQ} \div \frac{PP_1}{OP}$$
$$= \frac{CB}{OQ} \div \frac{AC}{QA} = \frac{CB}{AC} \times \frac{QA}{OQ}$$

Since ACB and AQD_1 are similar triangles, the expression CB/AC is equal to QD_1/AQ, and hence

$$E = \frac{QD_1}{AQ} \times \frac{QA}{OQ} = \frac{QD_1}{OQ}$$

[5] There are three exceptions to this – see below.

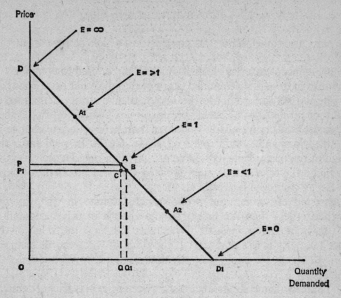

Figure 3.2 Values of price elasticity of demand range from infinity to zero

Since triangles AQD_1 and DPA are similar, $QD_1/OQ = AD_1/AD$, and therefore $E = AD_1/AD$.

Point A is located exactly half-way along curve DD_1, and so $AD_1 = AD$, giving a price elasticity value of one. At points on the curve to the left of the mid-point the coefficient of price elasticity will be greater than one. For example at A_1, $A_1D_1 > A_1D$ and so $A_1D_1/A_1D > 1$. Over the range of the curve to the right of the mid-point, price elasticity will be less than one. At A_2, $A_2D_1 < A_2D$, hence $A_2D_1/A_2D < 1$.

Where the curve cuts the price axis at point D, calculation of the coefficient of price elasticity requires us to divide DD_1 by zero, and so E is infinity. The fraction is reversed at point D_1, where price elasticity is found by dividing zero by DD_1, giving a value of zero.

Consequently, we cannot strictly say that a product has a specific value of price elasticity of demand, only that it has a value in relation to a specific change in price. In the case of a linear demand curve, price elasticity declines from infinity to zero along the curve from left to right.

There are some important conclusions which emerge from this analysis:

(*i*) The concept of price elasticity of demand is used to compare the response in quantity demanded of a good to different price changes, or alternatively to compare the response in quantity demanded of different products to a specific proportionate change in price. When a variation in price leads to a greater than proportionate change in quantity, demand is said to be **relatively elastic.** In such cases the value of the price elasticity will be greater than one. Hence we could say that if the price of L.P. records changed from £5 to £4 the demand for L.P.'s would be relatively elastic.

Alternatively, when the proportionate change in quantity demanded is less than the proportionate change in price, demand is said to be **relatively inelastic.** When this happens, the value of the price elasticity is less than one. If the price of L.P. records changed from £2 to £1, we could now say that demand would be relatively inelastic.

(*ii*) There are some important links between price elasticity of demand and total revenue or expenditure, where revenue is found by multiplying the number of units bought by the price of each unit. When the price of a good changes it is conceivable that total revenue will either increase, decrease or remain unaltered, with the actual effect depending on the value of the elasticity according to the following rules. When demand is relatively elastic, a fall in price will lead to an increase in total revenue, and a rise in price will lead to a fall in total revenue. These relationships are shown in Diagram 3.3.

We have already seen that demand for L.P. records is relatively elastic over the range from £5 to £4. When price falls from £5 to £4, total revenue from (or expenditure on) L.P.s increases. At a price of £5 total revenue is £5 × 100,000 = £500,000 and at £4 total revenue is £4 × 200,000 = £800,000. The reason for this increase in revenue is because the proportionate increase in quantity demanded is greater than the proportionate fall in price. In diagrammatic terms, total revenue is measured by the area of rectangles such as OPQR, or OSTV, since the distances OP and OS denote prices of £5 and £4 respectively, and OR and OV denote quantities 100,000 and 200,000 respectively. Rectangle OSTV is larger than rectangle OPQR, denoting the higher level of total expenditure on L.P. records when price falls from £5 to £4.

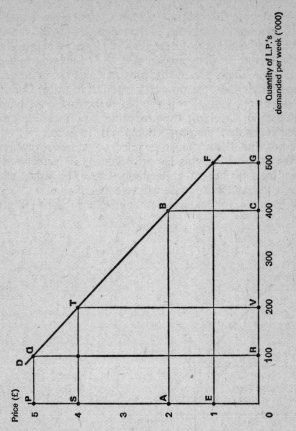

Figure 3.3 Relationships between price elasticities of demand and total expenditure or revenue

Conversely, when price rises from £4 to £5, total revenue falls from £800,000 to £500,000. This is because the proportionate fall in quantity demanded is greater than the proportionate rise in price when demand is relatively elastic.

When demand is relatively inelastic, a fall in price results in a fall in total revenue, and a rise in price results in a rise in total revenue. We have seen that the demand for L.P. records is inelastic over the range from £2 to £1. In Diagram 3.3 total revenue at £2 and £1 can be measured by the area of the rectangles OABC and OEFG respectively, of which the former is the larger. When demand is inelastic, therefore, a fall in price from £2 to £1 will lead to a decrease in total revenue simply because the proportionate rise in the quantity demanded is less than the proportionate fall in price. Conversely, a rise in price from £1 to £2 will result in an increase in total revenue; because demand is inelastic the proportionate decrease in quantity demanded is less than the proportionate rise in price.

(*iv*) It is possible that a change in price would leave total revenue exactly the same. When this happens demand is neither relatively elastic or inelastic but of **unitary elasticity.** The value of price elasticity of demand in this case will be equal to one.

In Diagram 3.4, for example, let us imagine a change in price of

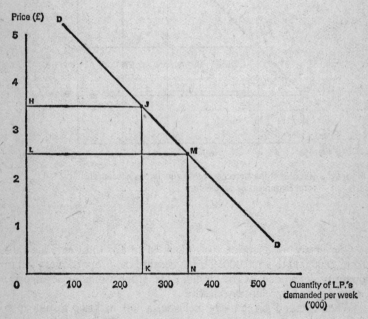

Figure 3.4 A price change leaves total revenue constant when demand is of unitary elasticity

L.P. records from £3.5 to £2.5, resulting in a change in quantity demanded from 250,000 to 350,000 per week. At both £3.5 (rectangle OHJK) and £2.5 (rectangle OLMN) total revenue is unchanged at £8,750,000. Using average values of price and quantity to compute price elasticity of demand,

$$E = \frac{100,000}{300,000} \div \frac{1.0}{3}$$

$$= 1.$$

where $\Delta Q = 100,000$
$Q = 300,000$
$\Delta P = 1.0$
$P = 3$

Since price elasticity of demand is equal to unity, the proportionate change in quantity demanded is just equal to the proportionate change in price, and so total revenue at each price is exactly equal (OHJK = OLMN). There are three limiting cases of interest which show the conditions under which price elasticity of demand is equal to zero, infinity and one throughout the whole length of a demand curve.

In Diagram 3.5(a), the demand curve DD is drawn as a vertical line. By inspecting this demand curve it can be seen that quantity demanded always remains the same (i.e. at OQ) at all price levels. If we computed the value of price elasticity of demand for any price change, the numerator in our formula would always be zero since no change in quantity demanded takes place. Hence the value of price elasticity of demand would be zero over all parts of the demand curve. When a price change results in no change in quantity demanded, demand is said to be **perfectly inelastic.**

In Diagram 3.5(b) the demand curve D_1D_1 is drawn as a horizontal line. We can infer from this that if price was set at a level of OP consumers would wish to buy all they could possibly get at that price. For any other price, the quantity demanded would be zero. Hence, if, for example, price changed from OP_1 to OP, quantity demanded would change from zero to an infinite amount, and so the value of price elasticity of demand would be equal to infinity. When the demand curve is horizontal it is said that demand is **perfectly elastic.**

The demand curve D_2D_2 in Diagram 3.5(c) illustrates the idea of **unitary elasticity** which we also dealt with in the previous section in relation to a point on a linear demand curve. However, the demand curve D_2D_2 is a special limiting case of unitary elasticity since this is the value of price elasticity over all ranges of the curve. For this to be so, any two rectangles under the demand curve must have the

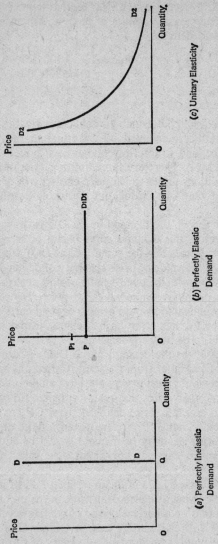

Figure 3.5 Three limiting cases of price elasticity of demand

same area since if price elasticity is always equal to one, total revenue must remain unchanged for any price change. The curve D_2D_2 has such properties, and is given the special name of a **rectangular hyperbola**.

Since we have now examined the definition and measurement of price elasticity of demand, we can summarise our findings in tabular form as shown in Table 3.2.

Table 3.2   **Range of Values for Price Elasticity of Demand**

Perfectly Inelastic $E = 0$	*Unit Elasticity* $E = 1$	*Perfectly Elastic* $E = \infty$
Relatively Inelastic $E < 1$ (a) Demand Curve downward sloping, where percentage price change > percentage change in quantity demanded. (b) Total revenue rises when price rises; total revenue falls when price falls.	*Relatively Elastic* $E > 1$ (a) Demand Curve downward sloping, where percentage price change < percentage change in quantity demanded. (b) Total revenue rises when price falls; total revenue falls when price rises.	

The Determinants of Price Elasticity of Demand

The most important determinant of the value of price elasticity of demand for a product is the degree to which it has available and acceptable substitutes. Goods which have many substitutes tend to have a relatively elastic demand, since a rise in their prices will induce consumers to switch to the available alternatives, resulting in a greater than proportionate fall in the quantity demanded. Goods which do not have ready substitutes tend to have a relatively inelastic demand. A given price change tends to lead to a less than proportionate change in quantity demanded because consumers cannot easily buy goods which perform similar functions.

Of course, much depends on how a 'product' is defined. The demand for food as a general category of product is extremely inelastic for the very obvious reason that substitutes are difficult to find. But beneath the general heading of 'food' we might expect to find some products with relatively higher elasticities of demand than others. When the United Kingdom first joined the European Economic Community, the price of beef rose suddenly. A large number of consumers responded by switching their purchases towards other forms of meat which were considered adequate substitutes. By contrast we would not expect the demand for cigarettes to respond very much to a change in price; demand is very inelastic since acceptable substitutes (including abstention) are few.

Price elasticity of demand can also depend on the proportion of consumers' incomes spent on the good. In the case of goods which account for an extremely small proportion of income, we would not normally expect that demand would be very responsive to price changes. Most people, for example, write a number of letters and postcards every year but their total outlay in stamps will be very small in relation to their total income. Hence a rise in the price of postage stamps will not have a very noticeable effect on the quantity of letters and postcards sent every year.

Price elasticity of demand can also vary with the period of time elapsing between a price change and its effects. Consumers often take time to adjust their pattern of purchases and discover the possibilities of substituting other goods for the one whose price has risen. Hence it may well be the case that the demand for some products becomes more elastic as time passes.

We can now analyse more effectively the example of the fare increase on Red Arrow buses illustrated at the beginning of the chapter. Remember that on each service revenue was estimated to have risen after a rise in the fare level from 6d to 9d. Now we have established that if revenue rises as a result of an increase in price, demand is relatively inelastic. There is therefore a good case for believing that the demand for Red Arrow bus services was relatively inelastic over this range of fare levels. The proportionate fall in the number of journeys undertaken must have been less than the proportionate rise in fares, thus increasing total revenue.

An incidental point of interest is that local authorities all over Britain often debate whether more revenue from bus services would be gained by raising or by reducing fares. At heart, these debates actually depend on the values of price elasticity of demand for bus services which are assumed to exist. Those who argue that more revenue would result from an increase in fares obviously believe that demand is relatively inelastic. Those who believe that increased revenue would occur through lowering fares must believe that the proportionate increase in the number of bus journeys undertaken would be greater than the proportionate fall in price, and hence that demand is relatively elastic.

Price Elasticity of Demand and Taxation of Goods

The concept of price elasticity of demand can be of great value in estimating the effects of levying a tax on products. The following example gives an illustration of this. Columns one and two of Table 3.3 show the quantity of L.P. records supplied at various prices. Now let us suppose that the government imposed a tax of £1 on every record sold, which in practice means that sellers would have to subtract £1 from the price of every record and pay this to the government in tax.

Table 3.3   Effect of £1 Tax on Supply Conditions for L.P. Records

1 Price (£)	2 Quantity Supplied	3 Revenue (£)	4 Desired Revenue After Tax (£)	5 Desired Price (£)
1	100,000	100,000	200,000	2
2	200,000	400,000	600,000	3
3	300,000	900,000	1,200,000	4
4	400,000	1,600,000	2,000,000	5
5	500,000	2,500,000	3,000,000	6

Column three shows the total revenue to *sellers* from sales at every price. For example, if records were to be priced at £1 each, 100,000 would be supplied per week and total revenue would be £100,000. After the tax is imposed, however, sellers would have to pay the government £100,000 in tax on sales of 100,000 and therefore to leave themselves no worse off than before they would like to achieve revenue of £200,000. This amount is shown in column four. The only way this level of total revenue could be obtained by sellers is if they offered 100,000 L.P.s for sale every week at a price of £2 instead of £1 as before. This new *desired* level of price is shown in column five.

Similarly, if the price of records had been £2 each, sellers' total revenue would have been £400,000. But sellers would have to pay £200,000 in tax on sales of 200,000, and so their desired level of total revenue would be £600,000 (£200,000 for tax and £400,000 to leave them just as well off as before). The desired price for sales of 200,000 in order to obtain total revenue of £600,000 would therefore be £3.

The overall effect, then, of a tax of £1 per unit is to change the desired level of price for each quantity of records offered for sale. In graphical terms (Diagram 3.6), the effects of plotting out the information in columns one, two and five can be seen as a parallel upward shift of the supply curve at every point, indicating that sellers would like to sell the original quantities for £1 more than the original price.

In Diagram 3.6, the supply curve shifts from SS to S_1S_1 as a result of the tax. This does not mean to say, however, that sellers are *able* to increase the price of records by £1 from the original equilibrium level of £3. A supply curve on its own merely signifies sellers' *intentions* – what quantities of a good they would like to sell at various prices. To find out what actually happens to the price and quantity of records bought and sold after the tax is imposed, we have to look at supply and demand together, as in Diagram 3.6. It can be seen that the price of records rises from £3 to £3.75 (i.e. by less than the full amount of the tax). Consumers therefore have to pay three-quarters of the tax in the form of higher prices, but the after-tax price received by sellers also falls by one-quarter of the amount of tax [i.e. from £3 to £2.75 (£3.75–£1)].

The extent to which a tax-induced price change is borne by consumers depends on the price elasticity of demand. If, for example, the demand for records had been much more elastic, as shown by the curve D_1D_1, then the market price would only have risen to £3.25 after the tax. Consequently only one-quarter of the tax would have been passed on to consumers in the form of higher prices, the remaining three-quarters being borne by sellers (after tax, the price received by sellers falls from £3 to £2.25). More generally, we can say that whenever the demand for a product is relatively inelastic, the majority of the tax will be passed on to consumers in the form of higher prices. When demand is relatively elastic, the majority of the tax will be borne by producers.

The limiting cases where the full tax is paid by consumers in the form of higher prices, or where the full tax is borne completely by sellers because price does not rise at all after the tax, are found where the demand for a product is completely inelastic or completely elastic. In Diagram 3.7, for example, we can see that the

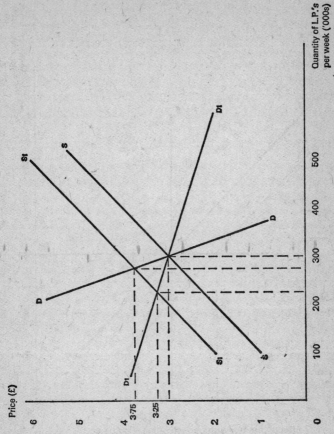

Figure 3.6 Effects of a tax with different price elasticities of demand

effect of the tax on a product whose demand curve is D_3D_3 (i.e. perfectly inelastic) is to raise price from £3 to £4, in other words by the full amount of the tax, with no change in quantity bought and sold (300,000 per week). Conversely, if the demand curve for a product was represented by D_4D_4 which is perfectly elastic, the

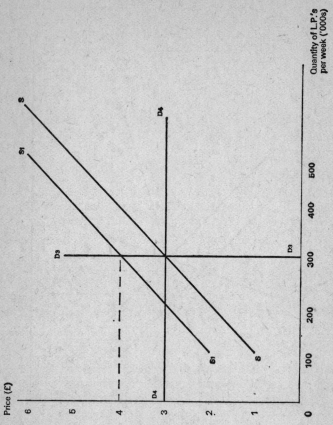

Figure 3.7 Effects of a tax with perfectly inelastic and elastic
demand

full tax would be borne by sellers since the price remains at £3 after
the tax is imposed, and record sales fall to 200,000 per week.

So far we have considered the incidence of a tax, or its effect in
raising prices paid by consumers and reducing producer receipts.
However, this is only one of the effects of putting a tax on a commodity. If we look at changes in the quantity of the good bought and
sold we can add another dimension to our analysis.

Except where demand is completely inelastic, a tax has the effect of lowering the quantity of the product bought and sold, as shown in the examples considered above. In response to the lower output being produced, sellers of the product may decide to reduce the number of people they employ, so the first wider economic effect of the tax might be to create some unemployment in the industry producing the good. Clearly, the more elastic the demand for the good the more the quantity supplied and demanded will fall and so the greater will be the effect on unemployment. Further, should the product have a close complement (e.g. records and record-players), there will be a fall in demand for the complement product, probably resulting in a fall in output in the industry making it as well.

Total revenue received by the government will also be affected. In the simple case which we are considering, the total revenue received by the government will be higher the greater the quantity of the good bought and sold. For example, in Diagram 3.6, the more inelastic the demand curve the higher will be the quantity bought and sold after the tax. Hence when governments are looking for revenue from taxes on products, they often choose to rely on products like cigarettes and whisky. Since such products have a relatively inelastic demand, consumers do not tend to switch their purchases to other goods due to the lack of acceptable substitutes.[6]

Other Elasticities of Demand

Although we have so far concentrated on the price elasticity of demand, it is often useful to know how demand may respond to changes in some of its other determinants such as income and the price of other products.

Income Elasticity of Demand

The concept of **income elasticity of demand** measures the response of demand to changes in consumers' *real* incomes (i.e. assuming that prices remain constant), and is given by the formula:

$$\text{Income Elasticity of Demand} = \frac{\text{Proportionate Change in Quantity Demanded}}{\text{Proportionate Change in Income}}$$

[6] For a further discussion on taxation, *see* G. H. Peters, *Private and Public Finance*, Ch. 10.

It should be noticed that income elasticities are normally positive – an increase in income results in increased demand. Our interest then tends to focus on the magnitude of the coefficient. When the proportionate rise in the quantity demanded of a good is greater than the proportionate rise in income, income elasticity will have a value of more than one and the demand for the good is said to be **income-elastic.** Conversely, when the proportionate rise in the quantity demanded of a good is less than the proportionate rise in income, income elasticity will have a value of less than one and the demand for the good is said to be **income-inelastic.**

In some cases, however, we may sometimes find a negative elasticity, with the quantity demanded actually falling as income rises. In the case of **inferior products** (referred to previously in Chapter 2) consumers have the opportunity, given a rise in income, of replacing their purchases of such goods with more desirable commodities fulfilling the same broad function. It is conventionally thought, for example, that margarine has a negative income elasticity since, as incomes rise, consumers decrease their purchases in favour of butter which is usually more expensive.

As consumers' incomes rise, fundamental changes in their purchasing habits can occur. At relatively low income levels, consumers tend to spend the bulk of their money on necessities such as food. As incomes increase, however, we would not expect the demand for foodstuffs to rise even proportionately to income.

It is sometimes argued that, as a general rule, the demand for necessities tends to be income-inelastic whereas the demand for luxuries tends to be income-elastic. We need, however, to be more specific about the word 'luxuries' because attitudes towards goods and services change at different income levels. Motor cars were once regarded as luxuries, but are now regarded as necessities by a high proportion of families in Britain. There is probably a critical income range which, when reached, transforms the demand for a good (and also the nature of a good) from a luxury to a necessity. Evidence of this has already been seen in the USA with the massive increase in demand for what are known as consumer durables – cars, fridges, TV sets, washing machines, etc. – in the 1950s and in Britain in the 1960s. While the demand for these goods is still rising faster than incomes, more recently some of the highest income elasticities of demand have been found in the service industries – banking, insurance, entertainment, hotels, etc.

Cross Elasticity of Demand

It is also useful to be able to analyse the effect on the demand for a product of a change in the price of other items. How can we measure the effect of a change in the price of cars on the quantity of car radios demanded? What will be the effect of a rise in the price of records on the sales of cassette tapes?

The concept needed is that of the **cross elasticity of demand** given by the formula:

Cross Elasticity = Proportionate Change in Quantity Demanded
of Demand   of Good A
           ————————————————————————————
           Proportionate Change in Price of Good B

The value of cross elasticity of demand may be either positive or negative, depending on whether the goods concerned are substitutes or complements. For example, if the price of gas rose we would normally expect an increase in the quantity of electricity demanded, on the assumption that gas and electricity provide rival forms of heating and so can be considered as substitutes. Hence the cross elasticity of demand in this case would be positive since the price and quantity changes move in the same direction. An increase in the price of electrical appliances such as hair dryers, cookers, electric heaters, etc., would tend to lead to a fall in the quantity of electricity demanded since electricity and electrical appliances can be regarded as complements. Hence the value of cross elasticity of demand would be negative since the price and quantity changes have opposite algebraic signs.

Whether or not the actual value of cross elasticity of demand is high depends on the strength of substitutability or complementarity between the two goods. The higher the degree of substitutability or complementarity the higher we would expect the value of cross elasticity of demand to be (both in positive and negative terms).

Elasticity of Supply

The concept of elasticity can also be used to measure the response of the supply of a product to a change in price. Elasticity of supply is then calculated according to the following formula:

Elasticity = Proportionate Change in Quantity Supplied
of Supply   ————————————————————————————
             Proportionate Change in Price

As long as the supply curve for a product slopes upwards from left to right, changes in price and quantity supplied will take place in the same direction, and so we would expect the values of elasticity of supply to be positive. Elasticity of supply would be infinity where the supply curve is perfectly elastic (i.e. a horizontal straight line), and zero where the supply curve is perfectly inelastic (i.e. a vertical straight line). A special case of unitary elasticity of supply is found where the supply curve is a straight line with a forty-five degree angle at the origin, because the value of elasticity of supply will be equal to one at all points on this supply curve.

Given these critical values, we can classify the elasticity of supply of a product according to whether its value is greater than or less than one. If the percentage change in quantity supplied is greater than the percentage change in price, elasticity of supply is greater than one and we say that supply is *relatively elastic*. Conversely, if the percentage change in quantity supplied is less than the percentage change in price, elasticity of supply is less than one and we say that supply is *relatively inelastic*.

Determinants of Elasticity of Supply

Elasticity of supply is primarily determined by the ease with which producers can adapt their plant and equipment to adjust to changes in the price of a commodity. In some cases, for example, producers have very quick access to the additional resources required to increase output, and so there might be a fairly swift response to a price rise. In other cases, however, adaptation may be less easy. This would occur if production required the use of precision-made capital equipment which takes time to order, install and set in operation. In such cases, we would expect that it would take longer for supply to respond to the price change.

Hence it is the passage of time (reflecting the ease or otherwise of adaptability) which will basically determine the extent to which the supply of a good is relatively elastic or inelastic. In short, elasticity of supply can be expected to take on different values as time passes. For this reason economists often make an analytical distinction between the three time periods – the market period, the short-run and the long-run.[7]

---

[7] A much fuller analysis of production conditions under different time periods is found in Chs. 7–9.

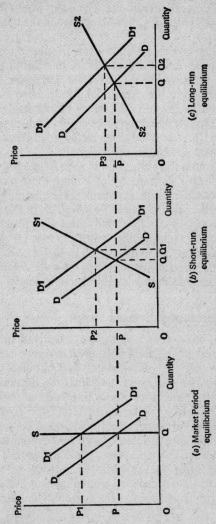

Figure 3.8 Elasticity of supply in different time-periods

Let us suppose that the demand for a product rises from DD to D_1D_1 as shown in Diagram 3.8(a). Now it may be that for some period of time the supply curve is completely inelastic (SS), indicating that producers are initially unable to expand supply at all to meet the new demand conditions. The effect would therefore be a rise in price from OP to OP_1, but no change in the quantity bought and sold (OQ).

After some time has elapsed, however, production plans may be adjusted, perhaps by employing more labour or asking the existing labour force to work overtime. The result is that the supply curve begins to shift round to the right, taking on a more elastic form as shown by S_1S_1 in Diagram 3.8(b). More output has now begun to be supplied (OQ to OQ_1) and the price is OP_2 – which is higher than the original price OP, but not as high as the price OP_1 reached when supply was inelastic in the market period.

When existing producers have had time to adjust fully their whole scale of operations – perhaps by extending their factories or installing more machinery – or new firms have entered the market – the supply curve becomes more elastic still (S_2S_2 in Diagram 3.8(c)). The quantity supplied (and bought) has expanded further still (from OQ_1 to OQ_2), and the market price is now OP_3 – still higher than the original price OP, but lower than the price in the previous two periods. Thus elasticity of supply is basically determined by the amount of time producers take to adjust to a change in price.

Empirical Measurement of Demand Curves

For many years now, economists have attempted to see whether demand curves resembling those postulated in theory can be observed in practice. Deriving 'real' demand curves is extremely useful for it enables us to analyse the extent to which the demand for certain goods is relatively elastic or relatively inelastic and to attach precise numerical values to the coefficient of elasticity. To conclude our two-chapter survey of supply and demand theory, it is worth mentioning some of the problems faced by economists who try to measure demand curves in practice. There are pitfalls surrounding the process and eager students who wish to try to trace out the demand curve for a product by obtaining real-life data relating quantities bought at different prices should be warned of their existence!

If, for example, we were to record the amounts of milk bought and sold annually at certain prices between 1970 and 1973,[8] we would derive points on a graph as shown in Diagram 3.9. Does this mean that we have discovered a product which provides an exception to the normal downward-sloping demand curve? The answer must be 'no', because of the fundamentally important fact that the observed data does not necessarily provide us with the type of information on which demand curves are based. It should be remembered that a demand curve is a schedule of consumers' *intentions*; it indicates the quantity of a good people would buy if various prices were to operate, assuming other determinants of demand remain constant. Thus though the actual data shows the amounts bought and sold at certain prices at particular points in time we can never be sure that price is the only operative variable. Basically any price and quantity combination which we observe represents only one point on both a demand curve and a supply curve, i.e. the equilibrium point. However, over the time-period which our observations cover, other determinants of demand (and supply) may have been changing. In fact there are two possible explanations of data such as that which we have seen for milk. These are illustrated in Diagram 3.10(*a*) and (*b*).

In Diagram 3.10(*a*), successively higher price–quantity observations (points A, B, C and D) have come about because, over time, the demand curve has been shifting out to the right intersecting an unchanging supply curve. In turn this might have been due to a host of factors such as changes in incomes, tastes, etc., as already shown in Chapter 2. So, in effect, we have the paradoxical result that our attempts to observe the demand curve for a product might result in our tracing out the path of the supply curve – SS in Diagram 3.10(*a*).

It could be the case, however, that each of our observations (such as points E, F, G, H in Diagram 3.10(*b*)) has resulted from the intersection of a series of demand and supply curves which are both shifting through time. Simply joining up these points of intersection does not reveal either a demand curve or a supply curve!

It can therefore be seen that there is sometimes great difficulty in actually identifying a demand curve for a product on the basis of data about prices and quantities, and not surprisingly economists refer to this difficulty as the **identification problem.**[9] The easiest

---

[8] Based on Milk Marketing Board, Annual Report and Accounts for year ended 31 March 1973, pp. 17, 18.

[9] The problem is further complicated in markets where the prices we observe are *not* equilibrium ones, but this difficulty is too sophisticated for treatment in this text.

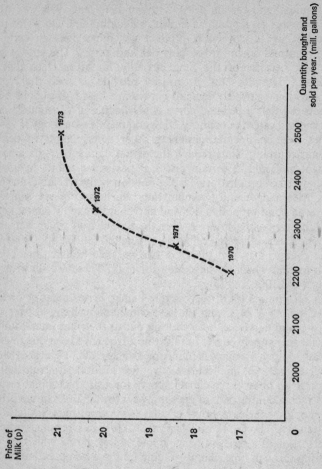

Figure 3.9 Price and quantity data for milk 1970-73

conditions for the identification problem to be overcome are often found in agricultural markets, where, as shown in Diagram 3.10(c), the price–quantity observations often arise from a shifting supply curve due to factors like harvest fluctuations and diseases, against a background of constant demand. Consequently the path of the demand curve is traced out.

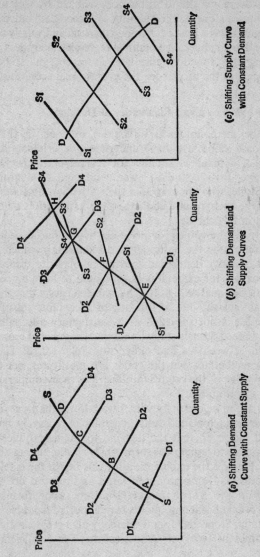

Figure 3.10 The identification problem

(a) Shifting Demand Curve with Constant Supply

(b) Shifting Demand and Supply Curves

(e) Shifting Supply Curve with Constant Demand

The successful estimation of demand curves relies on economists' ability to overcome the identification problem by isolating the influence of price alone on the quantity of a good demanded from data which might reflect a host of changing demand and supply conditions. A statistical technique called **multiple regression analysis** is capable of performing this function and has, in recent years, become an essential part of the toolkit for the professional economist.

Empirical Evidence about Elasticities of Demand

Despite the methodological difficulties outlined in the previous section, some economists have undertaken experiments to estimate the value of demand elasticities for several products. One of the most famous British studies[10] was conducted by a group led by Richard Stone, who concentrated their attention on food products. By and large their results confirmed the assumption of the theory developed in this chapter.

Virtually all the values for price elasticities had a negative sign, thereby confirming the basic demand relationship which illustrates price and quantity demanded moving in opposite directions. The demand for tea, for example was estimated to have a coefficient of price elasticity equal to —0.27. This value suggests that the demand for tea was inelastic due to the lack of acceptable substitutes (obviously coffee is not regarded as a satisfactory alternative by tea drinkers). Indeed Stone's study found that the value of cross elasticity of demand between tea and coffee was only +0.18. The positive sign confirms the fact that the goods are substitutes, but the smallness in the value of the coefficient illustrates their comparatively low degree of substitutability.

Most of the price elasticity values were lower than one, indicating that the demand for foodstuffs generally is relatively inelastic. It was found, however, that the demand for home-produced mutton and lamb (taken together) was surprisingly elastic, having a coefficient of —1.74. Perhaps the explanation for this lies in the categorisation of the products. Home-produced lamb and mutton do have close substitutes in the British market since the same forms of meat (although often of different quality) are imported from New Zealand and Australia. Stone also found relatively high cross elasticity values between different types of British meats. The coefficient between

---

[10] *Measurement of Consumers' Expenditure and Behaviour in the United Kingdom, 1920–38* (Cambridge University Press, 1954).

mutton and lamb on the one hand and beef and veal on the other hand was +1.61, suggesting quite a high degree of substitutability.

It was noted earlier that foodstuffs would tend to be income-inelastic, and this prediction was certainly borne out by Stone's work. Tea had a coefficient of income elasticity of only 0.04, while that for mutton and lamb was 0.7, suggesting that the quantity demand of these products increased less than in proportion to consumers' incomes.

Although most income-elasticity values were positive, margarine fitted into our inferior product stereotype with a negative coefficient of −0.16, indicating that consumers' preferences turned towards butter as incomes rose. Similarly, the income elasticity of demand for condensed milk was also shown to be negative (with a coefficient of −0.78), as a result, presumably, of many consumers of condensed milk transferring their purchases towards milk or cream.

Conclusion

Richard Stone's calculations represent one of the most successful attempts to derive values for the different types of elasticity of demand. Studies have been conducted in other countries and on a range of products other than foodstuffs, and readers who are interested in seeing how economists have tackled the problem of estimating 'real' demand curves can consult the references at the end of the text.

Chapter 4

Analysis of Consumer Behaviour

We have so far looked at the way in which economists analyse the working of a market. By considering the interaction of demand and supply, and their basic determinants, we were able to reach some important conclusions and predictions. Some of the most significant concepts in microeconomics, however, can only be discovered when we penetrate more deeply into the forces that underlie demand and supply.

In this chapter we will deal first with a more detailed analysis of consumer demand. Clearly, the simple concept of a downward sloping market demand curve leaves too many important questions unanswered. Why is it that consumers tend to buy more of a product at lower prices? Can we say whether a particular consumer is, in some sense, 'getting the most' out of his income by choosing a particular set of purchases? Might the consumer not be better off buying more of one good and less of another? To answer these questions we have to look at the methods by which economists analyse consumer behaviour.

At first glance, it might seem quite an heroic achievement, or a piece of impertinence, for economists to claim access to a theory of consumer behaviour. The word 'behaviour', after all, suggests that this might be a field better suited to investigation by psychologists. Indeed consumer behaviour is a legitimate and well-established area of psychological study. Consumers have basic physiological and psychological wants. Marketing divisions of companies spend large sums of money identifying these wants, and trying to convince consumers that their product fulfils them. Is human motivation not the proper corner-stone of a theory of human behaviour?

The answer really is 'perhaps', depending upon which particular aspect of consumer behaviour we wish to explain. The economist approaches the explanation of consumer behaviour from a different standpoint to that of the psychologist or the market researcher. For the economist, wants are usually placed under the general heading of 'tastes', which was discussed in Chapter 2, and assumed to be *given*. Admittedly, tastes may differ from consumer to consumer.

We know, for example, that the Scots consume more bread, cakes, scones and soup per week than the average for people in the United Kingdom as a whole. We also know that the Scots consume fewer vegetables (especially fresh vegetables) and fruit than the United Kingdom average.[1] But to the economist such differences in tastes are relevant only in so far as they affect the quantity of goods and services people are prepared to buy, and in the effect which changing tastes have on consumer demand. The economic theory of consumer behaviour is primarily concerned with the fundamental problem of choice – explaining how consumers, faced with limited resources of income, choose between the different types of goods and services which they could buy. But it is important to note that economists do make one fundamental general assumption about the motivation behind consumer behaviour. This is that consumers, in allocating their limited income between different goods and services, attempt to maximise the satisfaction derived from the variety of purchases which they can make.

The whole approach, then, of the economist in the field of consumer behaviour can initially be seen by setting out the question which the theory of consumer demand attempts to answer:

> Given certain assumptions about tastes and income levels, under what conditions will consumers arrange their purchases of all the goods and services available to them in order to maximise their satisfaction?

Utility

For over a hundred years, beginning with the work of economists such as Jevons and Walras, the theory of consumer demand has been rooted in the fundamental concept of **utility**, which means the amount of satisfaction a consumer derives from the goods and services he buys. Early attempts to clarify the concept were frequently confounded by a confusion between **total** and **marginal** utility. Total utility represents the satisfaction a consumer gains from his overall consumption of a certain good or service. By contrast, marginal utility (where the concept of the margin, widely used in economic analysis, means a small change in the quantity of some variable) denotes the satisfaction afforded by consuming a

---

[1] *See* C. D. Harbury, Ch. 1, for a fuller explanation of different consumer expenditure patterns.

little more or a little less of a commodity than the consumer already has. An example should make the distinction clear.

Let us imagine two consumers, A and B, who, amongst all their other purchases, buy a certain quantity of meat and records every month. It is likely that for both of them the total utility from meat consumption would be higher than the total utility of records bought. But we could not so easily predict how A and B would rate the marginal utility of an extra steak or an extra record per month. A critical determinant would be the current rate of consumption of the two products. For example, if consumer A was already eating meat on twenty-eight days of each month an extra steak might yield a low marginal utility, whereas the satisfaction gained from an additional record might be high if he was in the habit of buying only one per month.

Our expectation that the marginal utility of an extra unit of a good would be low when someone already has a large quantity but high when the quantity is small leads to the important **hypothesis of diminishing marginal utility.** This states that as a person's consumption of a product increases, the total utility derived will increase at a diminishing rate, i.e. marginal utility declines as extra units are bought. Recalling consumer A again, the above hypothesis simply proposes that if he increased his purchases of records from one to five per month, the total utility gained from five records would be greater than from one, but each *successive* record would make a smaller addition to total utility – the greatest increase in total utility coming from the first.

The hypothesis of diminishing marginal utility provides a general answer to the problem of specifying the conditions for an individual to maximise satisfaction from the purchase of a range of goods and services, and it also helps to explain why demand curves normally slope downwards. To discover the rule for maximising utility, let us suppose that consumer A was buying relative quantities of meat and records so that the utility from the last penny spent on meat was twice the utility gained from the last penny allocated to records. His total satisfaction could be improved by rearranging his expenditure so that he purchased more meat and fewer records. This would, in turn, lower the marginal utility of meat (since he would have more than before) and raise the marginal utility of records (since his stock would be lower). The gap between the marginal utility from the last penny spent on meat and records would thus narrow as he continued to buy more meat and fewer records until the marginal utility gained from the last penny allocated to each was exactly equal. Only when this happens will the consumer be unable to increase total utility by any further reallocation of expenditure and so his satisfaction will be maximised.

If we denote the marginal utility of the last purchase of meat by MUm and its price by Pm, and let similar measures for records be MUr and Pr, then we can express formally the condition for maximising utility as

$$\frac{MUm}{Pm} = \frac{MUr}{Pr}, \quad \text{or alternatively,}$$

$$\frac{MUm}{MUr} = \frac{Pm}{Pr}$$

Although we have dealt so far with only two commodities, it is easy to extend the logic of the expression above to cover more than this number. To obtain maximum utility from the consumption of many goods and services, a consumer will so allocate his expenditure that the marginal utility derived from the last penny spent on all goods and services is equal, i.e.

$$\frac{Mum}{Pm} = \frac{MUr}{Pr} = \ldots \frac{MUx}{Px}, \quad \text{where x denotes the number of commodities purchased.}$$

The second major contribution made by the hypothesis of diminishing marginal utility is in explaining the downward-sloping shape of demand curves. Let us assume that consumer A's expenditure on records forms a very small percentage of his total income, so that any marginal increase or decrease in his spending on records will not affect the marginal utilities gained from other goods and services. Now let us examine what would happen to the utility-maximising condition if the price of records fell. If A was allocating his expenditure on meat and records so that

$$\frac{MUm}{Pm} = \frac{MUr}{Pr}, \quad \text{a decrease in record prices will now mean that}$$

$$\frac{MUm}{Pm} < \frac{MUr}{Pr} \quad \text{(since Pr has become smaller, the expression MUr/Pr must be greater than before).}$$

If he wishes to achieve maximum utility again, we can see clearly that the value of MUr will have to be lowered until equality is reestablished. Of course this is easily done by buying more records, thereby diminishing their marginal utility. Hence a fall in the price of records would induce a higher level of record sales – a relationship expressed in the downward-sloping demand curve.

The Measurement of Utility

Although there would be general agreement about the logic of the propositions outlined above, economists are far from unanimous about the way in which the concept of utility might be measured. Basically, the debate revolves round the issue of whether it is possible to give a precise value to the quantity of satisfaction obtained from the consumption of goods and services. In other words, can 'units of utility' be measured in the same way as we measure units of money, weight, length and so on?

One school of thought argued that such quantification was possible, and based their case on what is known as the **cardinal approach** to the measurement of utility. This, for example, would enable us to say that consumer A derived ten units of utility from the first record bought, eight from the second, five from the third, etc. Hence not only could we give a precise figure to marginal utility, but, because units of measurement are additive, we could calculate the total utility of any number of records – e.g. 10 when 1 is purchased, 18 from 2 records, 23 from 3, etc. Cardinal measurement could also provide a standard of comparison because we could say, perhaps, that consumer A gets four more units of utility from the last penny spent on records than on meat.

A more modern approach to the theory of consumer behaviour, called the **ordinal approach,** believes that measurement of utility can only be done by a ranking system. Its proponents argue that we simply cannot measure directly the quantification of utility which goes on in people's minds. The ordinal system is based on a procedure of ranking the total satisfaction obtained from different combinations of goods and services according to whether they give a consumer higher or lower levels of satisfaction. Hence this approach rejects the claim that we could either measure how much satisfaction (in units of utility) was gained by a consumer from 4 records and 8 steaks per month or 5 records and 7 steaks per month, or even that we could say by how much 4 records and 8 steaks were preferred to 5 records and 7 steaks, or vice versa. It is only possible by the ordinal system to determine whether a consumer prefers the combination of 4 records and 8 steaks to that of 5 records and 7 steaks, or vice-versa, or whether he receives equal satisfaction from either combination.

The concept of utility, measured ordinally, is integrated into a theory of consumer behaviour to provide an answer to the question of the conditions necessary for a consumer to maximise satisfaction from his purchases of goods and services. It is based on an analytical technique called an **indifference curve.**

Indifference Curves

Let us suppose we wanted to know how a particular consumer would rank various bundles of two goods, chocolates and biscuits, according to the level of satisfaction obtained. We assume that the consumer will prefer any bundle which gives him more of one good and at least no less of the other good. In Diagram 4.1 the vertical axis measures pounds of chocolates per week, and the horizontal axis measures pounds of biscuits per week. The points A, B, C, D, E, F, G, H and X each represent a possible bundle of chocolates and biscuits. Suppose we asked this consumer how, on the basis of the level of satisfaction obtained, he would rank each of these bundles in relation, for example, to point X, where he would have 4 pounds of chocolates and 5 pounds of biscuits per week.

On the basis of the assumption just made he will prefer to be at points D, E and F than at point X. At point D, he would have more chocolates than at X (i.e. 6 pounds instead of 4 pounds) and just the same quantity of biscuits (i.e. 5 pounds). Point E would also give more satisfaction than point X since he would have more of both goods (i.e. 5 pounds of chocolates and 7 pounds of biscuits). He would also rather be at point F than point X since he would have just as many chocolates (4 pounds) but more biscuits (8 pounds instead of 5 pounds).

Conversely, we can say that he would derive more satisfaction from point X than either points A or H, both of which would give him less of both chocolates and biscuits. But what can we say about points such as B, C and G, where, compared with X, the consumer has more of one good but less of another? At B, for example, he would have more chocolates than at X (6 pounds instead of 4 pounds) but fewer biscuits (4 pounds instead of 5 pounds). It is possible that points B, C and G give more satisfaction than X, less satisfaction than X, or that the satisfaction from one or more of these points

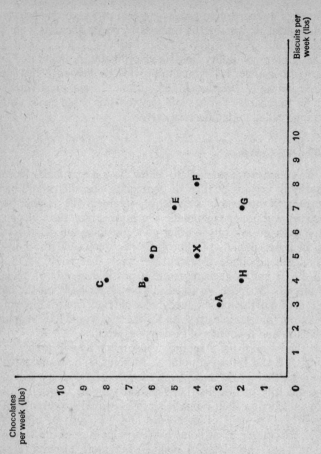

Figure 4.1 Combinations of chocolates and biscuits

and point X is exactly the same. Everything depends on the consumer's relative tastes for chocolates and biscuits.

Now if we knew this consumer's preferences between a very large number of bundles of chocolates and biscuits, the results might be as shown in Diagram 4.2. All the bundles of chocolates and biscuits preferred to X are located in the heavily shaded area, whereas all the bundles less preferred than X are found in the lightly shaded area. There will be a boundary between the two zones, and obviously on this boundary the consumer will derive equal satisfaction from each of the bundles of chocolates and biscuits. We say that the consumer is indifferent between X and any of the other points on the boundary line; and the boundary line which runs through X is called an **indifference curve** (II).

The indifference curve in Diagram 4.2 shows that this consumer would derive equal satisfaction from point X (4 pounds of chocolates and 5 pounds of biscuits), point B (6 pounds of chocolates and 4 pounds of biscuits), point G (2 pounds of chocolates and 7 pounds of biscuits) and every other point on the curve. Notice that by drawing a smooth curve, we have made the simplifying assumption that chocolates and biscuits are perfectly divisible.

The Shape of the Indifference Curve

The indifference curve in Diagram 4.2 is very steep at the left and becomes less steep until it is nearly horizontal. It is therefore said to be **convex** to the origin. As a consumer 'moves down' the indifference curve from left to right he is giving up chocolates but gaining more biscuits. The implication of the convex shape is that he retains the same level of satisfaction while sacrificing fewer and fewer chocolates per biscuit gained. The following example illustrates the point.

Along the indifference curve in Diagram 4.3, 4 bundles of chocolates and biscuits are represented by the points B, X, Y and G. By definition the consumer derives the same level of satisfaction from each bundle. Let us suppose the consumer actually had a bundle of 6 pounds of chocolates and 4 pounds of biscuits, as at point B. Our indifference curve tells us that if he wanted to change from B to X in order to have an extra 1 pound of biscuits without altering his level of satisfaction he would consider it worthwhile the sacrifice of 2 pounds of chocolates.

Diminishing Marginal Rate of Substitution

We could say that there is a marginal change (often denoted by the Greek symbol Δ) of 2 pounds of chocolates and a marginal change of 1 pound of biscuits in moving from B to X. Alternatively we can say that the consumer, in order to have one extra pound of biscuits, would have to give up 2 pounds of chocolates in his bundle of the two goods. The rate at which one good is substituted for the other

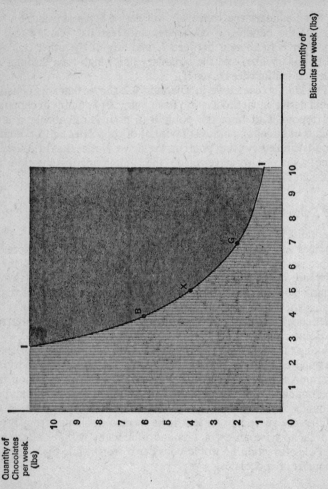

Figure 4.2 The indifference curve

good as a move along an indifference curve takes place is called the **marginal rate of substitution.** Therefore the marginal rate of substitution (MRS) of biscuits for chocolates along the indifference curve II between B and X is given by:

$$\frac{\Delta \text{ Chocolates}}{\Delta \text{ Biscuits}} = \frac{2}{1} = 2$$

[Strictly speaking, the value of MRS should be preceded by a negative

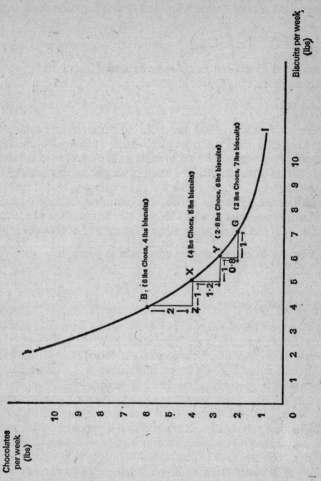

Figure 4.3 Marginal rate of substitution of chocolates for biscuits

sign, since a move along an indifference curve involves a reduction in the quantity of one good.]

Now consider a move further down the indifference curve from X to Y. For an extra 1 pound of biscuits, the quantity of chocolates which the consumer would be prepared to give up is 1·2 pounds. So the marginal rate of substitution of biscuits for chocolates from X to Y is:

$$\frac{\Delta \text{ Chocolates}}{\Delta \text{ Biscuits}} = \frac{1.2}{1} = 1\cdot2$$

Similarly the marginal rate of substitution of biscuits for chocolates in moving from Y to G would be:

$$\frac{0.8}{1} = 0.8$$

Therefore as a movement down the indifference curve takes place, the consumer is prepared to give up smaller and smaller amounts of chocolates for each pound of biscuits gained. In other words, the marginal rate of substitution of biscuits for chocolates declines from two to 1.2 to 0.8, etc. It is also worth mentioning that the slope of the indifference curve at a particular point, in geometric terms, will measure the marginal rate of substitution between the products. In Diagram 4.3, for example, the slope of the curve at B is given by

$$\frac{BZ}{ZX} = \frac{2}{1} = \text{MRS biscuits for chocolate at point B.}$$

A Map of Indifference Curves

So far we have looked at the choices open to a consumer along one particular indifference curve. We started, however, with a number of different combinations of chocolates and biscuits, and derived the indifference curve for all those combinations of chocolates and biscuits which gave the same level of satisfaction as point X in Diagram 4.1. But there were some points (like E) which contained more chocolates and biscuits, and therefore denoted a higher level of satisfaction compared to X. Hence, had we taken E as our starting point and traced a boundary line through it, denoting all combinations of chocolates and biscuits which would give the consumer the same level of satisfaction as E, we would have traced out another indifference curve.

Similarly, had we started with a point such as A (which denoted fewer chocolates and biscuits compared with X) we could have traced out an indifference curve representing all those combinations of chocolates and biscuits which would give the same level of satisfaction as point A. Indeed, if we assumed that chocolates and biscuits were completely divisible, there would be an infinite number of indifference curves on the same graph, each representing slightly different levels of satisfaction. Diagram 4.4 looks at three indifference curves, namely the original one through X and the two which have just been suggested.

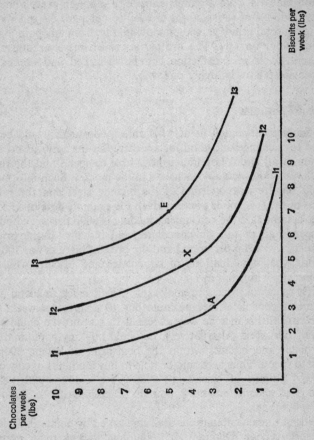

Figure 4.4 A set of indifference curves

I_1I_1 is the indifference curve through point A, and denotes all those combinations of chocolates and biscuits which give the consumer the same level of satisfaction as point A. Similarly, curves I_2I_2 and I_3I_3 represent the indifference curves through points X and E respectively. Notice that the ordinal approach to utility simply asserts that all points on I_2I_2 represent a higher level of satisfaction than all points on I_1I_1 and that I_3I_3 denotes a higher level of satisfaction than I_2I_2. No attempt is made to place an exact numerical value on levels of satisfaction, or even to compare the quantitative change in total utility gained by moving, say, from any point on I_1I_1 to any point on I_2I_2. The ordinal approach merely requires that different levels of satisfaction can be identified and *ranked subjectively* as relatively higher or lower.

Income Constraint

Indifference curves tell us at what rate a consumer would be prepared to exchange one good for another. But they give us no information at all about how much he is able to spend and the rate at which the goods actually exchange in the market. Such information would require a knowledge of his income level and the relative prices of the two goods concerned. In the example developed so far, let us assume that the consumer's income is 800p per week and that he spends all of this on chocolates and biscuits. If the price of chocolates was 80p per pound and the price of biscuits was 100p per pound, what combinations of chocolates and biscuits would his income allow him to buy?

First let us take two extreme cases. If he decided to spend all his income on chocolates then he could buy 10 pounds per week. Conversely, if all his income was allocated to biscuits, he could buy 8 pounds per week. Alternatively, he could buy any combination of chocolates and biscuits within the constraint of having 800p per week to spend. Thus he would be able to buy 2 pounds of chocolates and 6.4 pounds of biscuits ($2 \times 80 + 6.4 \times 100 = 800$); or 7.5 pounds of chocolates and 2 pounds of biscuits ($7.5 \times 80 + 2 \times 100 = 800$); etc.

Four of these combinations are represented by points P, Q, R and S respectively in Diagram 4.5. The line joining these points is commonly referred to as a **budget line** (or price-ratio line) and it represents the maximum combinations of the two goods which the consumer could buy with the income at his disposal. The slope of the budget line is the ratio of the price of biscuits to the price of chocolates. To explain this, consider that in Diagram 4.5 the slope

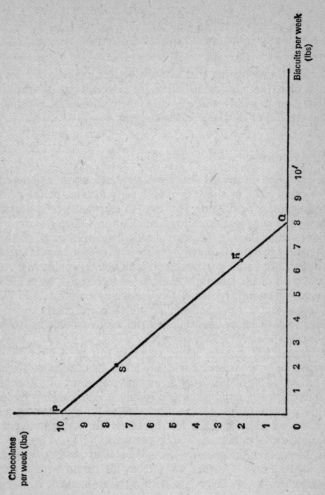

Figure 4.5 The budget line

of the line PQ is given by the ratio OP/OQ. If we denote the consumer's income by Y, and the price of chocolates and biscuits by Pc
and Pb then the distance

$$OP = \frac{Y}{Pc} \quad \text{and} \quad OQ = \frac{Y}{Pb}.$$

Hence $\dfrac{OP}{OQ} = \dfrac{Y}{Pc} \div \dfrac{Y}{Pb} = \dfrac{Pb}{Pc}$.

It is also worth noting that where a budget line just touches (i.e. is a tangent to) an indifference curve, the marginal rate of subsitution between the two goods will be equal to their price ratio. We shall see the importance of this later in the chapter.

Changes in Income

The budget line illustrated above will remain constant as long as no change takes place in either the consumer's income, or the price of either chocolates or biscuits. It is easy to see what would happen if the consumer's income doubled, from 800p to 1,600p per week and no change took place in the price of chocolates or biscuits. As shown in Diagram 4.6, if all of this new higher level of income was spent on chocolates, 20 pounds per week could be bought (point M). Alternatively if all of his income was allocated to biscuits, he could buy 16 pounds of biscuits (point N). By joining up points M and N, we have traced out a new budget line which corresponds to all the combinations of chocolates and biscuits which would be available at an income level of 1,600p per week.

An income fall, say to 400p per week, can be dealt with in a similar way. Our consumer could buy fewer chocolates and biscuits than before. If all of this level of income was spent on chocolates, 5 pounds per week could be bought (point J). Alternatively he could obtain 4 pounds of biscuits per week (point K) by spending all of his income on biscuits. Thus JK represents the budget line corresponding to an income level of 400p per week.

The effect, then, of a change in income is to *change the position* of the budget line – further away from the origin with a rise in income and closer to the origin with a fall in income. As long as there is no change in the relative price of the goods, such a change will always be parallel to the original budget line.

Changes in Relative Prices

Let us now assume that the consumer's income remains constant at 800p per week, but that the price of biscuits changes from 100p

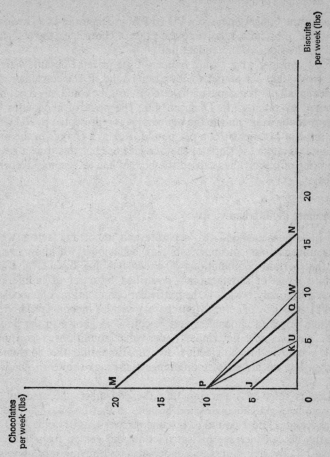

Figure 4.6 The budget line, with income and price change

per pound to 80p per pound. What would happen to the budget line? If the consumer spent all of his income on biscuits, he would be able to buy 10 pounds per week, represented by the point W in Diagram 4.6. Since the price of chocolates has not changed, the intercept on the vertical axis will, of course, remain unchanged at point P. Therefore the effect of a fall in the price of biscuits is to *change the slope* of the budget line, from PQ to PW in Diagram 4.6. The lower the price of biscuits, relative to the price of chocolates, the less steep will be the slope of the budget line.

Now consider what would happen if the price of biscuits were to rise from 100p per pound to 160p per pound. If the consumer now allocated all of his income of 800p to biscuits, he could buy 5 pounds, denoted by point U in Diagram 4.6. The price of chocolates has remained the same, and so the budget line is represented by PU when the price of biscuits is 160p per pound. Again, a change in the price of biscuits alters the slope of the budget line; but this time a rise in the price of biscuits has caused the budget line to become steeper in slope.

Consumer Equilibrium

We have now analysed two separate and important factors which will influence our consumer's buying behaviour. We know first of all that certain combinations of chocolates and biscuits give him certain levels of satisfaction – described by a set of indifference curves. Secondly, we know the particular combinations of chocolates and biscuits he can actually purchase, given his income level and the relative prices of chocolates and biscuits – as shown in the budget line. We can now determine under what conditions a consumer will maximise his satisfaction by superimposing the consumer's budget line on his set of indifference curves, as shown in Diagram 4.7.

Let us start by supposing that the consumer allocated all his income between chocolates and biscuits so that he buys 8.8 pounds of chocolates and 1 pound of biscuits per week, as at point A. Quite clearly, he can increase his satisfaction and get on to indifference curve I_2I_2 by giving up some chocolates and buying more biscuits. At point B, for example, he is on indifference curve I_2I_2 by buying 7.5 pounds of chocolates and 2 pounds of biscuits. It is still possible, if he rearranges his purchases, to get to a higher level of satisfaction at point E on indifference curve I_3I_3. He would now buy 4.8 pounds of biscuits and only 4 pounds of chocolates. But if he bought *more* biscuits, he would reduce his level of satisfaction by transferring back to a lower indifference curve. At point C, for example, he buys 7.4 pounds of biscuits and 0.8 pounds of chocolates, but has moved on to indifference curve I_1I_1.

Indifference curve I_3I_3 denotes the highest possible level of satis-

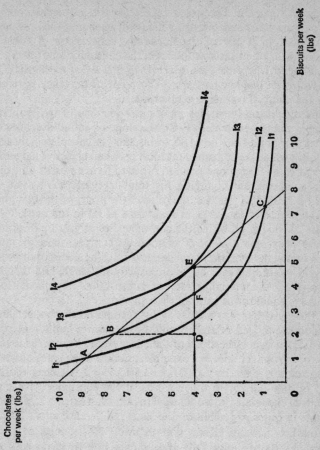

Figure 4.7 Consumer equilibrium at point E

faction which is attainable, given the income constraint and the relative prices of the two goods. It is, of course, impossible for the consumer to move to a higher indifference curve, say I_4I_4, unless there is some change in the position or slope of the budget line (*see* previous section on income and price changes). Point E is, therefore, extremely important because it represents the particular combination of chocolates and biscuits which will maximise the consumer's satisfaction. It is one of the important conclusions of consumer demand theory that satisfaction from the consumption of two goods is maximised where *the consumer's budget line just touches (i.e. is a tangent to) an indifference curve.* The point of tangency is referred to as the point of **consumer equilibrium.**

This conclusion illustrates the logical outcome of two important concepts already explained. First, the slope of an indifference curve at a certain point (i.e. the MRS of biscuits for chocolates) measures the rate at which the consumer (according to his subjective judgement) is prepared to forego one good in order to have an extra unit of the other good without changing his total level of satisfaction. The slope of the budget line (i.e. the ratio of the prices of the two goods) shows the rate of exchange in real terms as set in the market – the amount of one good which the consumer has to give up in order to acquire an extra unit of the other good. At point E, where the budget line is a tangent to the indifference curve I_3I_3, the slopes of the budget line and the indifference curve are exactly the same, and therefore, at point E, the marginal rate of substitution of chocolates for biscuits is equal to the ratio of their prices.

If the consumer was allocating his income on the budget line at any point to the left of E, he would be on a lower indifference curve than I_3I_3, at which the slope of the curve would be steeper than the slope of the budget line. For example, at point B the marginal rate of substitution is given by $BD/DF = 3.5/1.75 = 2$, whereas the price ratio is $10/8 = 1.25$. In other words, if the consumer gave up 3.8 pounds of chocolates he would wish to obtain an extra 1.75 pounds of biscuits in order to remain on the same indifference curve I_2I_2. But the market actually allows him to swop 2.8 pounds of biscuits (shown by the distance DE) and enables him to move on to the higher indifference curve I_3I_3.

Alternatively, at any point on the budget line to the right of E, he would again be on a lower indifference curve than I_2I_2 where its slope was less than the slope of the budget line. In this position the consumer would place a lower value on substituting biscuits for chocolates than the rate set in the market, and it would increase his satisfaction to give up some biscuits and increase his consumption of chocolates. Only when the marginal rate of substitution (subjective exchange rate) is equal to the price ratio (objective exchange rate) is it impossible for the consumer to increase his satisfaction by reallocating his expenditure on the two goods. In this sense, we can say that the consumer would be in equilibrium.

Conclusions

In the introductory section of this chapter we established that to obtain maximum satisfaction a consumer would allocate his expenditure so that the marginal utility from the last penny spent on all goods was exactly equal. For the simple case of two goods, a and b, this condition was expressed formally in the equation

$$\frac{MUa}{Pa} = \frac{MUb}{Pb}$$

or
$$\frac{MUa}{MUb} = \frac{Pa}{Pb}$$

Since we have also seen by the ordinal approach that for consumer equilibrium

$$MRS \text{ a for b} = \frac{Pa}{Pb},$$

then
$$MRS \text{ a for b} = \frac{MUa}{MUb}$$

The ordinal approach therefore arrives at the same general conclusion, although it does so by an alternative route since it rejects the possibility of cardinal measurement of utility.

Income and Substitution Effects

We have seen how a consumer maximises his utility from the consumption of two goods, under the assumption that income and relative prices remain constant. We now need to predict what would happen if income or prices were changed. How would the consumer adjust his purchases in order to continue to maximise utility?

Income Effect

First, let us assume that income is increased from 800p per week to 1,000p per week and that relative prices remain constant. In Diagram 4.8, such an income change moves the budget line from PQ to RS. We can now see that such an increase in income would take the consumer on to a higher indifference curve, $I_4 I_4$, on which point F

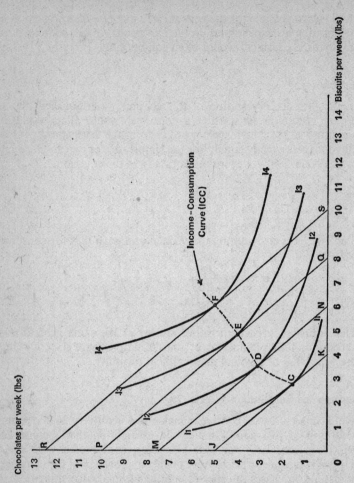

Figure 4.8 Effect of income changes on consumer equilibrium

(5 pounds of chocolates and 6 pounds of biscuits) would represent maximum utility.

The income effect, as it is called, enables the consumer to buy *more* chocolates and biscuits as his income rises.

We could draw several budget lines, starting at JK to represent successive increases in income, and link the points of tangency (C, D, E and F) as the consumer reaches higher levels of satisfaction. The path traced out, called the income-consumption curve (the dotted line ICC in Diagram 4.8), shows how a consumer adjusts his purchases of two products as income changes, given constant prices.

In Diagram 4.8, the income-consumption curve has been drawn sloping continuously upwards to the right, portraying the income effects that occur as the consumer reacts to increases in income by buying more of both commodities. It might well be, however, that the income-consumption curve for some goods slopes backwards at some point, as suggested by the curve ICC_1 in Diagram 4.9.

The curve ICC_1, for example, illustrates the hypothesis that after point F, the consumer reacts to an increase in income by buying fewer units of good B. At the new equilibrium point of X, only OQ_1 units of good B are consumed compared with OQ units before the rise in income takes place. The income effect in the case of curve ICC_1 is negative after a certain point has been reached. When the income effect is negative, then one of the products falls into that category called inferior goods – goods which are bought when the consumer has a low income level, but which are replaced by goods of higher quality when the consumer moves to a higher income level. In Diagram 4.9, good B would be classified as an inferior good. We have mentioned specific examples (e.g. margarine) in Chapter 2.

Changes in Price

Let us now examine what would happen to the consumption of a good (e.g. 'biscuits') consequent upon a change in its price, assuming that there was no change in the consumer's income or in the price of other commodities. Because the following piece of analysis attempts to show how we can derive the demand curve discussed in Chapters 2 and 3, we are going to generalise by letting the vertical axis represent expenditure on all goods other than biscuits.

If the price of biscuits fell from 100p per pound to 80p per pound, what consequences can we predict? We have already seen in Diagram 4.6 that the effect of a price change is to alter the slope of the budget line, from PQ to PF in Diagram 4.10(a). Similarly, if the price of biscuits was to continue falling, the budget line would become gradually less steep, say from PQ to PE to PG, etc.

If we now trace the effects of the successive decreases in the price of biscuits on their consumption (by means of a *price-consumption*

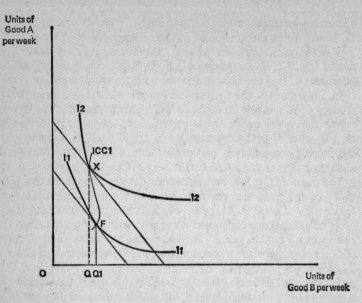

Figure 4.9 Negative income effect

curve – PCC – which joins the successive tangency points of budget lines and indifference curves) it can be seen that successively larger quantities are bought. This relationship between falling prices and greater quantities demanded, assuming incomes, tastes and the prices of all other goods to be constant, confirms the demand curve relationship, which is derived in Diagram 4.10(*b*) from the information on Diagram 4.10(*a*). Each point of tangency in Diagram 4.10(*a*) tells us how many biscuits would be bought at a series of prices and so we can transfer these relationships on to Diagram 4.10(*b*) where price is measured on the vertical axis and quantities of biscuits on the horizontal axis.

The reason why we expect consumers to buy more of a good when its price falls is really due to a combination of two factors – income effect and substitution effect. In order to see how these two effects can be isolated in the context of the examples of chocolates and

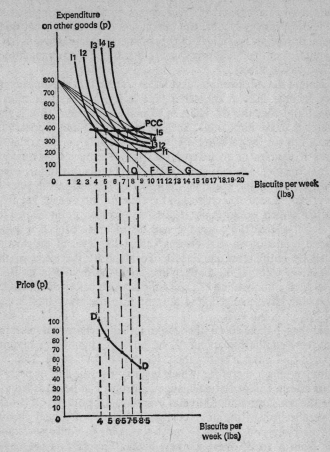

Figure 4.10 (*a*) Effect of fall in price of biscuits
          (*b*) Derivation of market demand curve

biscuits developed so far, let us assume that the price of biscuits falls. The effect of a fall in the price of biscuits relative to the price of chocolates is to give the consumer the opportunity of substituting the relatively cheaper good (biscuits) for the relatively more expensive one (chocolates). Also, the absolute fall in the money price of biscuits causes the consumer's *real* income to rise, meaning that his given level of money income can purchase a larger bundle of goods. We shall now show how much of the consumer's increased purchases of biscuits, after the fall in price, can be attributed to the substitution and the income effects.

To isolate the substitution effect let us assume that the consumer's money income falls at the same time as the price of biscuits is reduced, and that the net effect is to make movement to a higher indifference curve impossible. Such an occurrence may appear un-realistic, but for the moment it is worth following up the argument because it enables us to assume that the consumer's real income remains constant. We can then isolate the pure substitution effect. In Diagram 4.11, for example, the effect of the fall in the price of biscuits can be seen as a change in the slope of the budget line from PQ to PF which would make it possible to reach point Z on I_1I_2. Now suppose that the consumer had his income reduced to offset the price reduction so that he was still at the level of satisfaction denoted by indifference curve I_1I_1. To illustrate the effect of this reduction in income, the budget line could be drawn in at RS – parallel to the budget line PF, since the relative prices of chocolates and biscuits have changed, and tangential to the lower indifference curve I_1I_1 at point Y.

What has happened to the consumer's purchases of biscuits? At the new equilibrium point Y, he buys 4.2 pounds of biscuits, compared to 4 pounds before the price change took place. The pure **substitution effect,** therefore, which results from the fall in price of biscuits after a compensating change in income can be regarded as a rise in the consumption of biscuits from 4 to 4.2 pounds. Of course, the overall effect of the price change in biscuits, if money income were to remain constant, is to move the point of consumer equili-brium from X to Z, where the new budget line PF is a tangent to indifference curve I_2I_2. The fall in price of biscuits raises the con-sumer's level of real income, enabling him to buy more biscuits – diagrammatically, the budget line moves outwards from the origin to touch a higher indifference curve. The rise in the consumption of biscuits associated with the move from Y to Z (i.e. from 4.2 to 4.5) can be regarded as an **income effect.**

Analytically, therefore, we can assess the effect of the price change in biscuits as follows:

(*i*) An increase in the quantity of biscuits consumed takes place;

(*ii*) part of this increase (4 pounds to 4.2 pounds) is due to a

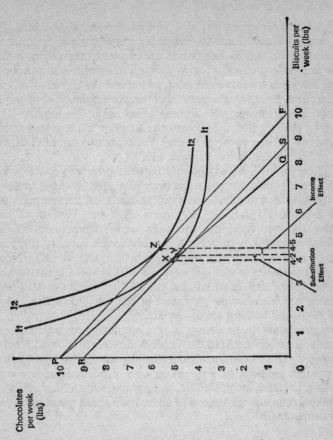

Figure 4.11 Income and substitution effects of a price change

substitution effect following the change in relative prices of chocolates and biscuits, (assuming income remains constant – i.e. the budget line swings from PQ to RS);

(*iii*) part of the increase (4.2 pounds to 4.5 pounds) is due to an income effect, following a shift outwards in the budget line (i.e. the budget line makes a parallel upwards shift from RS to PF).

In the example above, both the income and the substitution

effect led to an increase in the quantity of biscuits consumed. In such cases, the income and the substitution effects are both positive. Indeed, because indifference curves are convex to the origin, a fall in the price of a product will always result in a positive substitution effect. We cannot be so sure, however, about the direction of the income effect. It was mentioned earlier that for certain types of good, namely inferior goods, the income effect might be negative (as shown by the fact that the income consumption curve would slope 'backwards' for one of the products). The effect of a price fall for an inferior good is shown in Diagram 4.12.

In Diagram 4.12, let us suppose that the price of good B – an inferior good – falls relative to the price of a good A. It can be seen that the substitution effect results in an increased consumption of good B from OQ units to OQ_2 units. However, because of the negative income effect, the consumer moves from point M on indifference curve I_1I_1 to point N on indifference curve I_2I_2, representing a decrease in biscuit consumption from OQ_2 to OQ_1. Now the important point about this negative income effect is that it has not outweighed the force of the substitution effect, so that the consumer still increases his purchases of biscuits (OQ to OQ_1) as a result of the fall in the price of biscuits.

The conclusion to be drawn is that we have now provided an explanation of why demand curves slope downwards. Usually both the income and substitution effects resulting from a fall in the price of a product are positive. Even in the case of inferior goods where there is a negative income effect, the positive substitution effect is normally strong enough to lead to an increase in the quantity of the good demanded.[2]

Conclusion

The analysis of consumer demand based on indifference curves lies at the core of microeconomic theory. Many predictions made by economists about how consumers will react to changes in price and income are derived from the ideas presented in this chapter.

It should not be thought, however, that the formal relationships set out in this chapter are only of use in a theoretical context. On

[2] The only exception to this is found in a special class of inferior goods which accounts for a very large part of consumers' incomes. The term 'Giffen's Paradox' has been given to cases where the negative income effect is so large and exceeds the positive substitution effect, and therefore leads to a reduction in the quantity of the good demanded.

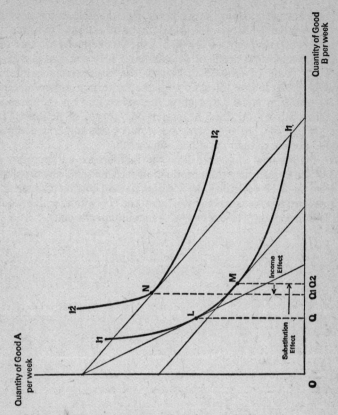

Figure 4.12 Income and substitution effects for an inferior good

the contrary, indifference curve analysis can often be of great assistance in the evaluation of important decisions in government and industry.[3] For example, when the government is planning a major new development such as a motorway or a new transport system, it is often useful to know something about consumers' preferences between different things such as the cost of the journey, journey speed, comfort and convenience, etc.

The approach can be extended to industry to discover decision-

[3] An application to indirect taxation is given in G. H. Peters, *Private and Public Finance*, Ch. 10, pp. 168–174.

makers' attitudes to certain problems. For example, a businessman might be faced with two possible courses of action – the first will result in a certain profit of £1,000 but the second has a fifty per cent chance of making a profit of £1,500 and a fifty per cent chance of making a profit of only £500. Now is the businessman indifferent between these courses of action, in the sense that either outcome would give him equal satisfaction (i.e. place him on the same indifference curve) or does he prefer one course of action to the other (meaning that one outcome would place him on a higher indifference curve than the other outcome)?

We shall see in Chapter 6 how the indifference curve approach can be used to analyse certain production decisions made by suppliers. And we shall be revisiting the ideas presented in this chapter at a later point when we come to investigate the conditions which would enable our economy to operate with maximum efficiency.

Chapter 5

Features Behind the Supply Curve

It is difficult to categorise the vast amount of activity which goes on in the everyday conduct of business. These activities involve the production of widely different types of goods and services, from oil, cars, chemicals, steel, beer, cigarettes, TV sets, and washing machines, to the provision of hotel accommodation, films, TV shows, insurance policies and hairdressing services. Business activity in Britain provides employment for nearly three-quarters of the working population.[1] The labour force is engaged in a wide range of working activity – some are involved directly in the manufacture of cars, steel, chemicals or in producing TV shows and films, some concentrate on selling products to consumers, others are employed purely in the management and administration of production and selling.

A short tour round any major city is enough to convince one of the great disparity in the size of business concerns – from the small newsagent's shop on the corner employing perhaps one or two people, to the shops in the high street which provide work for a few more people who specialise in selling one particular type of good such as electrical equipment, shoes, clothes or furniture, to the very large department store or supermarket providing a diverse range of goods for sale; from the small shoe repair shops to the huge factories where cars or chemicals are produced.

All of this business activity is represented in economic analysis by supply curves for certain products. A supply curve illustrates a relationship between the various quantities of a commodity that would be supplied to a market at various prices by all firms engaged in its production. At the end of this chapter, we shall pose the major lines of enquiry to be followed up in Chapters 6 to 9 which seek to explain the activities lying behind a market supply curve. We begin, however, by looking more closely at the meaning of a number of terms such as **firms, plants, industries,** and **markets,** which will

---

[1] The remainder being employed by central government, local authorities and nationalised industries. For further analysis of the operation of nationalised industries, *see* Ch. 12.

appear regularly in our discussion. It is important that their meaning in the context of economic analysis is quite clear.

Firms, Plants and Industries

An initial and useful distinction can be made between firms (or companies), plants and industries. A **firm** is the unit of ownership of a business activity or group of activities; a **plant** is an establishment within which a particular activity, or set of activities, such as production, packaging, etc., takes place; an **industry** consists of the collection of firms engaged in the production of some particular good or service.

Firms or Companies

There are three different types of ownership of firms in Britain – the single-owner firm, the partnership and the joint-stock company. In part, these three different types of ownership reflect the different sizes of the firms concerned. For example, the single-owner firm is a very well-known and common type of business organisation. It is the typical 'one-man' business, common in small-scale retailing (newsagents, grocers, etc.), in the service trades (electricians, decorators and painters) and in farming. In legal terms, the single owner is personally responsible for all the activities of the firm (including any debts which it contracts); in economic terms, the development of a small business depends to a large extent on how much money the owner actually has or can raise through borrowing, usually from his local bank. In the case of successful single-owner firms, of course, the profits received from sales provide a source of finance which can be 'ploughed back' into the business for further expansion.

Anyone requiring medical treatment from a general practitioner, legal advice from a lawyer, a check-up from a dental surgeon, or financial advice from a stockbroker will often go to a firm run on a partnership basis. The partners are recognised as being legally responsible for the affairs of the firm, and consequently they are liable for any debts which the firm may incur. In this respect, the partnership merely extends the legal liability for a firm's debts from one person to two or more.[2] It also extends the number of potential

---

[2] It is possible but rare for a partner to have 'limited liability', by which he is liable only to the extent of his financial contribution to the firm; in turn, it is common for such people to take no part in the day-to-day management of the firm.

sources of finance for the development of the firm, since more than one 'owner' will almost certainly have a stake in the business.

The third type of firm – the joint-stock company – represents the way in which most large private companies in Britain are organised. A joint-stock company issues shares which can be bought by the general public or by other firms or institutions, notably insurance companies, with the holders of shares becoming the owners of the company, entitled to some proportion of profits. The major legal difference between the joint-stock company on the one hand and the single-owner firm or partnership on the other hand lies in the recognition of the company as a legal entity, and in the fact that the owners have **limited liability.** This means that if the company goes so badly into debt that it becomes bankrupt, the owners will lose only that amount of money they have individually invested in the company.

In some joint-stock companies, especially where the business is small and a high proportion of the shares are held by a few people, ownership and control may be closely associated. Major share-holders may be in charge of the everyday business of the firm. But in the medium-sized and large joint-stock companies, where the number of shareholders is very much larger, it is usually impracticable for the owners of the firm actually to manage its affairs. The Court-aulds Company – a major textiles producer – has over 200,000 shareholders! Instead, a Board of Directors is elected at an Annual General Meeting which shareholders are entitled to attend, and this Board, in turn, appoints senior executives who are made responsible for the major areas of activity such as finance, production, marketing, personnel, etc. Hence, in most large joint-stock companies owner-ship and management are largely separated.

Firm Size

Economists have for a long time been interested in the relative size of firms. One such measure of size might be the value of sales in a given year. Looking at the value of the sales of some of Britain's best-known joint-stock companies in 1971–72, for example, we would find that the highest recorded value was that of the British Petroleum Company (BP) with sales of about £2,000 million. Also high in the league table were Unilever – the food and detergent manufacturer – with recorded sales of about £1,300 million, and the British Leyland Motor Corporation – car manufacturers – with sales of £1,000 million. Courtaulds – which has a long history in textile production, and more recently in man-made fibres – recorded sales of £660 million; Marks and Spencer reached £415 million; and Watney Mann, the brewers, had sales of £160 million.

Alternatively firm size can be measured in terms of labour employed. Of the companies mentioned above, the largest employer of labour in 1971–72 was the British Leyland Motor Corporation with 199,524 employees. Next came Courtaulds (160,000 employees) and Unilever (100,553 employees). The other firms employed substantially fewer people. Marks and Spencer's labour force totalled 34,372; British Petroleum's 27,200, and Watney Mann's 23,538.

Table 5.1

Year	Firms employing more than 10,000 people	Firms employing fewer than 1,000 people
	% of total employment	
1935	14	59
1963	32	37

It is also interesting to compare the size of firms in Britain over a period of time, as shown in table 5.1. If measured according to the number of people employed, then the number of firms employing a labour force of over 10,000 accounted for 14 per cent of total employment in 1935. By 1963, the number of firms employing more than 10,000 people accounted for 32 per cent of the total working population. The same picture emerges if we observe what happened to much smaller firms – those employing fewer than 1,000 people – over the same time period. Their employment accounted for 59 per cent of the working population in 1935, but only 37 per cent in 1963.

Plants

The concept of a **plant** (or an 'establishment', as it is sometimes called) refers to a site where certain activities are grouped together. A straightforward example would be a factory where machinery, raw materials and labour are combined in order to manufacture some product. On a larger scale, a steelworks can be defined as a plant since it involves the grouping together of a number of activities on a certain site to manufacture steel. Oil refineries, power stations, breweries and weaving mills are further examples of plants.

The reason for distinguishing between firms and plants is that any particular firm may well have many plants, each concerned with its own type of activity. The British Leyland Motor Corporation, for example, has fifty-nine plants in Britain. Some of these make components such as engines and gear boxes, others manufacture car bodies, while the function of others is to assemble the components and bodies into complete vehicles ready for distribution. In some firms, plants are engaged in more than one major activity. Breweries, for example, are organised both to make beer and to package it ready for distribution.

Table 5.2 **Distribution of Employment by Size of Plant, British Manufacturing Industry, 1935, 1951, and 1963**

Number employed in Plant	Percentage of Total Employment		
	1935	1951	1963
11–49	13.9	11.5	9.0
50–99	11.7	10.4	8.3
100–299	26.2	22.2	20.3
300–499	12.8	11.6	11.4
500–999	13.9	13.6	14.6
1,000–1,499	6.3	7.2	8.2
1,500 and over	15.2	23.6	28.2

Source: K. D. George, *Industrial Organisation*, London, George Allen and Unwin, 1971, p. 38.

Economists have also been interested in providing explanations for the increasing size of plants in Britain, which we will be looking at in Chapter 7. Some evidence about increasing plant size is given in Table 5.2, which shows the percentage of the working population employed in plants of various sizes in 1935, 1951 and 1963. In 1935, 13.9 per cent of total employment was provided in plants employing between 11 and 49 people, with 15.2 per cent being accounted for in the largest plants of 1,500 people and above. By 1963, however, the largest plants accounted for 28.2 per cent of total employment. In fact, as a very rough dividing line, plants employing fewer than 500 people have declined in significance whereas plants employing more than 500 people accounted for 51 per cent of employment in 1963 compared with 35.4 per cent in 1935.

Industries

In theory, the definition of an **industry** is relatively straightforward. An industry can be said to represent the combined activities of all firms producing the same good (or service), or goods (or services) which can be considered very close substitutes for one another. Looked at in this way, the definition of an industry is analogous to that of a market which we have been using so far. Industries would thus be regarded as groups of firms producing goods (or services) which had high mutual cross elasticities of demand – meaning that consumers view them as very close substitutes - and high cross elasticities of supply – which can be taken as a measure of inter-relationships on the production side.

Unfortunately one of the great practical problems is that some companies are engaged in activities which spread over several industries. The two major activities of the Rank Organisation, for example, are the provision of entertainments (cinemas, dancing, bingo), and the manufacture of Xerox copying machines. With such diverse activities it would clearly be impossible to allocate the Rank Organisation to one particular industry!

The definition of an industry in the Standard Industrial Classification – which forms the basis for government industrial statistics – is a good deal different from the one suggested above. Industries are defined on the basis of the 'principal product' made in plants (not by firms), where a principal product is that which accounts for the major proportion of sales from a plant. Further, principal products are classified on the basis of technological conditions of supply such as the nature of the process used (printing, weaving, etc.), and the common raw materials used in production. There is no mention of cross elasticities. Such a practice leads to difficulties of its own, notably when goods which can be regarded as close substitutes from the demand side are made in different industries. Thus the making of leather coats and woollen coats is attributed to different industries since their manufacture involves a different process, though they certainly appear as close substitutes in the minds of consumers.

We can bring together the concepts of firm, plant and industry by looking at information relating to changes in the size of firms and the size of plants in various industries. Looking first at the size of firms, there has been a tendency in virtually all cases for the numbers operating to fall (by implication leading to larger-size

Table 5.3

Industry Group	No. of Companies* Beginning 1961	End 1968
Food	63	39
Drink	106	51
Tobacco	8	7
Chemicals and allied industries	69	45
Metal manufacture	70	56
Non-electrical engineering	198	138
Electrical engineering	87	63
Shipbuilding and marine	22	17
Vehicles	61	41
Metal goods n.e.s.	98	80
Textiles	192	128
Leather and fur	11	11
Clothing and footwear	63	42
Bricks, pottery, glass, cement	73	44
Timber, furniture	40	34
Paper, printing, publishing	99	72
Other manufacturing	52	40
All manufacturing	1,312	908

Source: Board of Trade, Mergers, a guide to Board of Trade practice, (HMSO 1969), Appendix 3 to Annex 4.
 * Refers to companies having assets of at least £¼ million and with a Stock Exchange quotation.

firms), as shown in Table 5.3. During the 1960s the well marked trend was partly explained by the takeover of some firms by other firms in the same industry (an activity known as a merger). The trend towards larger-size plants illustrated in Table 5.2, can be shown by industry group as in Table 5.4.

Table 5.4 shows the proportions of the total labour force in each industry employed in the largest plants in each industry. In all but a few cases (e.g. footwear and rubber manufacture) there has been a significant increase in the importance of large plants. In the chemical industry, for example, the largest plants accounted for 30 per cent of employment in 1963, compared with only 18 per cent in 1935; and in metal industries the proportion of employment found in the largest plants more than doubled over the same period.

Table 5.4 **Percentage employed in largest plants, by Industry Group, British Manufacturing Industry, 1935, 1951 and 1963.**

Industry Group	Size of largest plants	Employment in largest plants as percentage of total employment*		
		1935	1951	1963
Food, drink, tobacco	1,500+	18	14	22
Chemicals	1,500+	18	25	30
Metal industries	1,500+	13	23	30
Engineering	1,500+	22	23	25
Shipbuilding	2,000+	n.a.	44	45
Electrical goods	1,500+	n.a.	47	51
Vehicles	1,500+	52	56	67
Aircraft	1,500+	52	67	77
Textiles	750+	19	16	19
Clothing	500+	19	16	18
Footwear	1,000+	15	11	8
Bricks, etc.	1,000+	10	18	22
Timber	400+	10	12	14
Paper manufacturing	500+	28	40	43
Printing and publishing	500+	33	33	33
Rubber	1,500+	44	41	38
All manufacturing industry	1,500+	15	24	28

Sources: Alan Armstrong and Aubrey Silberston, Board of Trade *Report on the Census of Production*, 1963, reprinted in K. D. George, *op. cit.*, p. 39.

  * Excluding plants employing 10 or less.

Main Features behind the Supply Curve

Against the background of this description of firms, plants, and industries there are several features which we will attempt to explain in Chapters 6 to 9. We shall make the simplifying assumption for the moment that all firms have a single plant so that the terms 'firm' and 'plant' can be used synonymously.

(*i*) **Combination of Inputs** How do firms decide on the combination of various inputs (such as labour, capital, raw materials) to be used in producing a certain level of output ? When we observe, for example, the amount of capital employed and the amount of labour employed by some firms, it becomes clear that quite different proportions of the two inputs are used. A company like British Petroleum employs capital worth £1,890,500,000 and a labour force of 27,000. The capital employed per worker is about £70,000. By contrast, Imperial Chemical Industries, the largest chemicals producer in the UK, has capital of £1,695,000,000 and a labour force totalling 194,000, giving a ratio of capital per employee of £8,740. An even greater contrast is provided by looking at Kraft, the food manufacturers, which employs capital worth £9,470,000 and a labour force of 4,186, so that £2,262 of capital is employed for every member of its labour force.

What influences the factor combinations used by firms in their productive processes? This is the first question to be taken up in Chapters 6 and 7.

(*ii*) **The Size of Firms and the Size of Plants** The fact that we can observe firms of every size, from the one-man business to the industrial giant like British Petroleum, requires an explanation. Why do some firms become very large, and what makes it possible for other firms to remain very small? Also, why is it that the size of plants making certain products is very large, whereas some other plants remain relatively small? The nature of this question forces us to analyse the information contained in Tables 5.2, 5.3 and 5.4, and to come up with some explanations.

(*iii*) **The Structure of a Market** By **market structure** we generally mean some measure of the number of firms in an industry and their relative size. In principle it is possible to imagine quite different market structures, from one in which the industry consists of a large number of firms each accounting for approximately the same proportion of total sales to one in which a few large firms supply similar proportions of total market output. The limit, of course, comes when one firm is the sole producer. There can also be markets which are supplied by a large number of firms, but where a relatively high proportion of total output is in the hands of a small number of larger firms.

Economists believe that in order to make important predictions about firms' behaviour it is necessary to classify the structure of the market in which they operate simply because different behaviour patterns could reasonably be expected in the various market environments outlined above.

(*iv*) **Volume of Output** What determines the volume of output produced by firms? To take a specific example, we know that in 1971 the Kellogg Company produced about 95,000 tons of breakfast cereals, but can we explain that particular level of output? One straightforward reason might be that Kellogg (and perhaps firms in general) simply produced as much as they possibly could within the productive limits of the inputs which they employed. This type of explanation would mean that Kellogg produced 95,000 tons of breakfast cereals in 1971 because that was the largest volume of output they were capable of producing, given the size and quality of their labour force and capital equipment. Or did they produce an output which was in accord with some *intended* level, and which was perhaps less than the volume which Kellogg was technically capable of producing?

To explain why firms choose certain volumes of output really requires us to specify some assumption about the motives which guide their behaviour.

The Assumption of Profit Maximisation

In developing a 'Theory of the Firm', we shall make an assumption which has a long history in microeconomic theory, namely that firms aim to **maximise profits** (where profits are the difference between the revenue gained from the sales of the firm's product and the costs of the resources used in making the product). Hence, in attempting to answer question (*iv*) above, we shall be looking for some method of identifying that particular level of output where the firm's profits would be maximised.

There has been considerable and continuous controversy amongst economists for over thirty years about the empirical validity of this assumption. This is hardly surprising when one considers that the theory which we are about to develop attempts to explain the outcome of the behaviour of an immense diversity of business organisations. Is it really valid to make the same assumption about the motives behind the decisions of all firms, from the smallest to the largest?

Critics of the basic assumption have directed their attacks both on the word **profits** and the word **maximise.** Some economists objected to the assumption because they claimed that profits were not the only factor guiding firms' decisions. It was pointed out that many firms go to some lengths to attract and retain customers' goodwill, even if it means sacrificing some profit; other firms are more concerned with their level of sales and their share of the market rather than in raising profits; and other objectives have also been noted. Another group of economists objected to the word **maximise** on the grounds that studies of decision-making procedures in firms showed that managers tended to settle for a **satisfactory** level of profit, rather than the highest level of profit obtainable.

We shall be considering the nature of these criticisms later on and asking to what extent they are valid, and to what extent they harm the theory which has been developed. For the moment, in the words of one famous economist, '. . . we shall retain the assumption that the firm aims at maximising its profit. But we shall regard this assumption as a working hypothesis rather than as a universal rule'.[3]

[3] T. Scitovsky, *Welfare and Competition*, Chicago 1951, p. 111.

Chapter 6

The Relationships Between Inputs and Outputs

'I think we shall probably end up with a little more labour and a little less equipment than some of the others, but I agree that we haven't got the right ratio by any means.' Those words were spoken by Mr John Barber, a Senior Executive in the British Leyland Motor Company in a newspaper interview.[1] He was contrasting the amount of capital employed per worker in his company with that in some of British Leyland's foreign competitors. In so doing, he gives us a clear introduction to the type of problem with which this chapter is concerned.

We shall be analysing the relationships between different quantities and combinations of inputs and the resulting level of output obtained. Another example, quoted in a little more detail, may give the reader an idea of the kinds of question which this chapter attempts to answer.

Studies[2] made of the oil industry in the USA illustrate one particular problem faced by oil producers. In oil pipe-lines the rate of flow is determined by two factors – the diameter of the pipe-line, and the amount of power used in pumping. Firms therefore have to decide on the diameter of the pipe to use and on the power input. Studies of the problem uncovered two important relationships which are shown in Diagrams 6.1(a) and (b).

In Diagram 6.1(a), the rate of flow of oil is measured on the vertical axis (in thousands of barrels per day); power is measured along the horizontal axis. The graph shows what happens to the flow of oil when successively larger amounts of power are applied to *pipe-lines of a certain diameter*. Line AB, for example, demonstrates the effect of increased power on the flow of oil through a pipe-line fourteen inches in diameter while lines CD, EF, GH and IJ show the relationship for other diameters.

One feature common to all the lines is that throughput rises as

---

[1] *Business Observer*, 20 May 1973.
[2] This example is based on 'Production and Cost Functions for Oil Pipe-lines' by L. Cookenboo, Jnr, in D. Watson (ed.), *Price Theory in Action*, Houghton Mifflin Co, Boston 1969, pp. 94–9.

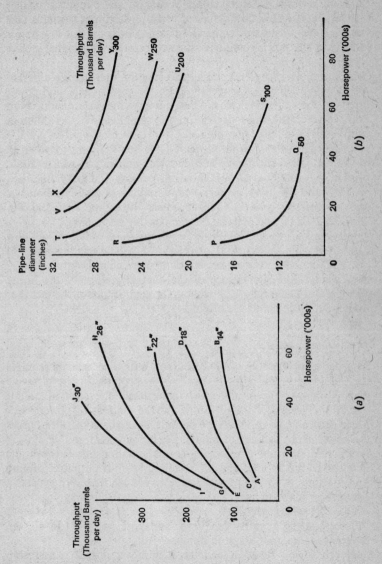

Figure 6.1 Relations between inputs and outputs for oil

extra power is applied, but the increase in flow produced by additional power which occurs at high levels of power input is smaller than the incremental flow achieved when power input is small. This feature is demonstrated by the steep slope of the lines at low power levels and the much shallower slope associated with higher power levels.

Diagram 6.1(*b*) presents similar information in a slightly different way. Pipe-line diameter is measured on the vertical axis, and power input on the horizontal axis. Thus the axes measure quantities of both inputs. The lines drawn on the graph show the different combinations of pipe-line diameter and power *required to produce any particular rate of oil throughput*. Thus line PQ joins together all those combinations of pipe-line diameter and power which would produce a throughput of 50,000 barrels per day. Similarly, lines RS, TU, VW and XY join together all combinations of pipe-line diameter and horsepower which would produce throughputs of 100,000, 200,000, 250,000 and 300,000 barrels per day respectively.

Diagrams 6.1(*a*) and (*b*) illustrate relationships which we will now seek to explain. What kind of relationship between the input of horsepower and the output of oil is demonstrated in Diagram 6.1(*a*)? And what is the significance of the changing slope of the lines? Similarly, in Diagram 6.1(*b*), what is the significance of the fact that the lines are convex to the origin?

Production Functions

In order to produce any level of output, a firm necessarily requires to feed some inputs into the production process. In the pipe-line example above, the inputs which determined the level of output were the diameter of the pipe-line and the amount of power used. More generally, we can revert to our initial classification of resources for convenient headings of inputs, i.e. labour, land and capital. A production function expresses a formal relationship between the quantity of inputs used and the resulting level of output, assuming that the state of technology is constant. We can therefore express a production function as:

$$Q = Q(I_1, I_2, I_3, \ldots In)$$

Where Q is the quantity produced, and I_1, I_2, I_3, ... In are the different inputs, totalling n in number.

A production function denotes a purely *technical* relationship between inputs and outputs. It relates physical output to physical inputs. Further, production functions denote the *maximum* potential output which can be obtained using certain quantities of inputs. We thus assume that if inputs are used efficiently in the technical sense it would be impossible for a higher output than that specified in the production function to be produced. If, for example, a very simple production function told us that a shirt manufacturer could make 100 shirts per week using 2 machines, 2 employees and 5 bundles of cloth, then we are assuming *technical efficiency*, i.e. the shirt manufacturer can and does make a *maximum* of 100 shirts per week, with this quantity of inputs and no more. It could be, of course, that fewer shirts would be produced if the manufacturer operated inefficiently – for example, by forgetting to have his machinery properly serviced and maintained so that it was operating below full potential – but this is a possibility which we rule out.

Fixed and Variable Inputs

For convenience in developing the theory, we are going to assume that inputs can be classified as **fixed** and **variable** – these are terms which apply to the ease with which inputs can be altered in order to change output levels. A fixed input is one whose quantity cannot easily be altered in response to a decision to change a level of output. By contrast, the quantity of a variable input can be changed easily and quickly. Such definitions must be somewhat arbitrary, and it is certainly not possible to pick out certain types of inputs and say that they can be classified as fixed or variable for all time in all situations.

Perhaps the best way of acknowledging the need for the distinction between fixed and variable inputs is to introduce another distinction which assumes great importance in the theory of the firm – the **short-run** and the **long-run**; the short-run is a period during which one (or some) inputs are fixed, and the long-run a period when all inputs are variable. These concepts introduce a time horizon to the firm's decision to change output levels, but it is a time horizon defined not so much in terms of days, weeks, months or years, but in terms of the way in which inputs can be changed in response to a decision to change output. Let us revert for a moment to the example of our shirt manufacturer. Suppose he wished to increase production of shirts to 150 per week. He may decide to increase the quantity of all his inputs – men, machines and cloth. But the time required to make adjustments to each of his inputs may well vary. He could, for example, increase output within a matter of days by advertising for an extra worker, interviewing and hiring someone. But it is highly unlikely that an expensive piece of precision machinery could be installed before some further time had elapsed. And it might be the case that in order to meet the extra output requirements, the manufacturer would have to move to larger premises. Again, an even longer time period would be needed.

We could say that in the short-run the input of machinery was fixed, and that output could only be expanded by increasing quantities of the variable input of labour. But in the long-run, output of shirts could be increased by using more of each input, i.e. the quantities of labour and machinery would be variable. As mentioned above, however, it should not be concluded that capital equipment is a fixed input and labour a variable input in the short-run. It might be the case that the shirt manufacturer used machinery which could be installed within a day of being ordered. And it might be the case (as an illustration of the way in which short-run and long-run refer to the variability of inputs rather than specific time-intervals) that in the short-run both labour and machinery were variable, and the fixed input was the factory in which production was carried out. On this definition, output could be increased in the short-run by increasing both the labour force and the number of machines, but only within the confines of the same factory. The long-run would now, by implication, refer to that period when further expansion of output could be achieved by employing more labour, buying more machines *and* moving to larger premises.

In practice, there are cases where the long-run may be a period of several years. The Central Electricity Generating Board, for example, is responsible for the supply of electricity in Britain. What would happen if, due to a sudden increase in purchases of electrical equipment, the demand for electricity rose? To meet the higher level of output required, the Board could obviously see how far it was possible to coax more electricity out of existing equipment. But in the short-run one type of input is certainly fixed and that is the number of power stations operating. Since it takes something like five or six years to build a new power station there is simply no question of meeting this extra demand in the short-run by building an extra station. Hence in this case the short-run may last as long as five or six years.

Short-Run Changes in Output

Let us now examine the way in which we would expect output to react to changes in the quantity of inputs used, assuming that one input is fixed and the other variable. In short, we are going to examine the relationship between inputs and outputs during a short-run period, when extra output can be produced only by adding more of the variable input to the same quantity of the fixed input.

Total Product

The most straightforward short-run production function is found by tracing out the relationship between the total output or **total product** (TP) obtained when different quantities of some variable input are added to a specific quantity of some fixed input. Let us consider the case of a firm producing cars.

In Diagram 6.2 output of cars is measured on the vertical axis, and quantities of labour appear on the horizontal axis. Since we are assuming that one input is fixed (in the case of the car firm, we take this to be capital equipment), any point on the graph will represent the maximum number of cars which can be manufactured using a certain quantity of labour and the fixed amount of capital equipment. Point A, for example, denotes that OQ_1 cars could be produced per week when ON_1 people are employed.

The curve labelled 'Total Product' in Diagram 6.2 shows the relationship between output and inputs which is held to exist whenever more and more of a variable input is added to a certain quantity of a fixed input. Notice the trend of the curve.[3] When a relatively small number of workers is employed in the firm, output of cars rises at an increasing rate as more workers are employed. For example, expanding the labour force from ON_2 to ON_3 raises total output from OQ_2 to OQ_3. This rise in output is greater than that (OQ_1 to OQ_2) following an increase in the labour force from ON_1 to ON_2. As more and more workers are employed, however, the rate of increase in production appears to slow down. When ON_4 workers are employed, OQ_4 cars are produced. By increasing the

[3] The fact that the curve is smooth and continuous means that we assume that the features being measured are infinitely divisible. There may be great practical objections to implying that we can talk about 'half a man', but we shall keep the simplifying assumption just now.

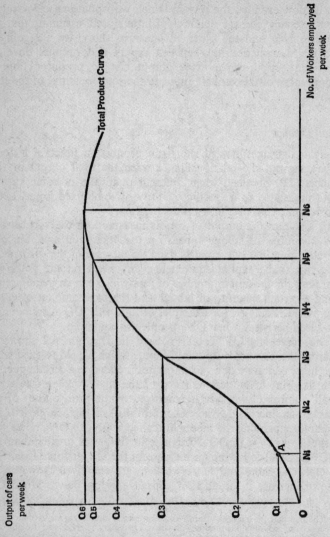

Figure 6.2 Total product curve

labour force to ON_5, output expands to OQ_5 which is again a smaller change than those considered at first. When employment is further expanded to ON_6, output of cars increases from OQ_5 to OQ_6 which is in turn a smaller increment than OQ_4 to OQ_5. When the firm is employing ON_6 workers, any further additions to the labour force seem to reduce total output. The reason for the shape of this total product curve lies in a long-established principle of microeconomics, called the **Principle of Diminishing Marginal Productivity** (sometimes known as the **Law of Diminishing Returns**). We will understand this more easily if the concepts of **average product** and **marginal product** are explained first.

Average and Marginal Product

By dividing total output at any level of input by that quantity of input we find that **average product** (AP) is given by:

$$AP = \frac{TP}{N}, \text{ where } TP = \text{total product, and } N = \text{quantity of labour}$$

Using this formula in our example of the car firm, we can see that by using ON_1 workers, the number of cars produced is OQ_1. The average product of ON_1 workers is therefore denoted by OQ_1/ON_1. Geometrically, this can be measured by the slope of a line OR_1 (called a **ray**) from the origin to point A, as shown in Diagram 6.3.

Using this geometric device, we can see instantly how average product changes with any change of input by drawing the appropriate ray, because average product will be greater the steeper the slope of the ray. Rays OR_2 and OR_3 have steeper slopes than OR_1, and so average product is increasing as the quantity of labour is increased from ON_1 to ON_3. But notice what happens when we measure average product when the quantity of labour is ON_4. The appropriate ray is OR_4, the slope of which is less steep than OR_3. We can therefore say that average product increases at first when the input of labour is relatively small, but declines after a certain point has been reached. This point is, in fact, reached when ON_3 workers are employed, because the corresponding ray measuring average product, OR_3, is a tangent to the total product curve at point B. OR_3 thus has the highest slope of a line from the origin to any point on the total product curve, and average product is highest when ON_3 workers are employed.

Marginal Product is the change in total output due to a one unit

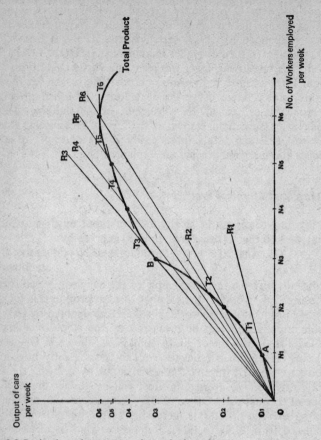

Figure 6.3 Derivation of average and marginal product

change in the quantity of input; hence in our example it can be defined as:

$$MP = \frac{\Delta TP}{\Delta N},$$ where ΔN stands for a (one) unit change in the quantity of labour used, and ΔTP measures the corresponding increment in output.

We can apply this definition to the example of the car manufacturer in order to see how marginal product varies as increasing numbers of workers are employed. In Diagram 6.2, we have already noted that when the number of workers increases from ON_1 to ON_2, total product rises from OQ_1 to OQ_2. Marginal product is therefore Q_1Q_2/N_1N_2, and a good approximation to this rate of change of total product as labour is varied is found by observing the slope of a tangent to the total product curve; such a tangent is shown by T_2 in Diagram 6.3.

By using a series of tangents to the total product curve, we can see how marginal product changes as labour is increased, since the steeper the slope of the tangent, the greater the value of marginal product. Tangent T_2 is steeper than T_1, and so marginal product is increasing when ON_2 workers are employed. But the slope of T_3 is less steep than the slope of T_2, and the slopes of T_4, T_5 and T_6 become even less steep until at T_6 the slope is zero. Thus the same general pattern emerges with marginal product as was the case with average product. At first marginal product rises and then falls, eventually becoming zero when ON_6 workers are employed, and negative thereafter.

It is interesting to compare the slopes of the rays and the tangents in Diagram 6.3, because this comparison indicates the relative values of average product and marginal product as the quantity of labour is increased. Since T_1 and T_2 have steeper slopes than OR_1 and OR_2 respectively, this must mean that marginal product exceeds average product when ON_1 and ON_2 workers are employed. However, the slopes of T_3 and OR_3 are exactly the same, and so when ON_3 workers are employed marginal product is equal to average product (and average product is at a maximum). When more labour is added, average product is greater than marginal product since the slopes of rays such as OR_5 and OR_6 are greater than the slopes of tangents T_5 and T_6.

The relationships between total product, average product and marginal product can be brought together again by drawing a curve to represent the way in which each varies as the quantity of labour is increased. The total, average and marginal product curves are illustrated in Diagram 6.4.

One general feature common to each of the curves in Diagram 6.4 is the way in which they rise as labour is increased over a certain range, reach a maximum point, and then fall with further additions of labour. The total product curve, for example, rises steeply when

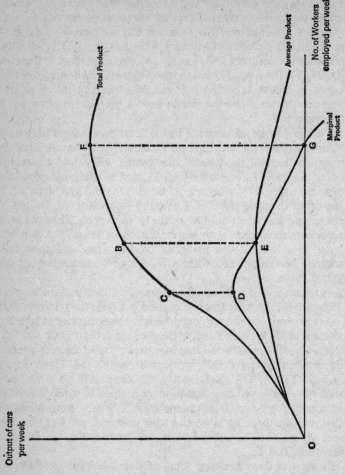

Figure 6.4 Total, average and marginal product curves

there is a relatively small labour input; the rate at which it rises most quickly is found where a tangent to the curve has the maximum slope, i.e. point C. In addition, the tangent at point C must also denote the highest possible value of marginal product (which measures the rate of change of total product), and so point C corresponds to that quantity of input which also signifies the highest point on the marginal product curve (i.e. point D). After this point, total product increases at a diminishing rate, and consequently the marginal product curve falls.

It has already been shown that the steepest possible ray to the total product curve is a tangent to the curve at point B. Therefore point B defines the highest value of average product (point E on the average product curve) and it is also the point where average product equals marginal product. After point E, the average product curve falls. When the total product curve reaches point F, the tangent at this point is horizontal, indicating that marginal product is zero (point G on the marginal product curve). Since the total product curve falls after point F is reached, the marginal product curve crosses the horizontal axis; marginal product becomes negative because any additional increase in labour lowers total product.

To explain the shape of our curves we can now turn to a long-standing principle of economics – the 'law' of diminishing returns.

The 'Law' of Diminishing Returns

The shape of both the marginal product curve and the average product curve in Diagram 6.4 illustrate the fact that as more labour is added to the fixed quantity of capital, the extra number of cars produced by successive additions of workers (marginal product) and the number of cars per worker (average product) eventually begins to fall. Both of these effects are described in the 'law' of diminishing returns, which predicts that as more and more units of a variable input are combined with a fixed quantity of another input the addition to output following from each successive unit change in the variable input, and output per unit of variable input, will eventually fall.

One word is particularly important in the above paragraph – 'eventually'. As we have seen in Diagram 6.4, there may be circumstances in which both marginal product and average product rise. Such conditions can be noticed, for example, in agricultural production. When a farmer is cultivating an acre of land, the successive application of relatively small amounts of fertilizer results in large marginal increases in crop production. But 'eventually' the addition of more fertilizer ceases to make as much impact on production as the initial applications, and so diminishing returns set in. Thus the 'law' of diminishing returns only makes the prediction that marginal and average product will fall sometime during the process of adding variable inputs to fixed inputs.[4]

It is now possible to revisit one of the situations described at the beginning of this chapter, and provide an explanation. Diagram 6.1(a) illustrated the effect of increased power on the throughput of oil in pipe-lines of fixed diameter. Here, then, is a case where successive quantities of a variable input are being applied to a fixed quantity of another input, and the lines AB, CD, EF, GH and IJ represent total product curves. These curves clearly demonstrate diminishing returns when relatively large amounts of power are applied in pipe-lines of different diameters; they also show that the marginal product of low quantities of power shows a faster rate of initial increase (i.e. before diminishing returns set in) the greater the diameter of pipe-line. This can be inferred from the fact that the total product curves for the widest pipe-lines rise most steeply.

Isoquants

Let us now move on to consider how we can analyse relationships between inputs and outputs under conditions when all or more than one of the inputs are variable. Such conditions could either be seen in the **long-run** (i.e. when all inputs are variable) or in the **short-run** when a firm uses many inputs, *two* of which are variable. We can revisit the example of the car manufacturer and pose the question, 'How does output respond to changes in the quantities used of both inputs, i.e. capital and labour?' One interesting feature of the reply to this question would be that any particular level of output could technically be produced by using different combinations of the inputs.

For example, the car manufacturer would probably find that in order to produce 100 cars per week *different proportions* of capital and labour might be technically feasible. It might be discovered that 100 cars per week could be produced by combining 500 workers with one machine, or 350 workers with two machines, or 280 workers with three machines, or 230 workers with four machines. One device

---

[4] In addition, there might well be some situations where diminishing returns occur immediately. In such cases, it is clear that the application of the first unit of the variable input gives the greatest return, and from that point, marginal product and average product both fall. Cases like this, of course, are still quite consistent with the prediction about diminishing returns, the only difference being that diminishing returns do not occur 'eventually', but from the outset.

often used to identify all possible combinations of inputs technically capable of producing the same level of output is called an **isoquant**. An illustration is given in Diagram 6.5 (and, of course, in Diagram 6.1(*b*)).

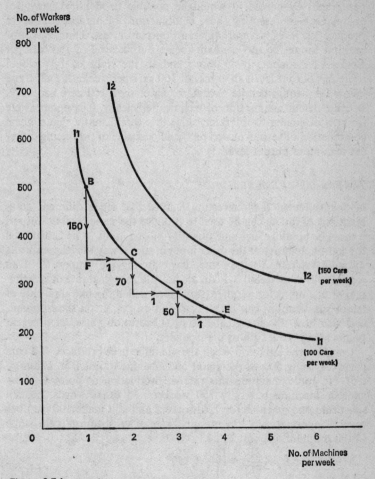

Figure 6.5 Isoquants

In Diagram 6.5 isoquant I_1I_1 denotes all combinations of capital and labour capable of producing 100 cars per week, where units of capital and units of labour are measured on the horizontal and vertical axes, respectively. The points B, C, D and E correspond to the combinations of capital and labour mentioned in the previous paragraph. Of course, it would be possible to identify many isoquants each representing those combinations of inputs required to, produce each of several different output levels. Thus I_2I_2, for example, might be the isoquant for an output level of 150 cars per week. All isoquants lying above and to the right of I_1I_1 would represent output levels in excess of 100 cars per week, and all those below I_2I_2 would denote outputs of fewer than 100 cars per week. Because of our assumption of technical efficiency, it is not possible for two isoquants to intersect, since this would imply that a given combination of resources was physically capable of producing different maximum output levels.

The Principle of Substitution

Isoquants reveal the interesting feature that since different combinations of inputs can be used to produce the same level of output, it must be possible for some quantity of one input to be substituted for a given quantity of the other input in such a way that the resulting output level remains the same. By analysing the properties of an isoquant in more detail, we can see how the **marginal rate of substitution** of one input for another (sometimes called the marginal rate of factor substitution) can be measured at any point on the isoquant, and also how this marginal rate of substitution varies at different points along the length of the isoquant.

Consider the situation when the manufacturer produces 100 cars per week using 500 workers and one machine (point B in Diagram 6.5). He could maintain this rate of production at point C using another machine but only 350 workers. In other words, he can substitute one machine for 150 workers and still make 100 cars per week. Diagramatically, the marginal rate of substitution is the slope of the isoquant at point B, i.e.

$$\text{MRS C for L} = \frac{\text{BF}}{\text{FC}} = \frac{150}{1} = 150$$

It can also be shown that as more capital and less labour is employed in the production at a given level of output, the marginal rate of substitution of capital for labour declines. Moving along the isoquant between points B, C, D and E involves a series of one unit increases in the quantity of capital used. The fall in the number of workers required to achieve the move from B to C is 150, from C to D it is 70, and from D to E it is 50. The marginal rate of substitution of capital for labour therefore diminishes from 150 to 70 to 50. In other words, less and less labour is replaced by each additional machine as a movement down the isoquant takes place. The reason for the convex shape of isoquants lies in the principle of diminishing marginal rate of substitution between inputs.

We can further explore the significance of the principle of substitution by linking it to the concept of marginal product. Given a move along an isoquant, the loss in output due to a decrease in the quantity of one input must be exactly offset by the increased output caused by the extra amount of the alternative input which must be used. Let us call the marginal product lost by employing fewer workers MP_L and the marginal product of an extra machine MP_C. Since total product is the same at points B and C on isoquant I_1I_1, then

$$MP_L \times BF = MP_C \times FC$$

or $\quad \dfrac{MP_C}{MP_L} = \dfrac{BF}{FC} = $ MRS capital for labour,

hence **the marginal rate of substitution of capital for labour is equal to the ratio of their marginal products.**

This relationship can be used to explain further the hypothesis of a diminishing marginal rate of substitution between the inputs. As the marginal rate of substitution of capital for labour declines, the value of the ratio MP_C/MP_L must also be falling. In turn, the reason might be either that MP_C is decreasing, MP_L is rising, or both. By recalling our analysis of product curves, it can be shown that MP_C is falling and MP_L increasing as a move down the isoquant takes place. When a large amount of labour is combined with a small amount of capital (e.g. point B) MP_C is high and MP_L is low.

But moving down the isoquant alters the relative proportions of capital and labour used to produce the same output level, combining relatively larger quantities of capital with relatively smaller amounts of labour. When this happens, MP_C (by the 'law' of diminishing returns) begins to fall whereas MP_L rises. In other words, the ratio MP_C/MP_L decreases, implying that there exists a diminishing marginal rate of substitution of capital for labour as more machines are substituted for workers.

Economic Region of Production

So far we have looked at what might be called 'normally-shaped' isoquants which fall continuously from left to right. It is just possible, however, that our car manufacturer, in estimating isoquants for several levels of output, discovers an isoquant map as portrayed in Diagram 6.6

The major difference between the isoquants in Diagram 6.6 and the isoquants which were analysed initially lies in those segments which bend backwards. Points P, Q, R, S, T, U, V and W mark the exact combinations of inputs where the isoquants begin to behave differently, and lines OX and OY have joined these points to form two boundaries. What, then, is the significance of the segments of the isoquants lying outside boundaries OX and OY?

The segments beyond OX and OY represent stages of production where the marginal product of one of the inputs is negative. For example, what would be the implications of a move from point Q to point N on isoquant $I_2 I_2$? Such a move means that increasing the quantity of capital used requires an accompanying *increase* in the quantity of labour used to maintain the same level of output of 150 cars per week. The reason for having to increase the quantities of both inputs could only be that the marginal product of one of them – in this case capital – was negative. Hence the fall in total product incurred by using more capital in the segment of isoquant $I_2 I_2$ above Q would require compensation by employing more labour, and not less. Similarly, moving from U to M denotes negative marginal productivity of labour, since increasing the quantity of labour would have to be accompanied by an increase in the quantity of capital used to maintain the same output level.

The **ridge lines** OX and OY are thus useful for separating those combinations of the inputs where the marginal product of both inputs is positive from those combinations of inputs where the marginal product of one of the inputs is negative. Hence all points on the isoquants above OX denote negative marginal product of capital, and all points on the isoquants below OY represent negative marginal product of labour. It follows that points P, Q, R and S define combinations of capital and labour where the marginal product of capital is zero, and points T, U, V and W define combinations of capital and labour where the marginal product of labour is zero. The appearance of negative marginal productivity in the

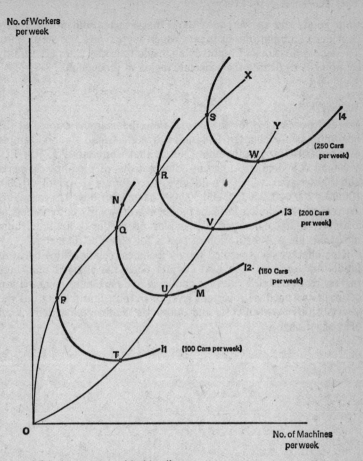

Figure 6.6 Isoquant map with ridge lines

case of one of the inputs might occur when so much of that input was being used in the production process (e.g. the number of men working at each machine) that some kind of saturation level is reached. To employ more of the input would literally do more harm than good, and so we can assume that firms would not seriously consider combinations of inputs which lay beyond the ridge lines. These combinations of inputs lying inside the ridge lines are said by economists to denote the **economic region of production.**

Conclusions

We can now revisit for the second time the example quoted at the beginning of the chapter. Diagram 6.1(*b*) illustrated a good example of isoquants for oil pipe-lines. Notice that isoquants PQ, RS, TU, VW and XY denoted different combinations of pipe-line diameter and horsepower which would give throughputs of oil of 50,000, 100,000, 200,000, 250,000 and 300,000 barrels per day. The isoquants are remarkably similar in shape to the ones drawn in our hypothetical example, and so demonstrate similar properties – a diminishing marginal rate of substitution of power for pipe-line diameter.

This chapter has specified purely technical relationships between inputs and outputs. The next chapter takes the analysis one stage further by developing rules for choosing one particular combination of inputs to produce a certain level of output, and tracing out the relationships between costs and output as the firm expands its level of production.

Chapter 7

Relationships Between Costs and Output

We shall begin this chapter by analysing the way in which a firm may choose one particular combination of inputs to produce a certain level of output. We shall then consider different levels of output and the costs incurred in producing them. The relationships which we shall develop between costs and output levels will form one part of the information needed in specifying which particular output level a firm should produce.

Choosing the Least-Cost Combination of Inputs

The isoquants illustrated in Chapter 6 showed the car manufacturer the different quantities of capital and labour which could be combined to produce a certain number of cars per week. How is he to choose which particular combination of capital and labour should be used to produce, say, 200 cars per week? Since we have made the assumption that firms attempt to maximise profits, it follows that the car manufacturer will choose the **least-cost** combination of labour and capital for any level of output, since to choose a more expensive combination of labour and capital would be inconsistent with the objective – some profit would be foregone. Thus the problem can now be put very simply. Given alternative methods of producing 200 cars per week, how can the manufacturer choose the least-cost method? To find this we need an extra piece of information, namely the **relative prices** of capital and labour. We can then calculate the total cost of each combination and select the one with the lowest total cost. An illustration is given in Table 7.1.

Table 7.1 shows the different combinations of capital and labour required to produce 200 cars per week, e.g. 1 machine and 620 workers, or 2 machines and 480 workers, etc. Given that the cost of each machine is £1,000 per week and the cost of labour is £20 in terms of man-hours per week, it is possible to calculate the total cost of producing 200 cars per week by each of the different input combinations. The calculations clearly show that the least-cost

Table 7.1

Number of Machines	Cost per Machine (£)	No. of Workers	Cost per Worker (£)	Combined Cost (£)
1	1,000	620	20	13,400
2	1,000	480	20	11,600
3	1,000	370	20	10,400
4	1,000	300	20	10,000
5	1,000	270	20	10,400
6	1,000	250	20	11,000

combination of capital and labour is 4 machines and 300 workers.

This argument and conclusion may also be shown graphically. The isoquant illustrating the different ways of producing 200 cars per week is drawn in Diagram 7.1. Also included in Diagram 7.1 are the lines BA and DC which denote all those combinations of capital and labour which can be purchased for £11,000 and £10,000 respectively. Lines such as BA and DC are called **iso-cost lines** and we can explain their construction as follows.

Let us consider for example point U. The total cost of the combination of labour and capital at U would be £11,000. It is possible to construct a line which joins together all those combinations of capital and labour which cost £11,000. For example, if £11,000 was spent only on capital, the car manufacturer could run 11 machines (each machine costs £1,000 per week), denoted by point A. Alternatively, £11,000 could be spent only on labour, in which case 550 workers could be hired, as shown by point B. Joining points such as A, U and B gives a line which shows those input combinations having the same total cost (or which can be purchased for the same expenditure), i.e. an iso-cost line. In principle, such lines could be drawn for any level of expenditure, as in CD which denotes the iso-cost line for an expenditure of £10,000. The further the position of the line from the origin, given the relative prices of the two inputs, the higher the level of total cost denoted by each point on any iso-cost line.

More generally, we can represent the total cost (TC) of any combination of labour (L) and machinery (M) by the equation:

$$TC = Mp + Lw,$$ where p and w represent the cost per machine and worker per week respectively.

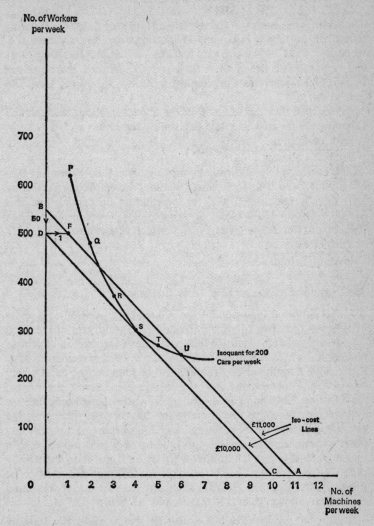

Figure 7.1 The least-cost combination of inputs to produce a
given output

Thus for a total cost of £11,000,

$$11,000 = 1,000 \times 5 + 20 \times 300$$

or $11,000 = 1,000M + 20L$

or $L = 550 - 50M$

The latter is the equation for the iso-cost line for £11,000,[1] showing that when no labour is bought 11 machines can be purchased (i.e. when $L = 0$, $M = 11$), when no machines are employed 550 workers can be hired (i.e. when $M = 0$, $L = 550$). When 5 machines are bought 300 workers can be employed (i.e. when $M = 5$, $L = 300$) and so on.

Notice also that the value 50 in the above equation measures the slope[2] of the iso-cost line, and is given by the ratio

$$\frac{\text{Price of Capital}}{\text{Price of Labour}} = \frac{1,000}{20} = 50$$

This can be seen graphically by moving down the iso-cost line BA. By moving from B to F, 50 fewer workers are employed (shown by BD) thereby releasing £1,000 for expenditure on capital, and this £1,000 will buy 1,000/1,000, or 1 machine (shown by DF). Thus the slope of line BA is given by 50/1, which is the ratio

$$\frac{\text{Price of Capital}}{\text{Price of Labour}}$$

Identifying the Minimum Cost Input Combination

By superimposing the isoquant for 200 cars per week on to a series of iso-cost lines (two of which, BA and DC, are drawn in Diagram 7.1), it is possible to identify that particular combination of labour and capital which will produce 200 cars per week at minimum cost. The cheapest combination of inputs will be found at the point where the isoquant touches the lowest possible (i.e. nearest the origin) iso-cost line. This point is shown by S, where the iso-cost line for £10,000 is a tangent to the isoquant for 200 cars. At this point, the car manufacturer uses 4 machines and 300 workers. If he chose any other combination of capital and labour, he would move on to a higher iso-cost line which implies a higher total cost than denoted by point S. Conversely, it is not possible for 200 cars per week to be produced for less than £10,000 since any iso-cost line representing expenditure lower than £10,000 would lie below (i.e. would not

[1] Readers who are unfamiliar with equations of straight lines should derive the equation for different iso-cost lines, e.g. £10,000, £9,000 etc. *See also* C. D. Harbury, *Introduction to Economic Behaviour*, Ch. 9.

[2] Iso-cost lines have similar properties to budget lines as analysed in Chapter 4.

touch) CD, and would specify combinations of labour and capital which are not capable of producing as many as 200 cars per week.

We can therefore conclude that given different technical methods of producing a certain level of output (as shown on an isoquant), the least-cost method is found at the point where the isoquant is a tangent to an iso-cost line (which reflects the relative prices of the two inputs).

Implications of the Tangency Point between an Isoquant and an Iso-cost Curve

At the point of tangency between an isoquant and an iso-cost line the slopes of the two curves must be exactly equal. We have already shown that the slope of an isoquant denotes the marginal rate of substitution of capital for labour, and the slope of an iso-cost line denotes the ratio of the price of capital to the price of labour. Thus the selection of the least-cost method of producing a certain level of output is achieved when

$$\frac{\text{Marginal Rate of Substitution}}{\text{(Capital for Labour)}} = \frac{\text{Price of Capital}}{\text{Price of Labour}}$$

Since an isoquant shows the rate at which one input technically substitutes for another input and an iso-cost line shows the rate at which one input can be substituted for another input given their money prices, it can easily be shown that these two rates must be the same for the least-cost method of production to be chosen.

Let us consider first point Q, denoting a combination of 2 machines and 480 workers. It would clearly be worthwhile for the car manufacturer to move from Q to R for the following reason. Between Q and R the marginal rate of substitution between capital and labour is 110, since one machine can be technically substituted for 110 workers in order to maintain production at 200 cars per week. But the ratio of the price of capital to the price of labour is such that the services of 2 machines can be obtained with the payments which would otherwise be made to 110 workers. In other words, doing without 110 workers saves the car manufacturer £2,200, and it is necessary technically only to substitute 1 machine costing an extra £1,000. Thus by moving from Q to R the total cost of production is lowered by £2,200 − £1,000 = £1,200.

Similarly, in moving from R to S, the marginal rate of substitution is 70 since 1 machine now technically substitutes for 70 workers. This ratio, however, is still higher than the ratio of the prices of the factors. It would therefore pay the car manufacturer to move from R to S since £1,400 would be saved by employing 70 fewer workers but only an extra £1,000 is required to run an extra machine, thereby reducing total costs of production by a further £400.

To go further down the isoquant beyond S, however, would only raise the total costs of production again. Since 1 machine technically substitutes for 30 workers in moving from S to T the marginal rate of substitution is now 30, which is less than the ratio of the price of capital to the price of labour. The saving of £600 in labour costs would be more than offset by the extra £1,000 needed to employ an extra machine.

In general, as long as the marginal rate of substitution between the two inputs is different from the ratio of their prices it will always be possible to lower the costs of producing any given level of output by substituting one input for another. Only when the marginal rate of substitution is exactly equal to the price ratio of the two inputs will the least-cost method of production be achieved.

Also, it was shown in Chapter 6 that the marginal rate of substitution between two inputs is given by the ratio of their marginal products, i.e.

$$\text{MRS (C for L)} = \frac{MP_C}{MP_L}$$

Therefore
$$\text{MRS (C for L)} = \frac{MP_C}{MP_L} = \frac{P_C}{P_L},$$

where P_C and P_L denote the price of capital and labour respectively.

Hence
$$\frac{MP_C}{P_C} = \frac{MP_L}{P_L},$$

which is simply a shorthand way of saying that in order to produce any given level of output, the least-cost combination of inputs is achieved when the marginal product per pound spent is the same for each input. Only when this condition is satisfied is it impossible to lower costs by rearranging the combination of inputs.

Changes in the Relative Prices of Inputs

So far, we have assumed that the prices of the factors are given and considered how the car manufacturer would choose one particular combination of capital and labour to produce 200 cars per week, given the technical possibilities as shown on the isoquant, and the relative prices as shown on the iso-cost line. Let us now consider what would happen if the relative prices of capital and labour changed. Suppose that the price of capital were to rise to £2,000 per week while the price of labour remained the same at £20 per week. Would 4 machines and 300 workers still be the least-cost combination of the 2 inputs, or would it pay the car manufacturer to substitute some quantity of one input for the other? Again, there are two ways in which we can answer this question, using Table 7.2 and Diagram 7.2.

Table 7.2

No. of Machines	Cost per Machine (£)	No. of Workers	Cost per Worker (£)	Combined Cost (£)
1	2,000	620	20	14,400
2	2,000	480	20	13,600
3	2,000	370	20	13,400
4	2,000	300	20	14,000
5	2,000	270	20	15,400
6	2,000	250	20	17,000

Table 7.2 shows the total cost of each combination of inputs required to produce 200 cars per week after the relative price change, and it is clear that the least-cost combination is now 3 machines and 370 workers when the prices of capital and labour are £2,000 and £20 respectively. In other words, the change in relative prices would force the car manufacturer to change his production method by employing relatively less capital and more labour than before.

By analysing the relative price change using isoquants and iso-cost lines we can see exactly why this substitution between the inputs would take place. If the car manufacturer continued to use 4 machines and 300 workers after the price of capital had risen to £2,000, the combined cost of the inputs would be £14,000 (4 × £2,000 + 30 × £20 = £14,000). As shown in Diagram 7.2, however, the iso-cost line for £14,000 (WV) is not a tangent to the isoquant for 200 cars per week at point S. Therefore we can say that point S is not now the least-cost method of producing 200 cars per week. If the car manufacturer substituted labour for capital and chose point R, where the iso-cost line XY (reflecting the new price ratio between labour and capital, since XY is parallel to WV) is a tangent to the isoquant, then point R would denote the least-cost method of

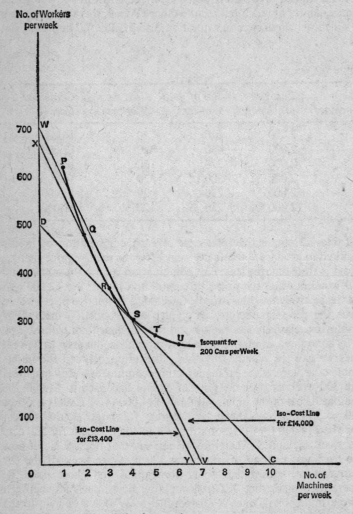

Figure 7.2 Change in relative input prices

producing 200 cars per week. By substituting labour for capital, the car manufacturer would now spend £13,400 (3 × £2,000 + 370 × £20), which is a lower total cost than he would have incurred by continuing to produce with the original factor combination.

Relationships Between Costs and Output

In a major investigation of production costs in a number of plants in various British manufacturing industries, a Cambridge economist, C. F. Pratten,[3] produced evidence to lend support to a long-standing theoretical relationship, namely that as the level of output in a particular plant is increased the total cost of production per unit tends to fall over a large range of output. We shall be examining some of the results in Pratten's study at the end of this chapter. First we shall trace out some general relationships between different levels of output and the costs of production associated with those levels, and then we shall see how far our theoretical relationships are consistent with some of the empirical evidence.

So far, we have considered the rules which the car manufacturer could use in choosing the least-cost combination of inputs to produce one particular level of output, i.e. 200 cars per week. But in setting up a plan for production the car manufacturer would surely also wish to consider other levels of output and the costs incurred in producing them. By drawing a set of isoquants, each representing a particular level of output, and a set of iso-cost lines, it is possible to trace out the least-cost combination of inputs for each output level, and in this way we may derive the total cost of each and every output level in which the manufacturer may be interested.

Diagram 7.3 illustrates isoquants Q_1, Q_2 and Q_3 representing output levels of 200, 250 and 300 cars per week respectively. The iso-cost lines DC, EF and GH are added and so from the tangency points S, J and K we can derive the least-cost combination of inputs required to produce each of the output levels mentioned, assuming that the relative prices of capital and labour remain constant. In fact by joining points S, J and K we can see an expansion path which denotes the combinations of inputs, and their combined costs, as output rises from 200 to 300 cars per week. To produce 250 cars per week, 5 machines and 330 workers would be used, giving a total cost of £11,600. The total cost of inputs would rise to £13,000 when

[3] C. F. Pratten, *Economies of Scale in Manufacturing Industry* Cambridge University Press 1971.

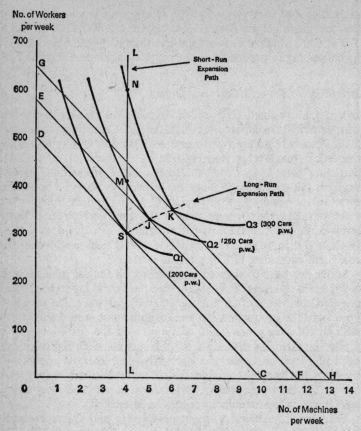

Figure 7.3 Short-run and long-run expansion of output

6 machines and 350 workers are used to produce 300 cars per week. The expansion path SJK is drawn on the assumption that the car manufacturer is able to vary the combinations of *both* capital and labour as output expands. It may be the case, however, that he finds it a much more difficult or a much longer process to vary the quantity of one input than to vary the quantity of the other. We need to

reintroduce at this stage the distinction between the short-run and the long-run discussed in the previous chapter. The path SJK denotes that long-run conditions are operating since the quantities of both inputs can be varied as output expands. There would, however, be an alternative expansion path if we assumed short-run conditions where the quantity of one input, let us suppose machinery, was fixed so that an expansion of output could only be achieved by adding more labour to the fixed quantity of machinery. What would such a short-run expansion path look like, and how would it differ from the long-run expansion path?

If we assume that the car manufacturer's quantity of capital is limited to 4 machines in the short-run, expansion of car production to 250 and 300 cars per week can only be achieved by moving along the vertical line LL in Diagram 7.3 and determining the points where LL intersects the isoquants Q_2 and Q_3, i.e. at points M and N respectively. In other words, in the short-run the car manufacturer would be forced to produce 250 cars per week using 4 machines and 410 workers, compared with 5 machines and 330 workers if both inputs had been variable in quantity. Similarly, 300 cars per week must be produced in the short-run by using 4 machines and 600 workers, compared with 6 machines and 350 workers on the long-run expansion path. Thus long-run and short-run conditions involve quite markedly different input combinations as output expands.

As a consequence of this difference, the total cost of producing any level of output other than 200 cars per week is greater under short-run conditions than under long-run conditions. We can understand this proposition in two ways. First we can compute the total costs of production incurred using the combination of inputs denoted by point M ($4 \times 1,000 + 410 \times 20 = £12,200$) and compare the total with the long-run input combination specified by J, which was £11,600. Similarly we could compare the costs of the input combination shown at N ($4 \times 1,000 + 600 \times 20 = £16,000$) and at K (£13,000). Alternatively, it can be seen from Diagram 7.3 that points such as M and N must lie on iso-cost lines which are higher than (and so not tangents to) the iso-cost lines which are tangents to the isoquants on which points like M and N lie. For output levels except 200 cars per week, therefore, total costs of production in the short-run will exceed total costs in the long-run.

Costs and Output in the Short-run

Let us now suppose that the car manufacturer decides on some particular scale of car production and sets up his plant and installs machinery accordingly. In the short-run, such inputs can be considered as fixed in the sense that any change in output within a given size of plant can only be made by employing more or less of the variable input, labour. Since the quantity of some inputs is fixed it follows that the total cost of those inputs is fixed in the short-run also. Hence the concept of **total cost of production** in the short-run is really an aggregate of two components – **total fixed costs** and **total variable costs,** where total fixed costs are the costs of the fixed inputs such as machinery, and total variable costs are the costs of labour at each possible level of output. Let us suppose that the car manufacturer builds a plant and installs machinery to manufacture 200 cars per week. From our analysis of long-run conditions, the cheapest combination of inputs for 200 cars per week would involve him installing 4 machines. Thus the cost of 4 machines (once they have been installed) becomes a fixed cost in the short-run, and we could specify the relationships between total costs and different output levels in the short-run, as shown in Table 7.3 and Diagram 7.4.

Table 7.3

Output	Total Fixed Costs (£)	Total Variable Costs (£)	Short-run Total Cost (£)
0	4,000	0	4,000
50	4,000	1,800	5,800
100	4,000	3,300	7,300
150	4,000	4,600	8,600
200	4,000	6,000	10,000
250	4,000	8,200	12,200
300	4,000	12,000	16,000

Table 7.3 shows that once 4 machines have been installed, a fixed cost of £4,000 is incurred irrespective of the level of output actually produced. In other words, if the car manufacturer wanted to change production from 200 cars per week to 250 cars per week, he could only achieve this by employing 110 additional workers at a cost

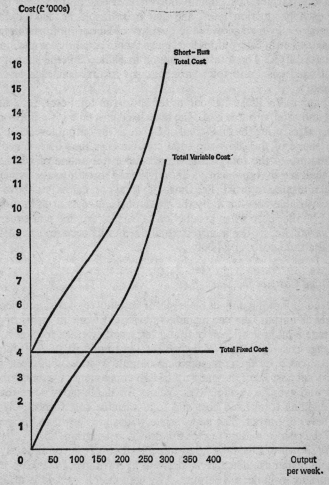

Figure 7.4 Short-run total cost, total variable cost, and total fixed cost

(variable) of £2,200. If he wanted to decrease output to 150 cars per week, he would still have to incur the fixed costs of the 4 machines, and even if production of cars fell to zero, the fixed cost for machinery would still have to be met. Hence the total fixed cost column in Table 7.3 shows the same value of £4,000 for each level of output. The total variable cost column illustrates the cost of the labour input for each production level, and can in principle be derived from Diagram 7.3 which showed the quantity of labour input required in the short-run at each output level given that the quantity of machinery remained fixed. The total cost column in Table 7.3 is the sum of the total fixed costs and total variable costs incurred at each level of output.

Diagram 7.4 illustrates curves for short-run total cost, total fixed cost and total variable cost. The total fixed cost curve is a horizontal line, representing the same total of £4,000 as the output level changes. The shape of the short-run total cost curve is thus determined by the nature of the total variable cost curve (the shape of which, as we shall see in a moment, is directly linked in turn to the principle of diminishing returns). The short-run total cost curve lies above the total variable cost curve by the value of fixed costs at each output level, so that even when production of cars is zero and consequently no variable costs are incurred, total fixed costs account completely for the total costs of £4,000.

Average Costs in the Short-Run

Instead of looking only at the levels of absolute total cost at different levels of output, the car manufacturer could work in terms of the **average total cost** of each output level, where average total cost (or average cost for short) is defined as the total cost of any output level divided by the corresponding output. Average total cost, just like total cost itself, is made up of two components – average fixed cost and average variable cost. Values for the latter two are found by dividing total fixed cost and to.al variable cost respectively by the level of output. The appropriate values are shown in Table 7.4 and the corresponding graphs are drawn in Diagram 7.5.

As shown in Diagram 7.5 average fixed cost falls continuously as output expands (since it is derived by dividing £4,000 by ever increasing volumes of output). Average variable cost falls at first, reaches a minimum point and then rises. The shape of the average variable cost curve is determined by the principle of diminishing returns. It has already been established in Chapter 6 that, in the short-run, adding more of a variable input to a given quantity of a fixed input will result in average product rising and then falling after a certain level of output. The average variable cost curve reflects the costs of the process of diminishing average product, and so the average variable cost curve takes the inverse shape to the average product curve. The declining part of the average variable cost curve corresponds to rising average product, and the rising part of the average variable cost curve to falling average product. To understand this relationship properly it is only necessary to remember that average variable cost is total variable cost divided by a certain output level:

$$AVC = \frac{TVC}{Q}$$
$$= \frac{N \times P}{Q}, \quad \text{where N is the quantity of the variable input, and P is the cost per unit of the variable input}$$

$\frac{NP}{Q}$ can be expressed as $P\left(\frac{N}{Q}\right)$, and the term $\left(\frac{N}{Q}\right)$ is the inverse of average product, since $AP = \frac{Q}{N}$

Hence the value of average variable cost varies in the inverse direction to the value of average product as output expands.

The shapes of the average fixed cost curve and the average variable

Table 7.4

Output	Total Cost (£)	Average Total Cost (£)	Average Fixed Cost (£)	Average Variable Cost (£)
0	4,000	—	—	—
50	5,800	116	80	36
100	7,300	73	40	33
150	8,600	57.3	26.7	30.6
200	10,000	50	20	30
250	12,200	48.8	16	32.8
300	16,000	53.3	13.3	40
350	21,000	60	11.4	48.6
400	28,000	70	10	60

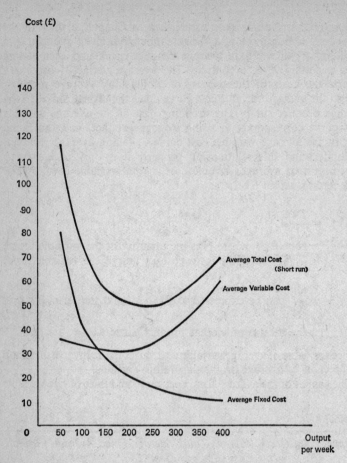

Cost (£)

140

130

120

110

100

90

80

70 — Average Total Cost
(Short run)

60 — Average Variable Cost

50

40

30

20

10 — Average Fixed Cost

0   50   100   150   200   250   300   350   400   Output
per week

Figure 7.5 Short-run average total cost, average variable cost and average fixed cost

cost curve help to explain why the average total cost curve in the short-run is 'U-shaped'. At relatively low levels of output, from zero to 200 cars per week, *both* average fixed costs and average variable costs are falling, so that average total cost must be falling. Even after average variable costs begin to rise after an output level of 200 cars per week, average fixed costs are still falling enough to offset this rise in average variable costs and so average total costs continue to fall until an output level of 250 cars per week is reached. After this point, the rise in average variable costs (due to falling average product) outweighs the continuous fall in average fixed costs and so average total costs begin to rise.

Marginal Cost in the Short-Run

The concept of **marginal cost** will assume great importance as we develop the theory of the firm. Marginal cost is defined as the incremental cost incurred by producing one extra unit of output. It is derived from the formula $\Delta TC/\Delta Q$, and since, in the strict sense, ΔQ is equal to one, the values for marginal cost can be derived by looking at the change in the levels of total cost as output expands by one unit. In our example, however, we have been looking at changes in output of 50 units, but we can approximate to the values of marginal cost by using the formula suggested and plotting the derived values on a graph at points midway between the 50 unit intervals. Thus the marginal cost as output expands from zero to 50 cars per week is given by $\dfrac{£5,800-4,000}{50} = £36$, and this value is plotted against an output level of 25 cars per week. The remaining values for short-run marginal cost are shown in Table 7.5 and the short-run marginal cost curve is illustrated in Diagram 7.6(b).

Table 7.5

Output	Total Cost (£)	Marginal Cost (£)
0	4,000	—
50	5,800	36
100	7,300	30
150	8,600	26
200	10,000	30
250	12,200	44
300	16,000	76
350	21,000	100
400	28,000	140

The short-run marginal cost curve falls over a certain range of output and then rises again. We can easily see why the short-run marginal cost curve must take such a shape, since the curve itself can be derived by drawing a series of tangents to the various points on the short-run total cost curve as shown in Diagram 7.6(a). The tangents T_1 and T_2 show that as output expands to 100 cars per week the slope of the short-run total cost curve declines, so that marginal cost must be falling. Tangent T_3 touches the short-run total cost curve at a point where its slope is least steep, and so at this point marginal cost is at a minimum. After that point tangents such as T_4, T_5 and T_6 become steeper again, indicating that marginal cost is rising.

We can also develop an important relationship between average cost and marginal cost. First, average cost is at a minimum when 250 cars per week are being produced. From Diagram 7.7(a) it can be seen that the ray and the tangent to the point on the total cost curve denoting 250 cars per week have the same slope. Therefore, marginal cost equals average cost when average cost is at a minimum, which can also be seen as the point of intersection of the two curves in Diagram 7.7(b). Also, when average cost is falling, marginal cost always has a lower value. At all output levels lower than 250 cars per week (i.e. when AC is falling) the marginal cost curve lies below the average cost curve, as shown in Diagram 7.7(b). An alternative way of understanding this relationship is to compare the slopes of the rays and the tangents in Diagram 7.7(a). At output levels lower than 250 cars per week, the slopes of the tangents (measuring MC) to the total cost curve are less than the slopes of the rays (measuring AC). It can also be seen from Diagram 7.7(b) that marginal cost is greater than average cost at output levels higher than 250 cars per week, and this relationship is confirmed in Diagram 7.7(a) where the slopes of the tangents to the total cost curve after the output level of 250 cars per week are greater than the slopes of the rays.

The explanation for this relationship between average and marginal cost is really arithmetical. A good analogy is a cricketer's batting average. When each additional score (marginal score) is less than his average score, then his average will fall; when each successive score is higher than his average, his average score will rise. Similarly if in a particular innings the marginal score is equal to the previous average the average will remain unchanged.

The total variable cost curve has also been drawn in Diagram 7.7(a). Notice that the similarity in shape between the short-run

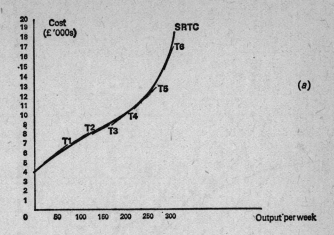

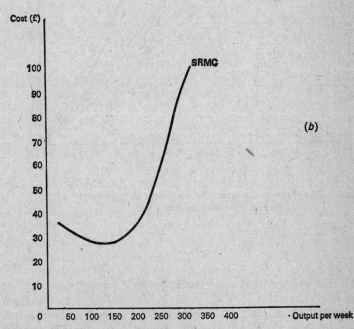

Figure 7.6 (a) Tangents to the short-run total cost curve
(b) short-run marginal cost curve

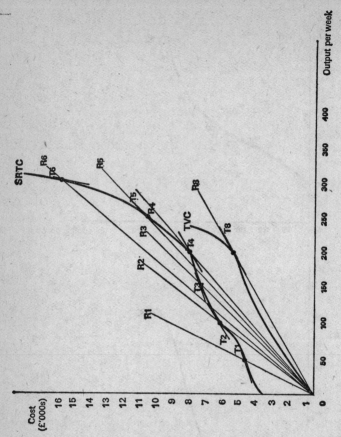

Figure 7.7 (a) Rays and tangents to the short-run total cost
curve and total variable cost curve

total cost and the total variable cost curve is simply due to the fact
that SRTC is equal to TVC with the constant fixed cost element
added at each output level. Hence at each output level both curves
have the same slope. For example, marginal cost for 200 cars per
week is given by the tangent T_4 or tangent T_8 to the total variable

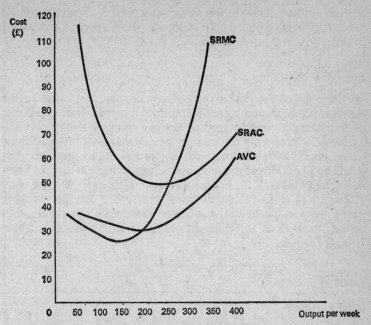

Figure 7.7 (*b*) The SRMC curve cuts the SRAC and AVC curves at their lowest points

cost curve. Since a ray to the TVC curve will measure average variable cost at any point, we can see that ray R_8 denotes average variable cost incurred by producing 200 cars per week. However, ray R_8 and tangent T_8 have the same slope, and since R_8 denotes the minimum level of AVC, we can therefore deduce that marginal cost will be equal to average variable cost when the latter has its lowest value. This is illustrated graphically in Diagram 7.7(*b*) where the average variable cost curve is intersected at its minimum point by the marginal cost curve.

Costs in the Long-Run

Let us now suppose that long-run conditions are operating and trace out some relationships between costs and output, assuming that the car manufacturer can vary the amounts of both capital and labour in order to expand production.

Long-Run Total Cost

We have already seen that the concept of total cost refers to the aggregate cost of inputs used to produce a certain level of output. In the example we developed at the beginning of the chapter the total cost of producing 200 cars per week under long-run conditions would be £10,000; the total cost of producing 250 cars per week would be £11,600; and the total cost of producing 300 cars per week would be £13,000. If the car manufacturer estimated the total costs of producing levels of output from zero to 350 cars per week, it would be possible to derive a curve illustrating the relationship between total costs and different output levels, as shown in Table 7.6 and Diagram 7.8(a).

Table 7.6

Output	Long-Run Total Cost (£)	Long-Run Average Cost (£)	Long-Run Marginal Cost (£)
0	0	0	0
50	3,500	70	70
100	6,000	60	55
150	8,200	54.6	45
200	10,000	50	36
250	11,600	46.4	32
300	13,000	43.3	28
350	15,000	42.9	40
400	18,200	45.5	64
450	24,000	53.3	116

Each point on the long-run total cost curve (LRTC) in Diagram 7.8(a) denotes a point of tangency between an isoquant and an iso-cost line, and therefore represents the least-cost combination of inputs required to produce each level of output. Thus points S, J and K illustrated in Diagram 7.8(a) correspond to the points S, J and K shown in Diagram 7.3.

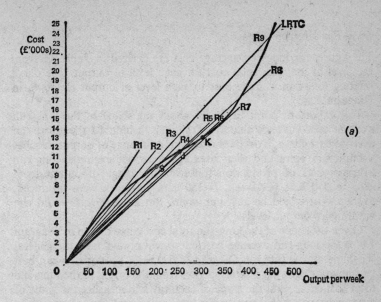

(a)

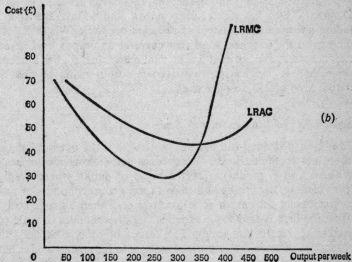

(b)

Figure 7.8 (a) Rays to the long-run. Total cost curve
(b) Long-run average and marginal cost curves

Long-Run Average Costs

The figures for long-run average cost are derived in Table 7.6 from the level of long-run total cost for each level of output. The curve relating long-run average cost to each level of output is shown in Diagram 7.8(b)

The important point to notice about the shape of the long-run average cost curve is that, in a similar fashion to the short-run average cost curve, it declines over a certain range of output, reaches a minimum point and then rises again. In our example, long-run average costs of production fall over the range of output from zero to 350 cars per week. If 350 cars per week were produced, average cost would be at a minimum. But average cost would rise with higher output levels.

Given the shape of the long-run total cost curve drawn in Diagram 7.8(a) the long-run average cost curve will always take the general 'U-shape' as indicated in Diagram 7.8(b). This proposition can best be shown by drawing a series of rays from the origin to the long-run total cost curve, and the slope of each ray will measure the value of average cost at each point on the total cost curve. Rays R_1 to R_7 in Diagram 7.8(a) have decreasing slopes, and so average cost is falling up to an output level of 350 cars per week. Where R_7 is a tangent to the long-run total cost curve at an output level of 350 cars per week, average cost has its minimum value. R_8 has a steeper slope than R_7, indicating that average cost is rising beyond the output level of 350 cars per week.

Economies and Diseconomies of Scale

The 'U-shaped' long-run average cost curve is the outcome of two important economic forces – **economies and diseconomies of scale.** When a firm is producing over a range of output where average cost is falling, the firm is said to be experiencing economies of scale (or increasing returns to scale); conversely, when average cost is rising the firm is said to be experiencing diseconomies of scale (or decreasing returns to scale). The forces of economies and diseconomies of scale are important enough to have generated a field of study all of their own, and we can only indicate here some of the features which may bring these forces into operation.

Economies of scale can arise through:

(*i*) **Division of Labour** As long ago as the eighteenth century, Adam Smith pointed out the significance of the division of labour, or specialisation, in factories which produced a large quantity of output. If a firm is small and employs only a few workers, each worker will probably have to undertake several different types of job in the production process. But larger output levels give the firm the opportunity to increase the specialisation of its labour force; to let workers concentrate on applying skills to particular jobs and thereby make for reduction in unit costs as output expands. Thus the larger firm can afford to hire workers who are proficient in the skills required at each stage in the manufacture of a product (the term 'skills' can equally well be applied to management, where the larger firm again has the opportunity of employing specialist types of management in the fields of accountancy, production, personnel, etc.).

Skills can also be increased by learning. The larger the production run the more a worker can learn about the nature of the job to be done, and so the more efficient the application of his skill is likely to be. Indeed a Dutch economist, P. J. Verdoorn, put forward the hypothesis that in some types of firms, especially those which manufacture their product using assembly-line techniques, learning through long production runs is a more important explanation of the different economies of scale observed between American and European plants than the sizes of plants themselves.

(*ii*) **Increased Dimensions** Some economies of scale derive from the effect on unit costs of the increased dimensions of some types of capital equipment. An oil tanker gives a good example of this type of scale economy. In absolute terms, larger tankers cost more than smaller tankers. But in terms of cost per unit (where 'units' refer to the capacity of the tanker in terms of oil), the increased costs of building larger tankers are roughly proportional to increases in the surface area of the tanker itself. But the productivity of the tanker is determined by its *capacity* which is proportional to the *volume* of the tanker. Thus the costs of increasing capacity rise less than in proportion to the increase in capacity itself, hence costs per unit decline. Economies of increased dimensions may be present in industries where containers such as furnaces, pipes, kilns, etc., are used.

Indeed in some industries, so predictable is the relationship between the increasing size of capital equipment and lower unit costs that engineers, especially in the chemical industry, often work with a rule-of-thumb known as **the 0.6 rule.** This rule briefly states that whenever the capacity of a piece of capital equipment is multiplied by a certain amount X, then the capital cost rises by $X^{0.6}$. More generally, economies due to increased dimensions can be expressed by the exponent **b** in the formula

   $C = aX^b,$

where C represents the capital cost, X represents output, **a** is a constant term, and **b** may be called the **coefficient of scale.** If the value of **b** is less than 1, economies of scale through increased dimensions are operating[4]; if $b = 1$, then capital costs per unit are rising in proportion to capacity; if **b** is greater than 1, then capital costs per unit are rising more than in proportion to capacity. In a study undertaken in America, two economists, Haldi and Whitcomb, analysed 678 types of manufacturing equipment and discovered that in 90 per cent of the cases the value of the scale coefficient was less than 1, with a very high proportion having a value between 0.5 and 0.7. We shall see later how important this type of scale economy is in two examples quoted in the study by Pratten mentioned at the beginning of this chapter.

(*iii*) **Economies to Firms** One reason for distinguishing between firms and plants in Chapter 5 was that in any discussion of economies of scale a distinction should be made between those economies purely affecting *plants* (in the sense of particular manufacturing establishments) and those economies that accrue to the *firm* which may have many plants. The reasons for economies of scale discussed so far refer to economies to the *plant* (since the analysis of cost curves is taking place within the context of a plant). Economies of scale to the *firm* may arise due to factors such as (*a*) **Bulk-buying** – where the large firm is able to obtain lower prices or discounts in the purchase of, say, raw materials or components for its product purely by virtue of its size and the size of the orders it can place; (*b*) **Finance** – where the large firm can receive loans to finance new developments at lower rates of interest than smaller and relatively less well-known firms which are considered greater risks than the larger company.

Diseconomies of Scale

When the long-run average cost curve begins to slope upwards, this

[4] Thus the 0.6 rule is one special case of the formula where b is believed to be 0.6.

means that diseconomies of scale are present. The major explanation for diseconomies of scale lies in the belief that managerial difficulties occur to such an extent once a certain output level has been reached that average costs begin to rise. There are many possible explanations for such management problems, e.g. difficulties in effectively controlling and monitoring the performance of such a large concern that inefficiency can go on unnoticed; difficulties in communication through the build-up of several layers of management so that decision-making becomes inefficient either in cases where decisions must always be referred to top management, or where delegation takes place but the quality of junior managers is poor.

Long-Run Marginal Cost

The definition of marginal cost is similar in long-run conditions as it is in short-run conditions – the change in total costs incurred by a one-unit change in output. Operationally, however, long-run marginal cost differs from short-run marginal cost in one important respect. In the long-run all costs are variable (and therefore marginal) by definition, whereas in the short-run we distinguished between fixed costs, which are not marginal in the sense that they remain unchanged by increases in output, and variable costs, which do vary as output increases.

Again, we can approximate to the values of marginal cost by using the formula suggested and plotting the derived values on a graph at points midway between the 50 unit intervals. Thus the marginal cost as output expands from zero to 50 cars per week is given by $\frac{£3,500-0}{50} = £70$, and this value is plotted against an output level of 25 cars per week. The remaining values for long-run marginal cost are shown in Table 7.6 and the long-run marginal cost curve is illustrated in Diagram 7.8(b).

As can be seen from Diagram 7.8(b), the marginal cost curve and the average cost curve stand in the same general relationship to each other in the long-run as in the short-run. As long as average cost is falling, marginal cost has a lower value. The marginal cost curve then cuts the average cost curve at its minimum point. When the average cost curve is rising the marginal cost curve lies above it.

Empirical Evidence About Cost Curves

The shape of the average cost curve (particularly in the long-run) has attracted a good deal of interest from economists. There are really two important questions which we should try to answer from the available evidence:

(i) Is there a general tendency for plants to exhibit long-run average cost curves which resemble those specified in theory? If the resemblance is confirmed, we shall be able to discover what level of output a par.icular plant would have to produce in order to achieve minimum long-run average cost. Such an output level is often referred to as the **optimum size** of a plant. In Chapter 8 the significance of this concept will be analysed in greater detail.

(ii) If long-run average cost curves in practice do bear some relation to long-run average cost curves in theory, what is the relation between the optimum level of output for a plant and the total quantity supplied to a market?

The reason for asking this question is that it will enable us to tell how much of a market would be supplied by a plant operating at the optimum scale. For example, it might be the case that in one industry the optimum size of plant would produce 50 per cent of the output to a market, and in another industry the optimum size of plant would account for only 5 per cent of the market output. Clearly this has implications for the number of plants of optimum size which can exist in any market. In the case where a plant of optimum size would produce 50 per cent of the market total, the industry could only sustain two plants operating at optimum size. In the case where the optimum size of a plant produced 5 per cent of the output to a market, 20 plants operating at optimum capacity could exist (presuming that plants had the same cost curves).

As we mentioned previously, the major investigation of the shape of long-run average cost curves in British manufacturing industries was undertaken by C. F. Pratten. The evidence which he produced tended, in most cases, to support the proposition that economies of scale exist over certain ranges of output. Pratten's investigations showed that for most firms average costs tended to fall continuously as output increased, or at least to remain constant after a certain level of output had been reached. In the latter event the firm is said to be experiencing constant returns to scale after economies of scale have been reaped, and the long-run average cost curve is said to be **L-shaped.** But Pratten found little evidence to suggest that diseconomies of scale existed.

For the purposes of his studies, Pratten used the term **Minimum Efficient Size** (MES) to denote that point on the long-run average cost curve beyond which further increases in scale would bring only a small reduction in unit costs. So the MES roughly corresponds to the minimum optimum size for the firm. To be strictly accurate, MES was defined as '. . . the minimum scale beyond which any possible subsequent doubling in scale would reduce total average unit costs by less than 5 per cent'.[5]

What, then are the implications of Pratten's investigations for the questions posed about the shape of cost curves? The following examples give illustrations.

Case 1 – The Chemical Industry – An Ethylene Plant In the chemical industry, the manufacture of ethylene gives an example of the economies of scale to be derived through increased dimensions. When the first plant to produce ethylene was set up in 1943, its capacity was limited to 12,000 tons per annum. Now it is possible to construct plants which would produce 450,000 tons per annum, the major source of economies of scale coming from the fact that although the fixed capital costs of ethylene plants are very high in absolute terms, capital costs do not rise in the same proportion as output. For example, it is estimated to cost £6 million to construct an ethylene plant capable of producing 100,000 tons per annum; but for a plant producing 200,000 tons per annum, the capital cost rises only to £10.8 million and then to only £13.3 for 300,000 tons per annum.

Pratten's estimates showed that the MES for an ethylene plant, as illustrated by point M in Diagram 7.9, is 300,000 tons per annum. At point M, cost per ton of ethylene is about £27.1. The dotted line past this point is an estimate of the pattern of average costs as plants are extended to output levels beyond 300,000 tons per annum. The curve flattens out because it is believed that potential economies of increased dimensions are not significant in the region of 450,000 to 500,000 tons per annum.

Also, if an ethylene plant was producing an output level of only half the MES level (point L), the increase in cost per unit would be £2.44, since cost per unit at point L is £29.54. In other words, a reduction of 8 per cent in unit costs is attainable by doubling the scale of plant from 150,000 tons per annum to 300,000 tons per annum. Further, since 300,000 tons per annum represents about 25 per cent of the UK output of ethylene, an ethylene plant of optimum size would provide about one quarter of the total market supply. We

[5] C. F. Pratten, op. cit., p. 278.

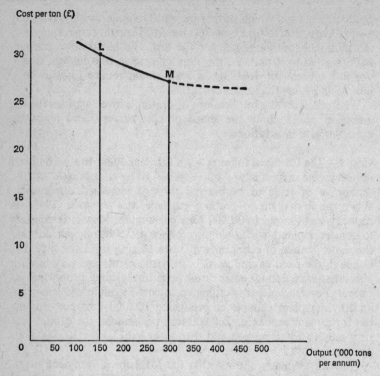

Figure 7.9 Economics of scale for an ethylene plant

could obviously interpret this as meaning that the UK market for ethylene is capable of sustaining only four ethylene plants operating at the optimum size.

Case 2 – Beer – Economies of Scale in Brewing Substantial economies of scale were found to exist in brewing. The sources are twofold – first, economies are reaped through increased dimensions as the size of the fixed capital costs for plant increase less than in proportion to the increase in output; secondly, specialisation of labour takes place as employees in breweries are able to operate more than one piece of equipment as the scale of plants increases. The results of the study are interpreted in Diagram 7.10.

The MES for a brewery was estimated at the time of Pratten's study at one million barrels per annum (point B in Diagram 7.10), although it was believed that economies of increased dimensions could exist for plants in the future operating at scales considerably above one million barrels per annum. If a brewery operated at half the MES (point A), the increase in unit costs would be about 9 per cent. Since the total output of beer to the UK market was about 31 million barrels per annum, a brewery operating at the MES would be producing about 3 per cent of the market output. One implication of this study, therefore, is that the beer industry is capable of sustaining a great number of plants operating at or near the MES.

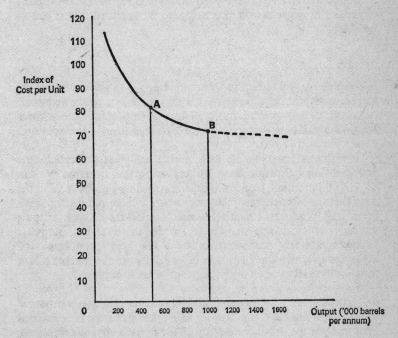

Figure 7.10 Economies of scale for a brewery

Chapter 8

Perfect Competition and Monopoly

In the following two chapters we shall develop a theory to show how a firm's revenue is affected by its level of output. Then by considering revenue in relation to costs we shall be able to specify the particular level of output which will maximise profits. In developing a theory of revenue, however, it is necessary to distinguish between the different types of market situation in which firms operate. The reason for this is that in order to make any sense out of the great diversity of business activity in the modern economy (referred to in Chapter 5), economists generally believe that there are three important aspects of industrial organisation which should be analysed. These are as follows:

Market Structure

In defining market structure we are looking for those features of the market environment which have a significant effect on the economic behaviour of firms in an industry. The most important factors which we shall consider in developing a theory about firms' behaviour are:

(*i*) **How many firms operate in a market and what proportion does each individual firm produce?** By answering this question we can begin to differentiate between industries (such as agriculture and the manufacture of some raw materials) where a large number of small firms each produces a relatively small proportion of total output; industries (such as the car industry) where the total UK output is almost completely accounted for by a few large producers; and industries in which one firm is so large relative to the market that it supplies virtually one hundred per cent of total output.

(*ii*) **What is the degree of substitutability between the goods produced by firms in a market?** This feature of market structure is concerned with whether the product made by all the firms is virtually the same, in which case the output of one firm is a very close substitute for the output produced by any other firm in the industry; or whether there are significant differences between the products of individual firms so that the types of goods produced in the industry cannot be considered as perfect substitutes for each other.

(*iii*) **How easy or difficult is it for potential new entrants to join the industry and begin production?** Are there barriers to entry which make it difficult or impossible for a potential new firm to set up in business should it be attracted, say, by a relatively high rate of profit being earned by the firms already in the industry?

Market Behaviour

It is widely believed that the three features of market structure mentioned above will influence firms' behaviour. In connection with behaviour we have two matters to consider in detail:

(*i*) **What policies can a firm adopt in relation to the price it charges for its product?** By looking for the answer to this question we are trying to establish the extent to which a firm has control over the price paid by consumers for the product it manufactures. Does the firm have virtually no control over the price it charges – simply accepting as unalterable the price set in the market by the general forces of supply and demand? Does the firm have control over the price of its product, unaffected by the actions of any other firms in the industry? Or does the firm have some control over its price but adapt its behaviour to the policies adopted by other firms?

The price behaviour of firms is largely determined by the market structure. We would intuitively expect, for example, that a market dominated by one firm will afford that firm more scope for controlling price than a market shared by a very large number of small firms.

(*ii*) **How does the firm behave in adapting its product to the needs of the market?** Some firms produce a good which is virtually identical to the output of all the other firms in a market. In other cases, however, depending upon market structure, firms may find it worthwhile to spend money on the packaging or design of the product in order to make it appear, in the eyes of consumers, to be slightly different from the goods made by competitors. In addition firms may spend money on advertising in the newspapers or on television in order to persuade consumers to buy their brand of the product in preference to all other brands.

Market Performance

When we have finished our analysis of market structure and the associated behaviour of firms we will attempt to set up criteria by which standards of performance can be assessed. In analysing standards of performance we will be concerned first with asking whether particular types of structure and behaviour help or hinder the attainment of an efficient solution to the basic economic problem considered in Chapter 1, namely the allocation of resources between the production of different goods and services in accordance with consumers' wishes. We shall be explaining a little later exactly how some appropriate measures of performance can be used to make such an assessment. We will also be concerned, in considering performance, with the study of wider economic objectives such as the full employment of resources, economic growth and the distribution of income.

The three factors – structure, behaviour and performance – can now be used as a framework for developing a 'theory of the firm'. We shall then be able to see how far the *predictions* of our theory are confirmed by empirical evidence, and whether the *predictions* imply a case for some kind of government intervention in specific types of market structure.

Perfect Competition

In studying the theory of the firm the normal starting point consists of analysing a particular type of market situation known as **perfect competition.** Though the restrictive, and abstract, assumptions made in defining perfect competition result in the theoretical model bearing little resemblance nowadays to any real-life industry, the concept has been retained by economists for an important analytical reason. If this type of market situation were to be present throughout the whole economy, then under certain conditions it could lead to the most efficient[1] allocation of the economy's resources. The characteristics of perfect competition in terms of market structure are as follows:

[1] We shall see in Chapter 11 how 'efficient' is defined.

(*i*) **Large Number of Firms** The first assumption is that there is a very large number of firms in the industry, the consequence being that each firm produces a level of output which is extremely small in relation to the total quantity sold in the market. One very important implication of the basic assumption is that each individual firm is unable to affect the market price of the product by varying its own level of output, since the level of output it can produce is very small in relation to the market total. Under conditions of perfect competition the firm has traditionally been called a **price-taker** because the price of the product is really determined for the firm by the general market forces of demand and supply, where the supply curve reflects the combined activities of a very large number of firms.

Diagram 8.1(*a*) illustrates the fact that the equilibrium price OP set in the market becomes the price at which each firm can sell the quantity of output it produces. Hence if *one* firm were to raise or lower its output, the resulting effect on the market price would be negligible because one firm's actions could not affect the position of the supply curve.

(*ii*) **Identical Products** The second characteristic of a perfectly competitive market structure is that all firms produce an identical product. This assumption really ensures that the first assumption about large numbers of firms, each with no control over the market price, becomes operational. Given identical products it simply would not pay a firm to raise its own price since consumers could quite easily go to one of the many other producers selling the same product at a lower price. Conversely, there would be no point in the firm lowering its price. By doing so it would only be giving up some profit because it could sell as many units as it wanted to at the market price.

It is important to remember that in making the assumption about identical products we are implying not only that the products are identical in physical terms, but also identical as seen in the eyes of consumers. If consumers believed that there was a difference between the product made by one firm and that of other firms then it would be possible for a firm whose product was regarded as better to have an influence over its selling price.

(*iii*) **Free Entry** The third assumption made about perfect competition is that there are no features, artificial or natural, about the market which make it difficult or impossible for new firms to enter the

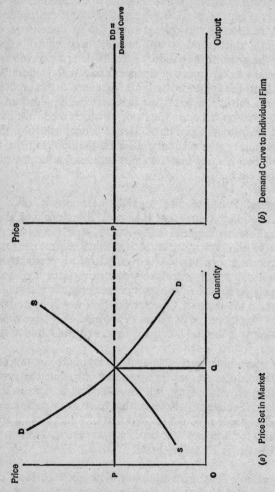

Figure 8.1 (*a*) Price Set in Market
(*b*) Demand Curve to Individual Firm

industry if they wish to do so. We assume, in other words, that it is impossible to exclude any potential entrant to the industry by means, say, of a legal patent enjoyed by the existing firms, by any association of firms in the industry designed to share the market and keep out new firms, or by some economic barrier to entry such as an extremely high cost of setting up a firm in the industry – high enough to discourage any new firm from trying. (We shall examine in detail later what form such barriers to entry might take.)

(*iv*) **Perfect Information** The final assumption we make about perfect competition is that consumers in all parts of the market have perfect knowledge of how the market as a whole is operating, i.e. that their knowledge of the market is not limited to the specific town or area in which they live, or to the activities of just a few firms in the market. This assumption ensures that the first two assumptions can operate. Clearly, if consumers in one part of the market had only partial information about what was happening in the market as a whole it might be possible for some firms to raise their prices above the level of market price without losing sales to firms in other areas simply because of consumer ignorance.

With these assumptions in mind, we can now develop a theory of how a firm operating in perfect competition will behave in terms of the quantity of the product it will produce in order to maximise profits. We have already developed a set of relationships between costs and output, and so in order to find this maximum profit output level we now need to relate revenue to output.

The Demand Curve for a Firm in Perfect Competition

Since we are about to draw up a set of relationships between revenue and output we must start by considering the nature of the demand curve facing an individual firm, from which we can calculate revenue from sales at different prices. The demand curve facing a firm in perfect competition has a unique shape, determined basically by the assumptions made about large numbers of firms and identity of products.

Each firm in perfect competition must accept the price set by the general forces of supply and demand in the market. This is shown as OP in Diagram 8.1(*a*). The firm's demand curve which we have drawn in Diagram 8.1(*b*) is a horizontal line meaning that the range of output which that firm is capable of producing could be sold at the same (market) price. Under our very restrictive assumptions our firm would clearly have no incentive to change price – an increase would reduce sales to zero; even a very small reduction in price would result in a flow of orders which it could not possibly meet!

Total, Average and Marginal Revenue

From the demand curve facing the individual firm in perfect competition we can derive a set of relationships for total revenue, average revenue and marginal revenue. These are illustrated in Table 8.1.

Table 8.1 Total, Average and Marginal Revenue

Output	Total Revenue (£)	Average Revenue (£)	Marginal Revenue (£)
0	0	10	10
1	10	10	10
2	20	10	10
3	30	10	10
4	40	10	10
5	50	10	10
6	60	10	10
7	70	10	10
8	80	10	10
9	90	10	10
10	100	10	10
⋮	⋮	⋮	⋮
20	200	10	10
⋮	⋮	⋮	⋮
30	300	10	10
⋮	⋮	⋮	⋮
40	400	10	10
⋮	⋮	⋮	⋮
50	500	10	10

Let us suppose that a price of £10 per unit is set in the market. **Total revenue** is found by multiplying the total quantity of the product sold by the price of each unit. As output expands from zero to 50 units per week, total revenue always goes up in direct proportion (from £0 to £10 to £20, etc.) since the price of each unit sold remains the same.

Average revenue is found by dividing the total revenue at each level of output by the number of units in that output level. Total revenue per unit is simply another way of defining the price of the product, and so the values for average revenue for a firm in perfect competition remain constant over the range of output capable of being produced by the individual firm. The values for average revenue are shown in Table 8.1 and the average revenue curve is drawn in Diagram 8.2.

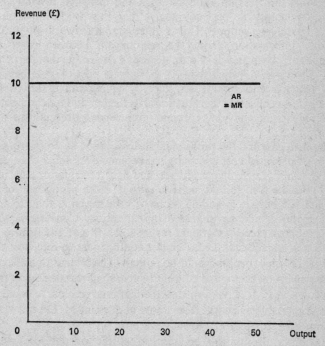

Figure 8.2 Average and marginal revenue curve

Marginal revenue is defined as the change in total revenue brought about by a one unit change in output. Since total revenue under conditions of perfect competition always rises by the same amount when the quantity sold is increased, marginal revenue has a constant value; and since the change in total revenue as a result of one more unit being sold is the same as the price of that extra unit, then in perfect competition marginal revenue equals average revenue. The values for marginal revenue are shown in Table 8.1 and the marginal revenue curve is identical to the average revenue curve shown in Diagram 8.2.

Price and Output Policy in the Short-Run

Given this information about average and marginal revenue, how would we expect the perfectly competitive firm to decide upon its profit-maximising output? This is quite straightforward. By putting together information about the relationship between costs and revenues at varying levels of output, we can determine that particular level of output at which there is the largest possible gap between total revenue and total costs, thereby giving maximum profits. Initially let us consider the situation of a firm in perfect competition in the short-run, which has cost and revenue conditions illustrated in Diagram 8.3.

The firm can find the profit-maximising output by comparing the values of marginal cost and marginal revenue over small changes in output levels. Logically, whenever marginal revenue exceeds marginal cost the firm should increase output; since production of the last unit of output is adding more to total revenue than to total cost, profits would be increased by expansion. Conversely, when marginal cost exceeds marginal revenue, it will pay the firm to cut back on production; if the last unit is adding more to total cost than to total revenue, profits would be falling. (These conditions depend on the marginal cost curve cutting the marginal revenue curve from below, i.e. at E. It is possible that the marginal cost curve could cut the marginal revenue curve from above as at point M, but this would not represent a maximum profit position.)

Maximum profits will be attained at the output level where **marginal cost equals marginal revenue,** i.e. when the last unit produced adds just as much to total revenue as it adds to total cost. This rule for finding the maximum profits level of output lies at the core of the theory of firms' behaviour, and we shall be able to apply it to firms in all kinds of market structure. In terms of Diagram 8.3 if

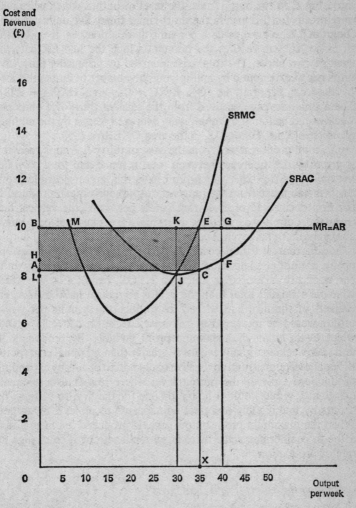

Figure 8.3 Profit-maximising output for perfectly competitive firm in the short-run

the firm in perfect competition wished to maximise profits, what level of output should it produce?

It can be seen from Diagram 8.3 that the marginal cost curve cuts the marginal revenue curve at point E, and so by extending a vertical line from E to the output axis, the level of output which will maximise profits for this firm in the short-run is thirty-five units per week (point X). The average cost per unit at this point is given by the distance XC, where C is the point at which the line EX cuts the average cost curve. The total cost incurred by producing thirty-five units per week is found by multiplying the number of units produced by the cost per unit, i.e. OX × XC = the area OXCA = £287. The average revenue received from the sales of thirty-five units per week would be found by multiplying average revenue by the number of units sold, i.e. EX × OX = the area OXEB = £350.

The total profit received from the sales of thirty-five units per week is given by the difference between total revenue and total cost, i.e. the area ACEB = £63, which represents the largest possible profit the firm can make from the range of output levels it can produce. If the firm decided to produce forty units per week, the vertical line from the output axis at forty units cuts the marginal cost curve above the marginal revenue curve, so that in this case the extra output is adding more to total cost than to total revenue, and therefore profits are not at a maximum. Profits made by producing forty units per week are measured by the area HFGB, i.e. £1.4 × 40 = £56, which is a smaller total than the profits contained in ACEB. Alternatively, if the firm had wished to produce thirty units per week, profits would be measured by the area LJKB, i.e. £2 × 30 = £60, which again is not the maximum profit possible. By producing 30 units per week, marginal revenue is greater than marginal cost (point K lies above point J) and so the firm could add to profits by expanding production. Only at the output level where marginal cost equals marginal revenue would it be impossible for the firm to increase its profits by making any marginal adjustments to its level of output. When the maximum profit output level is produced the firm is said to be in equilibrium, since there is no tendency for it to change its rate of production.

A Note on the Terms 'Profit' and 'Loss'

In analysing the behaviour of firms, we define cost in the sense of opportunity cost as outlined in Chapter 1. Cost, in other words, does not necessarily measure the value of the financial flows actually recorded when the firm pays for the use of inputs; cost really measures the value of inputs in their next best alternative use had they not been used to produce goods and services for the firm. As an example of this point, let us consider exactly how the cost of running a machine might be measured. Suppose a firm installs the machine and pays £1,000 per week for using it. The sum of £1,000 does not measure the full opportunity cost per week of the machine because the firm could use the £1,000 in another way, say investing it in a financial organisation at a six per cent rate of interest per annum. The opportunity cost of the machine is the £1,000 weekly price plus the six per cent per annum rate of interest given up – a sum which measures the value of the resource in its next best alternative use.

By measuring costs in terms of opportunity costs, we shall be using the words **profit** and **loss** in a slightly different manner from the way in which they are used by accountants. If, for example, the total revenue from the sale of a quantity of goods exceeds the total (opportunity) costs of production, we can say that the profits earned measure a return in excess of the return which could be gained by using the resources in the next best alternative way. Such profits are labelled **supernormal.** If the total revenue from the sale of a particular level of output exactly matched the total cost of producing it, then we can say that by using resources to produce that output level a return is received which is equal to the return which could be gained by using the resources in the next best alternative way. When this happens we say the firm is earning **normal profits.**

Notice here how normal profit, in economic terms, is consistent with an excess of revenue over cost in strict financial terms; this financial return, however, is no better and no worse than could have been obtained by using the inputs in an alternative activity. Likewise, if the total cost of some output level is greater than the total revenue received, we can conclude that losses are incurred in the sense that the returns are lower than would have been received by using the resources in the next best alternative activity. Hence when we define costs as opportunity costs, losses are not necessarily negative financial returns – the firm may still receive more money than it pays out in cash, but this return is lower than the return obtainable by using the resources elsewhere.

Applying this idea to our analysis of the firm's short-run maximum profit position, normal profit is included as a *necessary component of average cost.* We can therefore see that the area ACEB represents profits in excess of the return which could be obtained if the firm employed the resources at its command in the next best alternative activity. We sha!l return to this distinction between normal and supernormal profits when we analyse the firm's behaviour in the long-run.

The Short-Run Supply Curve of the Firm

A firm's supply curve illustrates a relationship between the quantity of a good that it would offer for sale at various possible prices. What would such a relationship look like for the perfectly-competitive firm? In Diagram 8.4, several average revenue curves denoting a series of possible price levels from £4 per unit to £11 per unit have been drawn.

Let us suppose that the price of the product as set in the market was £11 per unit (denoted by DD_6). By looking at the point where marginal cost equals marginal revenue, we can easily see that the firm's level of output would be 37 units per week. At a price of £10 per unit (denoted by DD_5), the firm would produce 35 units per week. If the price was £8 per unit (denoted by DD_4) output would be 30 units per week, and at this level of price the firm would be earning a return equivalent to the best return on the resources elsewhere, i.e. normal profit (since average revenue = average [opportunity] cost). What would happen if the price was £7 per unit, shown by demand curve DD_3? By applying the strict logic of the MC = MR rule, the firm ought to produce 27 units per week. But at point P, where MC = MR, average revenue is less than average cost and so total revenue would be lower than total cost. It does not follow, however, that the firm would necessarily cease activity in all cases where average revenue is less than average cost.

It is certainly true that by producing 27 units per week, the firm would be accepting a lower return than could be obtained by employing the resources in the next best alternative activity. In the short-run, however, the firm would have to pay its *fixed costs* (e.g. plant and machinery) irrespective of the level of output produced; even if the firm stopped producing in the short-run it would still have to meet its overheads. But by producing 27 units per week the firm's total revenue would be greater than total *variable* costs (point P lies above the AVC curve) and so the firm could meet all its variable expenses and still have some money left to cover part of its fixed costs. Hence by producing 27 units per week, the firm would

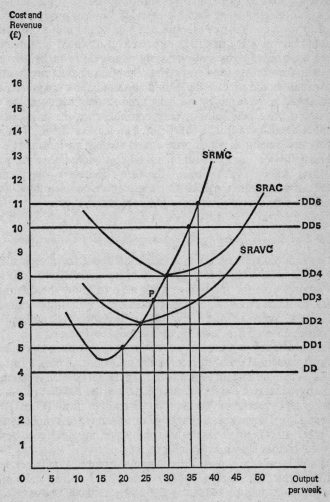

Figure 8.4 Derivation of short-run supply curve for firm in perfect competition

incur a smaller loss than it would do by producing nothing, because zero output would provide no revenue to cover any part of fixed costs.

The lowest price at which it would be worthwhile for the firm to produce would be £6 per unit (as shown by DD$_2$), where £6 is just enough to meet average variable costs. If the firm produced at any price lower than that (for example at £5 or £4 per unit as shown by demand curves DD$_1$ and DD respectively) it would be unable to cover its variable costs and obviously be unable to make any contribution towards its fixed costs. Hence producing at a price less than £6 per unit would involve the firm in sustaining an even greater loss than would be incurred by stopping production altogether. We can say that if price falls below average variable cost, the firm will not produce at all even in the short-run. The feasible range of output begins at the point at which price equals average variable cost.

The points on the short-run marginal cost curve above the point at which AR = AVC represent the firm's **short-run supply curve,** since the points on the SRMC curve denote those output levels which the firm would produce at different levels of price.

Short-Run Supply Curve of the Industry in Perfect Competition

Let us suppose we have some information about the marginal cost curves for all the firms in a perfectly competitive market. To find the supply curve for the industry, we need to know the quantities which would be supplied at various prices by all firms in the industry. These are easily obtained by adding together the appropriate quantities on each firm's short-run marginal cost curve.

The SRMC curve of the firm we have been analysing in this chapter so far is presented on a different scale in Diagram 8.5(a) (Firm A). Let us further assume that Firm A has a marginal cost curve identical to the marginal cost curves found in 10,000 of the 20,000 firms in the industry. The marginal cost curve of another firm (Firm B) is illustrated in Diagram 8.5(b) and we can assume for simplicity that the other 10,000 firms in the industry have marginal cost curves identical to that shown in Diagram 8.5(b).

At a price of £6 per unit, Firm A would supply 24 units per week and Firm B would supply 30 units per week, and so the total market supply at £6 would be 240,000 + 300,000 = 540,000 units per week (as shown by point A in Diagram 8.5(c)). When the price is £7 per unit, Firm A would supply 27 units per week and Firm B would

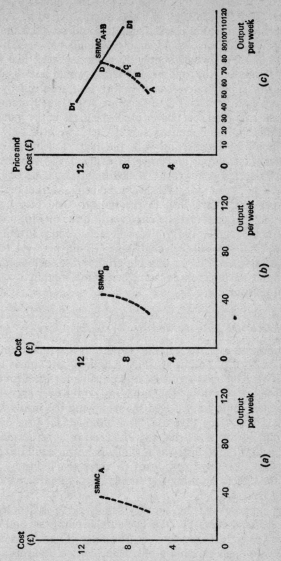

Figure 8.5 Derivation of short-run industry supply curve in perfect competition

produce 35 units per week, meaning that the total market output would be 270,000 + 350,000 = 620,000 units per week. At a price of £8 per week, the total market supply would be 700,000 units per week since 10,000 firms would supply 30 units per week like Firm A, and 10,000 firms would supply 40 units per week like Firm B. If the price was £10 the total market supply would be 780,000 units. The industry supply curve can therefore be traced out by joining points such as A, B, C and D in Diagram 8.5(c), i.e. by adding horizontally the marginal cost curves of all the firms in the industry.

Given this short-run industry supply curve, we need only to look for the point of intersection with the market demand curve to discover market output and price. If demand was represented by D_1D_1 in Diagram 8.5(c) then 770,000 units would be bought and sold since equilibrium is established at point D. Market price would be £10 per unit. Each firm in the industry will face horizontal average and marginal revenue curves at a price of £10, and Firms with cost curves similar to Firm A's will each produce 36 units weekly while the remainder will each contribute 42 units per week to market output. All firms will be maximising profits since each firm's output level denotes an intersection point between a marginal cost and a marginal revenue curve.

Equilibrium of the Firm and Industry in the Long-Run

In the short-run we have seen that the firm is in equilibrium when it produces a level of output at which marginal cost equals marginal revenue. We have also seen that it is possible for the firm to enjoy supernormal profits in the short-run, i.e. profits over and above the return which could be achieved by employing the firm's resources in the next best alternative use. Now although the firm may be in equilibrium in the short-run, the existence of supernormal profits will mean that the industry as a whole is not in equilibrium. High returns will encourage new firms to enter the industry. We can predict the effects by using the simple supply and demand curves shown in Diagram 8.6.

Let us suppose that the industry supply curve is denoted by SS and the demand curve by DD. The equilibrium price and quantity would be OP and OQ respectively. The entry of new firms, attracted by the level of supernormal profits being earned by firms at a price of OP, would push the supply curve outwards to S_1S_1, resulting in an expansion of output to OQ_1 and a fall in price to OP_1. The effect of entry into the industry for the individual firm is shown in Diagram 8.7.

As firms enter the industry, the market price of the product is forced down and we can see that the effect of this is to lower the level of supernormal profits being earned by the individual firm. Eventually when price reaches the level of £8 per unit, the average

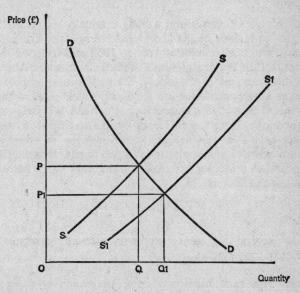

Figure 8.6 Effect on market price of entry by new firms

revenue curve is a tangent to the long-run average cost curve at its lowest point, indicating that normal profits are being earned. Once this situation occurs, the level of profits in the industry ceases to be attractive to potential entrants and the industry would be in equilibrium.

The conclusion we reach about the market performance standards in perfect competition is that in the long-run normal profits will be earned. Each firm will be selling its output at a price which is exactly equal to marginal cost (since in perfect competition AR (price) = MR = MC). We can also see from Diagram 8.8 that the long-run equilibrium position for a firm in perfect competition ensures that the level of output is produced in a plant of optimum size, since MR = MC at the minimum point of the average cost curve, indicating that all possible economies of scale have been reaped. We shall be examining in more detail later just how significant these performance standards are.

Monopoly

The Monopolies Commission, a body originally set up in 1948 to investigate industries dominated by one very large firm,[2] studied the manufacture of cellulosic fibres in 1968 and reported that the behaviour of the major supplier, Courtaulds, illustrated 'one of the classic disadvantages of monopoly, the limitation of supply to the level most advantageous for the producer, which is below the level which would be met in a competitive situation'. We shall see what the Monopolies Commission meant by this statement in analysing structure–behaviour–performance relationships in the market situation known as monopoly, and this will provide a useful frame of reference when we look more closely at the work of the Monopolies Commission in Chapter 13.

Structure

There are several important features about market structure under conditions of monopoly:

(*i*) **Single Firm** In a situation of complete monopoly, there is only one producer controlling the total market output. Such a position puts the monopolist producer in the opposite position to a firm in perfect competition because the monopolist will be able to affect the market price by his own actions. By definition, if the monopolist is the only producer of a particular good the market demand curve is the monopolist's demand curve. Since the market demand curve will be downward-sloping the monopolist is able to raise or lower price by contracting or expanding output.

(*ii*) **Lack of Substitutes** In the pure case of monopoly, theory demands that there should be no substitute for the monopolist's product (otherwise rivals might appear and the monopolist would no longer

[2] Or a group of firms acting in unison.

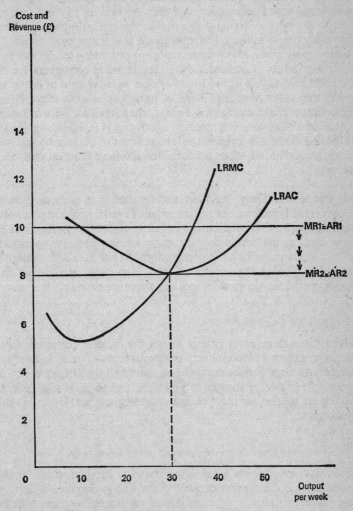

Figure 8.7 Long-run equilibrium for a firm in perfect competition

be a monopolist). We have to interpret this condition with care. It certainly must be the case that there is a severe lack of substitutes for the monopolist's product, but, in an indirect way, products made in other industries can sometimes be regarded as imperfect substitutes. For example, it needs no insight into economic theory to understand that a gas cooker will only operate on gas and that an electric fire needs electricity to provide warmth. Although gas and electricity supply in the UK are each operated under what appear to be monopoly conditions,[3] there are many situations where gas and electricity indirectly compete. For example, when consumers are on the point of deciding what kind of cooker or what kind of heater to install they often have the choice of using gas or electricity. When builders are constructing new houses, they have a choice between central heating systems run on gas or electricity. We might also say that, at the end of the day, even the unique product of the monopolist has to compete with all other products for the limited income of consumers.

(*iii*) **Barriers to Entry** We also assume that in a pure monopoly situation the production of the monopolist's good is closed to all but the monopolist. Complete barriers to entry exist either in the form of some legal ruling forbidding the entry of new firms, a patent to protect the monopolist's right to produce the good, or some extreme economic disadvantage (such as very high costs relative to the monopolist's) which would affect any potential entrant.

Monopolist's Behaviour

Given these three assumptions about the market structure, how would we expect a monopolist to behave in terms of price and output policy? As with perfect competition, we shall first of all derive a series of revenue relationships and then put them alongside cost curves to determine the profit-maximising output level for the monopolist.

Total, Average and Marginal Revenue under Monopoly

Since we have already established that the demand curve to the monopolist is the market demand curve and is downward-sloping, and, since we also know that the average revenue curve will be

---

[3] Since the industries are nationalised they are often called **public monopolies.**

identical to the demand curve, we can easily understand the linkages between total, average and marginal revenue shown in Table 8.2.

Table 8.2   **Total, Average and Marginal Revenue**

Output	Total Revenue (£)	Average Revenue (£)	Marginal Revenue (£)
0	0	18	0
1	16	16	16
2	28	14	12
3	36	12	8
4	40	10	4
5	40	8	0
6	36	6	−4
7	28	4	−8
8	16	2	−12

The first major point to notice from Table 8.2 is that total revenue does not rise proportionately with output, as happened under perfect competition. Total revenue under conditions of monopoly rises at first, reaches a maximum point and then declines. The second interesting point follows logically from this. Marginal revenue under monopoly does not have a constant value equal to average revenue, as was the case in perfect competition. As indicated by the path of total revenue, marginal revenue always declines and eventually becomes negative. Thirdly, the values of average revenue and marginal revenue are not the same (c.f. perfect competition); indeed, after the first unit of production marginal revenue is always less than average revenue. The corresponding curves for total revenue, average revenue and marginal revenue are illustrated in Diagram 8.8(a). (Points on the marginal revenue curve are plotted between the intervals on the output axis, in the same way as we constructed the marginal cost curve.)

Let us first consider the relationship between average revenue and marginal revenue under monopoly. Suppose the monopolist is selling 3 units per week at a price of £12 each. Total revenue is therefore £36. By increasing output to 4 units per week the price must be lowered to £10 each. Total revenue is now £40, and the marginal revenue obtained by selling the fourth unit is £4. The price, however, of the fourth unit is £10, and so the value of marginal revenue is less than average revenue. The reason for this divergence

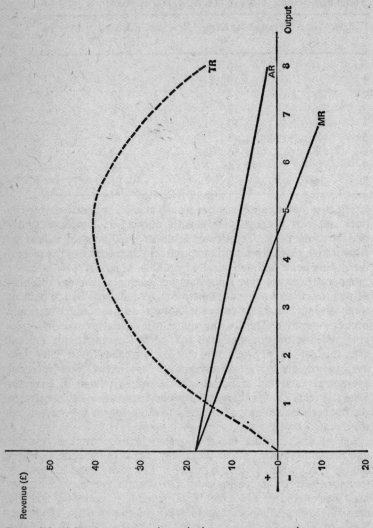

Figure 8.8 (a) Total, average and marginal revenue curves under monopoly

between average and marginal revenue lies in the fact that, in order to increase sales from 3 to 4 units per week, the price becomes £10 not only for the fourth unit but for all the previous units as well. Thus the monopolist is involved in a game of gain and loss. By selling the fourth unit he receives the price of that fourth unit (£10) as extra revenue; however, he also drops the price of the previous 3 units by £2 each (£6) and so the net addition to revenue is £10−£6 = £4. We can see this point clearly in Diagram 8.8(b), which shows the addition to revenue measured by area QRST (where QR is the extra unit and RS is the new price) and the loss of revenue on previous units measured by area ABTC (where BT measures the number of units and AB measures the fall in price).

Secondly we can analyse the reasons for the marginal revenue curve under monopoly eventually becoming negative. It will be remembered from Chapter 3 that values of price elasticity of demand were related to changes in total revenue as a move along a demand curve (average revenue curve) took place. To revise briefly the conclusions stated in Chapter 3, when demand is elastic (i.e. $E > 1$), a fall in price leads to an increase in total revenue. When demand has unit elasticity (i.e. $E = 1$) total revenue remains unchanged after a fall in price. When demand is inelastic (i.e. $E < 1$) a fall in price leads to a decrease in total revenue. Now since we have seen that under monopoly total revenue rises and then falls, and since marginal revenue is derived from the changing values of total revenue, then the values of marginal revenue must depend upon the values of price elasticity of demand.

As can be seen by referring back to Table 8.2, and illustrated in Diagram 8.9, whenever total revenue is increasing as price falls, marginal revenue is positive, and when total revenue is increasing elasticity of demand is greater than one. Hence when marginal revenue is positive (at output levels up to 4.5 units per week) demand is relatively elastic. When total revenue remains unchanged when price falls, marginal revenue is zero and when total revenue is unchanged elasticity is unitary. Therefore when marginal revenue is zero, elasticity is equal to one. When total revenue falls when price falls, marginal revenue is negative, and when total revenue falls demand is relatively inelastic. So when marginal revenue is negative, elasticity of demand is less than one (at output levels beyond 4.5 units per week).

We can generalise the above relationships between the demand

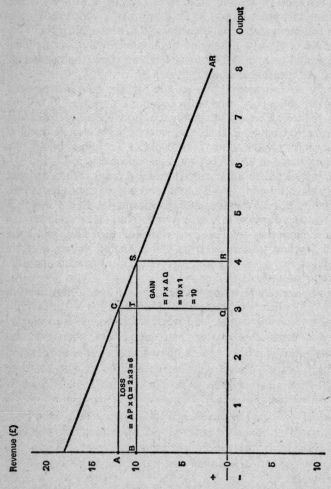

Figure 8.8 (b) Marginal revenue less than price under monopoly

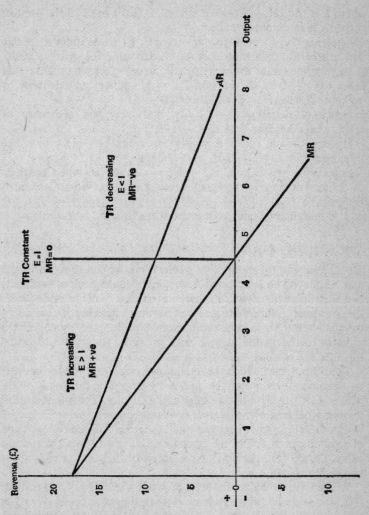

Figure 8.9 Relations between elasticity of demand and average and marginal revenue curves

curve (i.e. average revenue/price), marginal revenue and price elasticity of demand in the following equation:

$$MR = P\left(1 - \frac{1}{E}\right),$$

where E is the value of price elasticity, P is the price of the product and MR is marginal revenue.[4]

Applying this formula to our example, let us consider a specific and a general application. Let us take a value for price elasticity at some point on the average revenue curve $= 3$. Using the formula $MR = P(1 - 1/E)$, the fraction $1/E = \frac{1}{3}$, and we can generalise by saying that whenever $E > 1$, then $1/E < 1$.

Hence $(1 - 1/E) = (1 - \frac{1}{3}) = \frac{2}{3}$, and we again generalise by saying that whenever $E > 1$, $(1 - 1/E) > 0$.

Hence if the value for P is positive, the term $P(1 - \frac{1}{3}) > 0$, and so whenever $E > 1$, $P(1 - 1/E) > 0$, i.e. $MR > 0$.

Similarly when $E = 1$, $P(1 - 1/E) = 0$, and so when elasticity of demand is unitary, marginal revenue is zero. When demand is inelastic, i.e. $E < 1$, $P(1 - 1/E)$ will be negative since $(1 - 1/E) < 0$, and so marginal revenue is negative when demand is inelastic.

Short-Run and Long-Run Price and Output Policy under Monopoly

Turning now to the monopolist's behaviour, we can show how price and output will be determined. Sometimes people speak of monopoly as a situation where 'you can charge as much as you like and squeeze the consumer'. While there may well be some squeezing of consumers, we shall see that, in order to maximise profits, the monopolist is unlikely to charge the highest price possible. Diagram 8.10 brings together the revenue and cost curves for the monopolist.

The output level which the monopolist ought to produce in order to maximise profits can be found by applying the logic of the $MC = MR$ rule developed earlier in the chapter. The intersection of the marginal cost and marginal revenues comes at point E. Output will be OQ (i.e. 3 units) per week and the price charged for each unit of this output is found by extending QE to the average revenue curve, i.e. QS (£12 per unit). Note, in particular, that price is above marginal revenue.

We can also calculate the level of profit as follows. Total revenue from the sale of 3 units per week is given diagramatically by OQ × QS, i.e. the area OQSP = £36. Total cost incurred in producing

[4] *See* Appendix at the end of the chapter for the derivation of this formula.

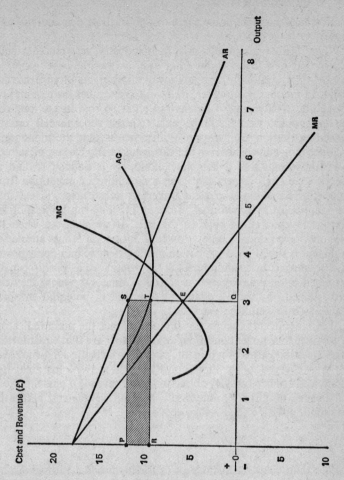

Figure 8.10 Profit-maximising output for a monopolist

3 units per week is OQ × QT (where QT measures the average cost per unit), i.e. the area OQTR = £28.5. Hence profits are denoted by the shaded area PSTR = £7.5. The reader can prove, by taking any other output level, that PSTR is the largest area of

profit which the monopolist can earn, given these demand and cost curves.

When supernormal profits exist in an industry, we would normally expect that new firms would enter and, as was the case in perfect competition, eventually compete away all elements of supernormal profit. In monopoly, however, we have to remember the assumption about the effectiveness of barriers to entry so that in the long-run the monopolist would still be able to earn supernormal profits. Indeed in the long-run the only difference is that the monopolist will face long-run cost curves indicating his ability to vary all inputs.

To the extent that a complete monopoly is difficult to find in practice, we might expect that even some indirect competition from competitors making somewhat imperfect substitutes will eat into the monopolist's supernormal profits in the long-run by shifting his average revenue curve back to the left. As we shall see when we examine government policy towards monopoly, one strand of argument is that a good indication of the extent of monopoly power can be gauged by examining how far supernormal profits can be sustained in an industry over a period of time – the more they can be sustained, the more evidence of the lack of potential entrants' ability to break into the market.

We can conclude this section by noting that the main indicators of performance under conditions of monopoly are that supernormal profits can be earned both in the short-run and the long-run; that the price charged for the monopolist's output is above marginal cost (since average revenue lies above marginal revenue); and the profit maximising output is produced at a level of average cost above the minimum point on the average cost curve.

Price Discrimination

Rather than charging a single price for his product throughout his market, there may be occasions when a monopolist can distinguish several quite independent and separate markets. Assuming the monopolist wishes to maximise profits, it might then pay him to discriminate between the several markets by charging a different price for the same product. One very common example of price discrimination is provided by drug companies who charge different prices for the same products in different countries. In cases like this markets can be considered as separate purely on a geographical basis. Similarly the possibility of separate markets can also occur because of very high transport costs needed to carry the good from one sub-market to another within a country. Also, consumers in one part of the market may not know about conditions in other parts of the market; or the good itself may be of such a nature that it is impossible for consumers in different parts of the market to exchange quantities of it. A well-known example of the last feature is found in the case of doctors in private practice who might charge two clients different fees for an operation; it would not, for obvious reasons, be possible for the person charged the cheaper fee to undergo the treatment twice and sell one dose to the other patient. In all of the examples the important point is that the markets are separable in the sense that it is extremely difficult to transfer the good produced by the monopolist between the different sub-markets. If this condition is met the scene is set for price discrimination.

There is however a further condition which must be satisfied if price discrimination is to be worthwhile, which is that demand conditions must be different in each category of the market, so that the monopolist can charge different prices according to the different attitudes of different groups of consumers towards his product. Instead of charging a uniform price to each group, it will pay the monopolist to divide his output between the markets in such a way that the *marginal revenue in each market is equal*. Only when this condition holds will it be impossible for him to increase total revenue by any rearrangement of the output levels between the markets.

Let us imagine that a monopolist was faced with two separate markets, whose average and marginal revenue curves are illustrated in Diagram 8.11(a). The different slopes of the curves AR_1 and AR_2 show that the demand conditions in the two markets are different (since the scale on the axis is the same for both), and so it will pay the monopolist to charge a discriminatory price. How can this be done in order to maximise profits? We can analyse the situation as follows.

First the curves AR_1 and AR_2 can be added together (similarly $MR_1 + MR_2$) to give the aggregate market average revenue and marginal revenue curves shown in Diagram 8.11(b). The curves in Diagram 8.11(b) can then be considered alongside the monopolist's marginal cost curve as shown in Diagram 8.12(c).

The total quantity of the product which the monopolist should produce is given at the intersection of the marginal cost and market marginal revenue curves, i.e. an output level of OQ. The marginal revenue associated with this output (i.e. the addition to total revenue

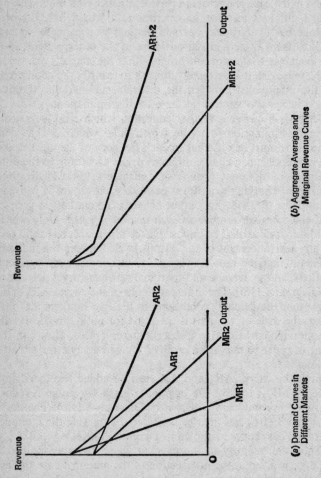

Figure 8.11 (a) Demand curves in different markets
(b) Aggregate average and marginal revenue curves

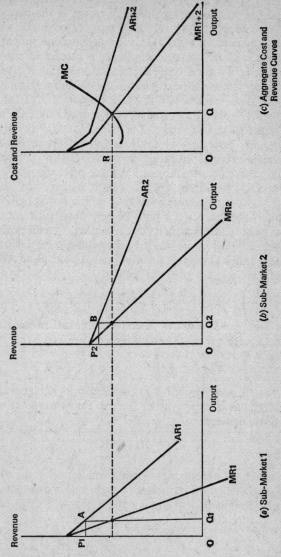

Figure 8.12 Price discrimination under monopoly

gained by selling the last unit in either market) is measured by OR. By extending a horizontal line from R back through Diagrams 8.12(*b*) and (*a*), which show the revenue curves in the two separate markets, we can apply the rule that output should be allocated between the markets in order that marginal revenue should be the same in each market. If marginal revenue is greater in one market than in another it would be possible to increase total revenue by reallocating output into the market with the higher marginal revenue.

When marginal revenue is OR, the total quantity of the mono-polist's output supplied to sub-market 1 is given by OQ_1 and the quantity supplied to sub-market 2 is given by OQ_2, where $OQ_1 + OQ_2 = OQ$. By extending a line from Q_1 and Q_2 to the average revenue curves in each sub-market we can see how price discrimina-tion would take place. In sub-market 1 the price charged per unit for output OQ_1 would be OP_1, which is higher than the price charged for output OQ_2 in sub-market 2 which would be OP_2.

Since price discrimination is possible only where different demand conditions exist in different parts of the market, we can explain why price would be higher in sub-market 1 than sub-market 2. If elasticity of demand is lower at point A on AR_1 than at point B on AR_2, then using the formula in the previous section,

$$P_1\left(1 - \frac{1}{E_1}\right) < P_2\left(1 - \frac{1}{E_2}\right), \quad \text{since} \quad E_1 < E_2.$$

Since the monopolist requires to equate marginal revenue in each sub-market, i.e. to satisfy the condition

$$P_1\left(1 - \frac{1}{E_1}\right) = P_2\left(1 - \frac{1}{E_2}\right),$$

the only way this can be done is to ensure that P_1 is higher than P_2; in other words to charge a higher price in the sub-market with the more inelastic demand.[5]

Conclusion

The quote from the Monopolies Commission Report at the beginning of the monopoly section was founded on a well-known comparison of the behaviour and performance standards of a firm in perfect

[5] At point A on AR_1, $E = \frac{1}{3} \div \frac{1}{26} = 8\frac{2}{3}$

At B on AR_2, $E = \frac{2.5}{4} \div \frac{1}{23} = 14$

Hence at A demand is more inelastic than at B.

competition and a monopolist. The main differences have been outlined in this chapter. First, in perfect competition price is equal to marginal cost, whereas under monopoly price is greater than marginal cost since average revenue is greater than marginal revenue. This means that consumers pay a monopolist a price greater than the value of extra resource costs needed to produce the last unit of output. Secondly, in long-run equilibrium a perfectly competitive firm will produce at the minimum point on the average cost curve, while a monopolist's profit-maximising output is produced at a unit cost higher than the minimum. Thirdly, the long-run equilibrium position of a monopolist shows that supernormal profits can exist unaffected by the entry of new firms, whereas a perfectly competitive firm earns only normal profits in the long-run.

We shall be looking at the implications of these comparisons when we consider theories of welfare and efficiency, and government policy towards monopolies. For the moment, we turn to an analysis of two further types of market structure–behaviour–performance relationships which lie somewhere in between the two extremes of perfect competition and monopoly.

Appendix

Relationships between Marginal Revenue, Average Revenue and Elasticity

The formula for price elasticity of demand is

$$E = \frac{\Delta Q}{Q} \div \frac{\Delta P}{P}$$

In order to derive the value of E at a particular point on a demand curve, it is necessary to calculate E for a very small change in price, and this small change is denoted by the letter d instead of the symbol Δ. That is, for a very small change in price,

$$E = \frac{dQ}{Q} \div \frac{dP}{P}$$

$$= \frac{dQ}{dP} \times \frac{P}{Q} \quad \text{...} \quad (1)$$

Total revenue is found by multiplying price by quantity sold,

i.e. $TR = PQ$ .... (2)

Now assume that a very small change in price occurs (dP) and as a result quantity sold changes (dQ). The new level of total revenue can be expressed as

$$TR_1 = (P + dP)(Q + dQ)$$

i.e. $TR_1 = PQ + dPdQ + dPQ + dQP$ .... (3)

The change in total revenue resulting from the price change is denoted by dTR, and so

$$dTR = TR_1 - TR$$

Subtracting (2) from (3)

$$dTR = dPdQ + dPQ + dQP$$ .... (4)

If dP and dQ are each extremely small numbers, say 0.00005 and 0.00001 respectively, then the expression dPdQ approaches zero and so can be ignored in (4).

We therefore have

$$dTR = dPQ + dQP$$

i.e. $dTR = QdP + PdQ$

Dividing both sides by dQ, we have

$$\frac{dTR}{dQ} = \frac{dPQ}{dQ} + P$$

The expression dTR/dQ is equivalent to marginal revenue (MR). Hence,

$$MR = \frac{dPQ}{dQ} + P$$

$$= \left(\frac{dP}{dQ}\right) Q + P$$ .... (5)

Since, as shown in (1), $E = \dfrac{dQ}{dP} \times \dfrac{P}{Q}$;

$$\frac{1}{E} = \frac{dP}{dQ} \times \frac{Q}{P}$$

i.e. $P\left(\dfrac{1}{E}\right) = \dfrac{dP}{dQ}\ (Q)$ .... (6)

substituting (6) in (5)

$$MR = P\left(\frac{1}{E}\right) + P$$

$$= P\left(1 + \frac{1}{E}\right)$$

Since E is normally a negative number,

$$MR = P\left(1 - \frac{1}{E}\right)$$

Chapter 9

Monopolistic Competition and Oligopoly

The theories of perfect competition and monopoly can be seen as two extreme points on a spectrum which describes different forms of market structure. On the one hand, a perfectly competitive market is assumed to contain an extremely large number of firms, while on the other hand a monopoly is controlled by only one producer. In this chapter, we examine two further types of market structure which lie between these two extremes. These are known as **monopolistic competition** and **oligopoly.** The following examples illustrate some of the features present in such market situations which this chapter attempts to explain.

(*i*) The Monopolies Commission (referred to in the previous chapter), investigating the market for breakfast cereals, commented that 'the market is seen by the industry as one in which the manufacturers compete through the appeal of different brand products and through constant search for new brand sales'.[1] We know that the creation of many different brands of a certain type of product is a common activity in many industries besides breakfast cereals. For example, firms in the soap and detergents industry manufacture a range of products which includes Daz, Lux, Camay, Knight's Castile, Palmolive, Omo, Surf, Ariel, Radiant, Fairy, Persil, etc., and spend over 30 per cent of the annual value of their sales on advertising and promoting these products.

A famous American economist, Joe S. Bain, produced evidence to show that the creation of many different brands of products means that it is extremely difficult for any new firms to enter the markets in which such activities take place. Further, in an investigation into the supply of detergents, the Monopolies Commission found that a potential new firm would be dissuaded from entering the market because of the high selling and promotional expenses which would have to be incurred to bring the product to the public's

[1] The Monopolies Commission, *A Report on the Supply of Ready Cooked Breakfast Cereal Foods* (HMSO, 1973) p. 19.

notice. Why should firms seek to compete in this way, and what might be the economic implications of such behaviour?

(ii) In its report on breakfast cereals, the Monopolies Commission commented on the fact that 90 per cent of the total quantity of cereals supplied was accounted for by only three firms. The Commission considered that one important consequence of this market structure was that 'Any significant reduction (or failure to follow a general increase) in prices would therefore be seen by a manufacturer as likely to be matched by his competitors, since they would not be able to risk the consequence of having their own prices too far out of line . . . We consider that the fear of price competition . . . arises from the fact that supply to so large a proportion of the market is concentrated in so small a number of manufacturers.'[2]

How do we account in theory for such a market structure, and do the predictions of the theory about firms' behaviour and performance in such market situations lend weight to the arguments of the Monopolies Commission in the above extract?

Monopolistic Competition

The theory of monopolistic competition received its classical exposition by an American economist, E. H. Chamberlin.[3] As the term implies, monopolistic competition has some of the features of a monopoly situation and other features which are nearer to perfect competition. But the predictions which the theory of monopolistic competition makes about standards of performance turn out to be very similar to those of monopoly. The characteristics of market structure under conditions of monopolistic competition are:

(i) A large number of firms, each producing a differentiated product

The assumption about the existence of a large number of firms seems to reflect the competitive aspect of monopolistic competition. Each firm, however, makes a product which is slightly different to the products made by all other firms in the industry. The way in which each firm differentiates its product is by making alterations to its design or packaging, and usually by incurring some advertising expenses to convince consumers that its particular product is superior to all others in the market. Firms in monopolistic com-

[2] Op. cit. p. 25.
[3] E. H. Chamberlin, *The Theory of Monopolistic Competition* (Cambridge, Mass., Howard University Press, 1933).

petition give considerable thought to the production of a brand image as well as to the production of the good itself.

In practice, this assumption really ensures that each firm actually has some of the characteristics of a monopolist. Since each firm's product is slightly different from other firms' products, each firm will have some power to influence its selling price by varying its level of output. Each firm will face a downward-sloping demand curve, and the more differentiated each firm can make its product the less elastic its demand curve will be.

(*ii*) **Free Entry** The second major assumption about monopolistic competition (in direct contrast to monopoly) is that any new firm can enter the industry if it so wishes. As in perfect competition, there can be no barriers to the entry of new firms who may be attracted by the level of supernormal profits. When each new firm joins, it will also play according to the 'rules of the game' and manufacture a product which is similar to the products made by all the other firms but is differentiated in style, design, packaging or some other way. The important implication of the assumption of free entry in monopolistic competition is that we shall be able to make a distinction between the equilibrium position for a firm in the short-run and in the long-run.

The example of laundrettes provides a reasonable illustration of monopolistic competition. There are many laundrettes in Britain, although each laundrette tends to have a slightly different appearance and may use different types of washing machine. Some laundrettes advertise in local newspapers; some try to differentiate their service by stressing the efficiency and cleanliness of their equipment; some highlight the fact that they provide chairs and automatic coffee-vending machines for their customers. Whatever the method of differentiation, there is little doubt that many laundrettes are successful in promoting a brand image which captures the loyalty of some customers who believe it is different from other laundrettes. Also, it is relatively simple for someone to enter the market and open a laundrette, if the person concerned has the available cash and can buy the necessary premises.

Given these elements of market structure, how would we expect the individual firm in monopolistic competition to behave? Since each firm will face a downward-sloping demand curve which is a contributory part of the total market demand curve,[4] each firm

---

[4] There is a problem in defining a 'market demand curve' precisely because products

accounts for only a small percentage of market output. Assuming the firm wishes to maximise profits, the price and output chosen will be those indicated by the equality of marginal cost and marginal revenue. The diagram which shows the short-run profit-maximising position for a firm in monopolistic competition looks exactly like the equilibrium position for a monopolist.

In Diagram 9.1, the firm's marginal and average revenue and cost curves have been drawn so that the equilibrium position is at E, where $MC = MR$. The level of output produced would be ON_1 units and the price charged OP_1. Notice that, like the monopolist, the firm in monopolistic competition may be capable of earning supernormal profits in the short-run because price is greater than average cost. The level of supernormal profits is denoted by the area P_1RQS. This situation, however, does not represent equilibrium in the industry as a whole. The existence of supernormal profits will act as an incentive for new firms to enter the industry in the long-run. As more firms enter, each firm will have to accept a reduced proportion of the total demand for the product and this will be reflected in a backward shift of the firm's average revenue curve showing that at each price which might be charged the firm is now able to attract fewer customers than before. It is also likely that the firm's demand curve will become more elastic as the range of substitutes is widened by the entry of new firms.

As can be seen in Diagram 9.2, the effect of the entry of new firms is to move the average revenue curve AR back to the left. Logically, new firms could keep entering the industry as long as supernormal profits exist (i.e. as long as price is greater than average cost). In the long-run, the industry will be in equilibrium when the marginal firm faces a demand curve in position AR_1, i.e. just a tangent to the average cost curve. The profit-maximising output would now be on ON_2, and the price, OP_2, would be just sufficient to cover average cost so that each firm would be earning only normal profits.

The predictions which the theory of monopolistic competition makes about the performance of the industry can be appreciated by looking again at Diagram 9.2. First, price will be above marginal cost (as was the case with monopoly) since average revenue is greater than marginal revenue, i.e. point R_1 lies above point E_1.

Secondly, when the industry is in long-run equilibrium, each firm is operating on its average cost curve at a point to the left of the

---

are differentiated, but for simplicity we can imagine a market demand curve for the general class of product.

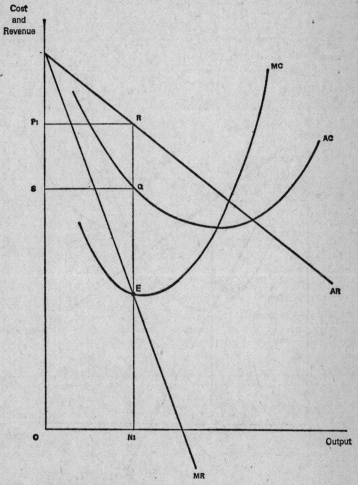

Figure 9.1 Short-run profit maximisation for firm in monopolistic competition

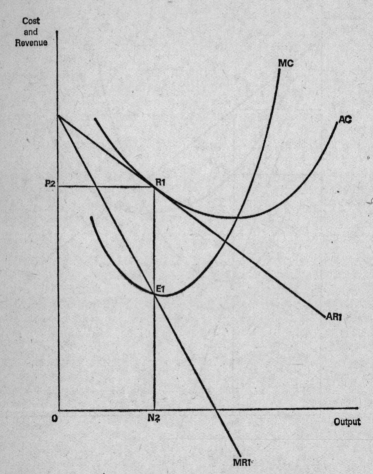

Figure 9.2 Long-run profit maximisation for firm in monopolistic
    competition

minimum. Such a situation has been called **excess or unused capacity,** reflecting the fact that the economies of scale offered by the plants being used are not fully gained since average cost is not a minimum. The only way, of course, for excess capacity to be utilised would be to expand output to the minimum point on the average cost curve, but such a move would produce an output level where marginal cost was greater than marginal revenue, and this would conflict with the assumption that the firm attempts to maximise profits.

The theory of monopolistic competition was developed in the 1930s to account for the phenomenon of product differentiation. In the modern economy product differentiation is still a prevalent feature in most markets. But where it does exist, it is common to find that only a few firms share the market and not a large number as assumed in the theory of monopolistic competition. Virtually all of the well-known brands of soap powder and detergents referred to at the beginning of this chapter are produced by two firms, Lever Brothers and Procter and Gamble. Similarly, the output of industries such as cars and tobacco is noted for the amount of differentiation between the many products on sale, but the output itself is in the hands of just a few firms. To find an explanation for this type of market situation we now turn to a theory of oligopoly.

Oligopoly

Oligopoly is defined as a market situation in which the output is produced by a few (usually large) firms. Although many people might think of oligopoly as a relatively recent feature of the modern economy since the best-known examples are in the markets for goods such as cars, soap powders, and electrical goods (fridges, TV sets, washing machines), etc., in fact the problem of oligopoly was considered as long ago as 1838 by a French economist, A. A. Cournot. Since that time, various economists have researched into the relationships between structure, behaviour and performance under oligopoly, but it is true to say that no single, widely-accepted theory of oligopoly has been developed so far.

The reason for this seemingly unsatisfactory state of affairs lies in two important aspects of oligopoly situations. The first is that each firm by definition produces a sufficiently large proportion of the total output for its behaviour to affect the market share of the other firms in the industry. Firms are said to exist in a state of **mutual interdependence.** Secondly, because of mutual interdependence and close rivalry between the firms in an oligopoly, the behaviour of one firm is conditioned not just by what its rivals are doing but what it thinks its rivals might do in response to any initiative of its own. Behaviour under oligopoly is therefore said to take place under conditions of **uncertainty** since each firm's policies are based on estimates of what its rivals' possible reactions might be. These two features – mutual interdependence and uncertainty – hold the key to the absence of a unique oligopoly theory, since it is possible that a large number of behaviour patterns are consistent with different hypotheses about how oligopolists might behave under certain circumstances. Equally, different theories can predict the same behaviour.

Most theories of oligopoly behaviour have been based on some assumption about the thinking behind each oligopolist's policies. For example, one hypothesis which enjoyed some influence for a period was based on the so-called **kinked-demand curve,** which provided some explanation of why many oligopolistic industries experienced significant stability of prices over a period of time.

Briefly, the kinked-demand curve hypothesis runs as follows. Let us suppose that an oligopolist's price is set at OP in Diagram 9.3. In considering whether he should raise the price of his product to OP_1, he takes into consideration the likely reaction of his rivals. He considers the most likely reaction to his increased price will be for rivals simply to leave their prices unchanged, and so his market share would significantly decline (as would his total revenue) from OQ to OQ_1. Graphically, the oligopolist believes that above the level of OP, his demand curve is relatively elastic. In considering a possible lowering of his price, from OP to OP_2, the oligopolist believes that his rivals would also cut their prices in retaliation. The demand curve below OP is believed by the oligopolist to be relatively inelastic, because the price cut would induce only a slight increase in quantity sold and cause a fall in total revenue. The major prediction of the kinked-demand curve hypothesis is that price under oligopoly will tend to stabilise at OP. From empirical observations we know that prices in many (but certainly not nearly all) oligopoly situations remain stable over periods of time. But the problem with the kinked-demand curve hypothesis is that it does not explain how price came to be fixed at OP in the first place; the hypothesis simply specifies what would happen after the interactions between the firms resulted in price actually settling at a particular level.

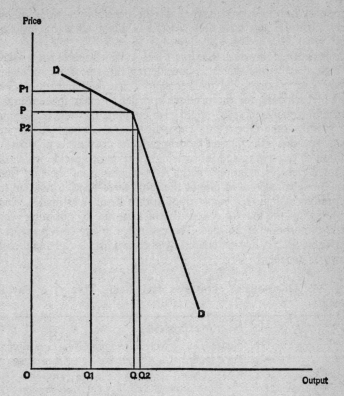

Figure 9.3 Kinked-demand curve

Game Theory

A more recent approach towards a general theory of oligopoly has been seen in the application of the principles of game theory, made famous initially by the economists, Von Neumann and Morgenstern. Game theory treats the oligopolist's behaviour in similar fashion to a game such as chess (although the game often involves more than one opponent, which makes the number of possible reactions to each player's moves even more numerous). In making any decision the oligopolist has to consider what all the possible reactions of his rivals might be and how these reactions might affect his level of sales.

Consider the following situation. Firm A, which shares the market for a product with Firm B, is considering three possible strategies designed to maximise its market share.[5] It could introduce new types of packaging for the product in order to make it seem more attractive to consumers; it might also combine the new packaging policy with some advertising expenditure; or it could go for an all-out assault on the market by dropping the price of its product in addition to packaging and advertising. In trying to decide which of the three policies to adopt, Firm A is conscious of the fact that Firm B might respond in one of the same three ways in relation to the product it makes. Let us suppose that Firm A estimates what percentage of the market output it could capture by adopting each of the three possible policies. The estimates might be represented as in Table 9.1. (A market shared by only two firms is a special case known as **duopoly**.)

Table 9.1   Oligopolists' Strategies and Game Theory; a Payoff Matrix.

		Firm B's Strategies		
		New Packaging	*New Packaging +Advertising*	*New Packaging +Advertising +Price Reduction*
Firm A's Strategies	*New Packaging*	45	40	20
	New Packaging +Advertising	50	45	40
	New Packaging +Advertising +Price Reduction	60	55	45

Figures represent expected Market share (%) for Firm A

Reading across Table 9.1, we can see that if Firm A were to adopt the policy of new packaging alone it could expect to gain 45 per cent

[5] This objective is not necessarily the same as profit maximisation; see section on 'Alternative Hypotheses about Firms' Objectives.'

if Firm B did exactly the same, 40 per cent of the market if Firm B went one step further and advertised as well as designed a new package, and only 20 per cent of the market if Firm B combined the new packaging with advertising and a price cut. Table 9.1 is often referred to as a **payoff matrix** because it relates the effects of each of the possible outcomes to each of the possible policies as seen from the viewpoint of one of the participants in the 'game'. Can we tell from Table 9.1 which of the three policies Firm A would adopt?

If Firm A simply designed new packaging, it is estimated that Firm B could cut Firm A's market share from 45 per cent to 40 per cent by packaging and advertising. However, Firm A could then restore its prospective market share to 45 per cent by similarly adopting a policy of packaging and advertising. But in response to this, Firm B is capable of cutting Firm A's market share back to 40 per cent by implementing a price cut in addition to its packaging and advertising policy. The only alternative left if Firm A wants to be sure of keeping its market share at 45 per cent will be to adopt a policy of packaging, advertising and price cut. Thus Firm A and Firm B would both end up at the right-hand bottom corner of the payoff matrix, although both firms would have been no better and no worse off had they both simply introduced new packaging. Basing policies on what one firm thinks the other might do has forced both to escalate their policies without either gaining a real competitive advantage.

Let us examine this game a little more closely to see why we would expect such a result to come about. First, the example illustrated is only one of a large number of game situations, but it is a very special case known as a **two-person zero-sum game.** The 'two-person' element in the title is easy enough to understand. 'Zero-sum' refers to the fact that gains in market share to Firm A represent losses in market share to Firm B, i.e. if A's market share increases by 5 per cent from 45 per cent to 50 per cent, B's market share falls by 5 per cent from 55 per cent to 50 per cent. Another way of expressing the fact that the gains and losses are equal is to say that the sum of the gains and losses (or **payoffs** as we termed them above) is equal to zero, i.e.

A's gain of 5 per cent = B's loss of 5 per cent
A's gain of 5 per cent + B's loss of 5 per cent = 0.

This is what is meant by a 'zero-sum' game.

In such a game, interest centres on the criteria which could and should be used by each firm to choose one particular strategy. In advocating a criterion that **should** be used, the assumption is made that there is some **rational** way for each firm to behave, where **rational** means that the firm behaves in a way which is consistent with some clearly stated objective which each firm desires to achieve. What might such an objective be? Given the uncertainty, inter-dependence and conflict inherent in the example above, game theorists believe that a rational behaviour pattern for Firm A would involve attempting to maximise its market share on the assumption that Firm B will attempt to do precisely the same. In other words, Firm A should expect that Firm B will choose that strategy which is worst from A's point of view, and on this assumption Firm A should choose that strategy which will maximise its market share.

The criterion used to achieve such an objective is called the **maximin criterion.** The term **maximin** conveys the impression that the firm will choose the best strategy (max) from the worst possible outcomes (min). We can again see why from Table 9.1, using the maximin criterion, Firm A would have the payoff represented in the bottom right-hand corner of the matrix. The worst possible outcomes of each of the three strategies for Firm A are 20 per cent, 40 per cent and 45 per cent respectively. The best of these worst outcomes is 45 per cent, and so the maximin criterion would suggest that Firm A chooses the strategy involving new packaging, advertising and price reduction.

There are many other examples of games where the structure is not as simple as the case of the two-person zero-sum game. There are also other criteria developed by game theorists which would suggest a different choice of strategy in certain situations. Game theory has now become a very large field of study in its own right, and for the reader who is interested in probing further into this field some references are given at the end of the book.

Direct and Indirect Collusion

One slightly different approach towards developing a theory of oligopoly starts by recognising the difficulties of developing hypotheses at the level of the individual firm, since, as we have seen, each oligopolist's behaviour is shaped by a large number of assumptions about its rivals' behaviour. It might, however, be possible to say something useful about oligopoly behaviour if we assume that oligopolists taken as a group and living in an atmosphere of mutual interdependence and uncertainty will adopt common policies designed to limit the area of uncertainty surrounding their decision-making, and to provide more security for their share of the market and for the market as a whole. It is believed, for example, that one way of limiting uncertainty and increasing security is by oligopolists adopting a policy of **joint profit maximisation,** whereby each oligopolist behaves in a way designed to help maximise the profits of the industry as a whole and then accepts whatever market share he can get.

Oligopolists can behave in accordance with the aim of maximising profits for the industry by various forms of **collusion** – agreements between the firms in an industry about the terms of sale of the good in question. Sometimes collusion can be direct and explicit – where, for example, each firm decides to apportion the market on some agreed quota system, or agrees to charge a common price (perhaps close to the level which would be charged by a profit-maximising monopolist thereby ensuring joint profit maximisation.) Such forms of collusion, however, have been illegal for some time in the United Kingdom.[6] But more indirect and 'undercover' forms of collusion still remain, since firms operating in oligopolistic markets occasionally exchange information about price and product policy, and also practise **price leadership** by which each oligopolist responds to the price increases or decreases of the mutually recognised leader in the market.

Barriers to Entry

Each oligopolist's share of the group's profits will be enhanced the greater are the barriers to entry into the industry, and it is believed that barriers to entry are very typical features of oligopolistic industries. Barriers to entry can be listed under three general headings:

(*i*) **Economies of Scale** We have already noticed the existence of economies of scale in Chapter 6, and they can be of great significance as barriers to entry into some types of oligopolistic industry. For example, in industries where the minimum point on a firm's long-run average cost curve (or the minimum efficient size) is reached only where a large proportion of the market output is supplied it will be very difficult for a new firm to enter the industry and compete on equal terms.

[6] See Chapter 13.

In Diagram 9.4, for example, let us suppose that the long-run average cost curve for an oligopolist is as shown with an MES at point X. By looking at the shape of the curve to the left of X, it can be seen that economies of scale are reaped as output expands. Now let us further suppose that the profit-maximising output of ON represents one-third of the total quantity supplied to the market,

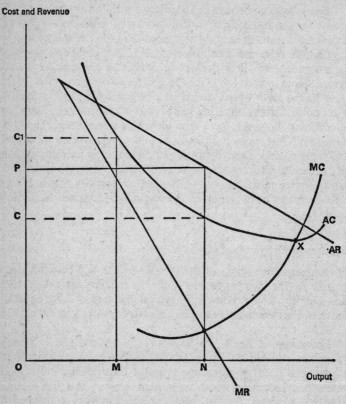

Figure 9.4 Economies of scale as barriers to entry

and that there are three firms each supplying ON units, at a price of OP.

At an output level of ON each oligopolist is making supernormal profits and so the industry is potentially attractive to entrants. But the new entrant would find survival in this type of industry a very precarious existence for several reasons. First, in order to compete on completely equal terms, the new firm would have to capture 25 per cent of the total market output. In practice, new firms usually enter industries on a much smaller scale, but the penalties for doing so in the present example would be considerable. Let us imagine that a new firm entering the industry would be able to capture initially a small market share, denoted by OM. Because of the significance of economies of scale the new entrant's unit costs would be considerably higher than those of existing firms (OC_1 compared with OC). Such a cost disadvantage might deter entry into the market.

Economies of scale can thus be an effective barrier to entry where two conditions hold:

(*a*) The minimum efficient size for a firm must be associated with an output level which is very large relative to the total market output. This condition makes it extremely difficult for a new firm to operate near the output level where all economies of scale have been reaped.

(*b*) The long-run average cost curve must fall sharply over a large range of output until the minimum efficient size has been reached. The sharper the fall of the LRAC, the greater will be the cost disadvantage suffered by firms supplying a relatively smaller proportion of the market than the output produced at a minimum efficient size.

The extent to which these two conditions hold is often said to denote the **height** of barriers to entry into an industry. The larger the proportion of market output denoted by the MES and the sharper the fall of the LRAC curve until the MES is reached, the greater is the height of the entry barriers. In oligopolistic industries where such entry barriers exist, conditions will allow the individual firms to coexist in pursuit of joint profit maximisation without the fear that entry of new firms will compete away some of their profits.

The study conducted by C. F. Pratten on economies of scale (referred to in Chapter 6) provides some good examples of the importance of such barriers to entry in oligopolistic industries. In the newspaper industry, for example, Pratten estimated that in order to achieve the MES, a newspaper would have to achieve sales equal to the total sales of all newspapers in a particular class (e.g. the *Daily Express* would have to sell copies equal to the total number of national popular daily newspapers sold, in order for costs of production to be at a minimum). Such a condition is hardly conducive to the success of a new firm about to enter the industry! Further, costs per unit rise by more than 20 per cent for firms with a circulation of less than 50 per cent of the total sales in any class of newspaper. Indeed, the tendency in the newspaper industry in recent years has been more towards monopoly, which is hardly surprising given the importance of economies of scale.

(*ii*) **Absolute Cost Differences** Firms in oligopolistic industries may be protected by the existence of a second type of barrier to entry, which is a lower unit cost of production than potential entrants at all output levels – often called an **absolute cost advantage.** There is an important conceptual and practical difference between this type of entry barrier and entry barriers due to economies of scale.

In Diagram 9.5, each existing firm has a long-run average cost curve as shown, but a new entrant has a long-run average cost curve which lies above the existing firm's curve regardless of the level of output at which the new firm might produce. Thus even though there may be no scale disadvantage facing the new entrant (i.e. MES could be small), existing firms would be able to produce any level of output more cheaply. Absolute cost advantages can arise from several sources. Sometimes existing firms have access to the most efficient production techniques by virtue of superior 'know-how', control of the supply of a raw material essential to the production of a good, or they can borrow funds for building plant and buying machinery at considerably lower interest rates than new firms.

(*iii*) **Product Differentiation** Entry into oligopolistic industries may be discouraged by existing firms having long adopted a policy of product differentiation backed up with heavy advertising expenditure. For example, one of the principal reasons why firms in the detergents industry make so many brands of the same type of product and spend over 30 per cent of sales revenue on advertising is that such policies make it extremely difficult for any new firm to set up in business, even though the industry is one in which there are no barriers due to technical economies of scale. The following example illustrates the point.

Let us suppose that in an oligopolistic industry consisting of

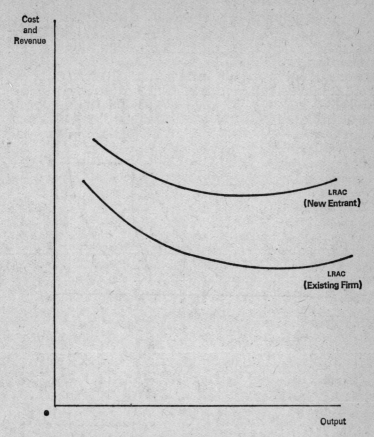

Figure 9.5 Absolute cost difference as barrier to entry

three firms, the long-run average cost curve for each firm is denoted by LRAC (Production) in Diagram 9.6(*a*). If the scale used on the axes means that LRAC (Production) illustrates a lack of economies of scale, a new firm could enter the industry and produce OM units of output compared with ON units of output at the optimum firm size without suffering much of a cost disadvantage. Now let us suppose that the existing firms each produce a range of brands of

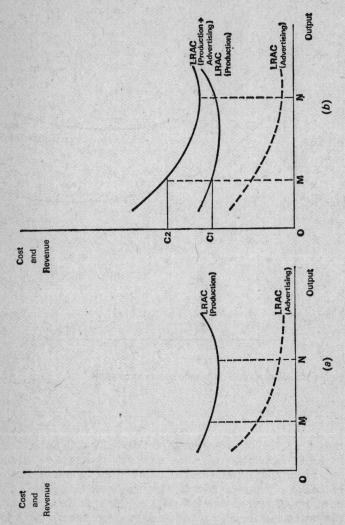

Figure 9.6 Advertising expenditure as barrier to entry

the good in question and incur heavy advertising expenditure in order to bring each individual brand into the public eye. It is known from experience in many industries that a minimum (often very large) critical size of advertising expenditure is needed to begin to be effective, and so advertising expenditure is really like a large block of fixed costs which can then be spread over a large range of output. Only when the level of sales is relatively high will advertising costs per unit be relatively low. The diagrammatic representation of such a policy can be seen in the curve LRAC (Advertising) which is high at low levels of output but declines continuously as output expands.

Existing firms now have two important components of long-run average cost. They have long-run average production costs and long-run average advertising costs, and by adding these two sets of cost together we derive the long-run average total cost curve as shown in Diagram 9.6(b). The effect of product differentiation and advertising is to raise the height of the long-run average cost curve at lower levels of output, and so policies designed to increase product differentiation and advertising costs can create economies of scale. Comparing Diagrams 9.6(a) and (b), it can be seen that a firm planning entry at a scale of OM would be operating under a considerably greater cost disadvantage when advertising expenditure in the industry is high. Unit costs would be OC_1 without advertising, but OC_2 with advertising.

Conclusion

The treatment of the theory of oligopoly has not been as straightforward as the treatment of the theories of perfect competition, monopoly and monopolistic competition. To restate the problem quoted at the beginning of this section: in a situation of mutual interdependence and uncertainty an oligopolist's behaviour is shaped by his assumptions about rivals' actions, and so the theories of economists must be based on hypotheses which state their assumptions about the oligopolist's assumptions! As yet, there is no agreement amongst economists about a set of general assumptions, and so, as we have seen, one strand of oligopoly theory is based on different explicit assumptions about the possible reactions of firms under specific circumstances (e.g. the kinked-demand curve, game theory) and another strand is based on a rationalisation of some well-known aspects of oligopoly behaviour in practice.

Alternative Hypotheses about Firms' Objectives

The theories which we have developed about perfect competition, monopoly, monopolistic competition and oligopoly all attempted to specify what price and output policy would be adopted by individual firms in a variety of market structures on the assumption that firms aimed to maximise profits. There has been considerable controversy in the economics profession in recent years about the validity of this assumption, and it is to this controversy that we now turn. Before stating the main alternative assumptions which have been proposed, it is worthwhile clarifying two points concerning the profit-maximisation assumption. First, when we look at the historical development of the theory of the firm it is clear that the assumption of profit maximisation is not based on any empirical foundation. In other words, when economists first expounded the theories we have been looking at, no one had conducted a large-scale survey of firms and found that all of them (or even 90 or 80 per cent) aimed at maximising their profits. It is, however, in the nature of theories in all branches of science that very general assumptions are put forward which may not exactly fit certain specific cases. The real test of whether an assumption is adequate lies in the extent to which the predictions which the theory makes can be tested against the facts of the real world. Secondly, it has sometimes been argued that the profit-maximisation assumption is misleading because firms do not in fact use the tools of marginal analysis in reaching their decisions about what price to charge and what level of output to produce. Firms, it is said, simply do not equate marginal cost with marginal revenue partly because they do not know what these terms mean (not all businessmen have been trained in economics!) or because the relevant values are difficult to quantify. Whether or not these charges are correct is beside the point. The theory of the firm as we have outlined it was not intended to describe or analyse the way in which individual firms actually reached decisions. Rather it was intended to show what the outcomes of those decisions would be if firms aimed at the objective of profit maximisation and reached their goal in some way or another.

The alternative theories of the firm advanced in recent years have arisen because of dissatisfaction with one or other of the two points mentioned in the previous paragraph. We shall look briefly first of all at those theories which, because of the alleged lack of reality about the profit-maximisation assumption, put forward an alternative hypothesis about the target which firms aim to maximise. Secondly, we shall consider a group of theories which argue that the only way to inject some realism into the theory of the firm is to study the way firms actually behave in coming to decisions. Not surprisingly, the latter group of theories are known as **behavioural theories of the firm.**

There have been four important rivals to the profit-maximisation assumption in the recent theories of the firm. It should be noted that each of these can be regarded, in part, as a response to the unsatisfactory nature of oligopoly theory, and a recognition of the fact that in oligopolistic industries the people who own the firm (perhaps a large number of independent shareholders) are *divorced* from the people who actually run the firms (the senior managers). Since the managers are actually in control of the firms, and since they (if they are not the major shareholders as well) may have different aspirations from the shareholders, it is argued that we would normally expect firms in oligopolistic industries to maximise some variable other than profits, although some target level of profits will have to be earned.

The Hypothesis of Full-Cost Pricing

Following some empirical investigations into firms' pricing policies by two economists, Hall and Hitch, in the 1930s, a hypothesis known as **full-cost pricing** has enjoyed popularity as an explanation of firms' pricing behaviour. The hypothesis is partly a rejection of the profit-maximisation assumption and partly an attempt to describe how businessmen actually fix prices in the absence of good information about demand and cost conditions. Briefly, the hypothesis states that businessmen will calculate the full costs of producing some level of output (i.e. overheads plus variable costs) and then add on some profit margin to arrive at the final price.

The hypothesis is largely concerned with *averages*, e.g. the full costs per unit of output and profit margin per unit of output, since there was considerable evidence in Hall and Hitch's study to show that businessmen did not use the concepts of marginal cost and marginal revenue in reaching price and output decisions.[7] Having calculated the level of full costs and an acceptable profit margin,

[7] See previous section for the reason why this does not necessarily harm the conventional theory of the firm.

the firm will then sell as much to the market as it can at the price level set.

It must be admitted that there is a great shortage of empirical evidence about the validity of this hypothesis, and in particular about the way in which a profit margin is estimated and the forces which may cause it to change over time. But the idea that pricing is conducted on a cost-plus basis does lend some support to the notion that oligopolists may create entry barriers. For example, whether or not barriers of the type mentioned in the previous section are present, firms may try to ensure the exclusion of potential entrants by adopting a policy known as **limit pricing**. This pricing policy would mean that existing firms might have to forego some profit in the short-run in order to set a price (lower than the profit-maximising level) which would virtually ensure that any new entrant would earn less than normal profits.

In Diagram 9.7 let us imagine that each oligopolist in an industry had similar costs and was selling OX units of output at a price of OP. A new firm might be tempted to enter the industry and be capable of selling OY units. For a time the new firm would certainly be at a cost disadvantage due to the existence of economies of scale. But suppose the new entrant was convinced he could survive. One way of preventing the survival and even the entry of the firm is for the existing oligopolists to set a **limit price** of, say, OP_1. This price would lower the level of supernormal profits earned by existing firms, but it would mean that by selling OY units at a price of OP_1 the new firm could make a loss since price would be less than average cost.

In its investigation into the market for breakfast cereals, the Monopolies Commission found evidence of limit pricing. The Commission reported that 'Kellogg told us that the company avoided setting its prices at such a high level that new competition would be attracted into the industry. When fixing its prices, therefore, Kellogg has as an objective the preservation of its share of the market against potential competitors.'[8]

Maximising Sales Revenue

An American economist, W. T. Baumol,[9] has put forward the hypothesis that firms aim at maximising sales revenue within the

[8] The Monopolies Commission, *A report on the Supply of Ready Cooked Breakfast Cereal Foods* (HMSO 1973) para. 86, p. 26.
[9] Baumol, W. T., *Business Behaviour, Value and Growth* (New York: Harcourt, Brace and World, Inc., 1967).

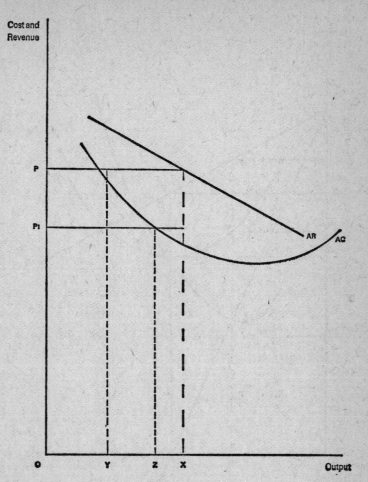

Figure 9.7 Limit pricing as barrier to entry

constraint of earning some *acceptable* level of profit. Let us consider how the price and output policy would be determined for a *sales revenue maximiser* and how this price and output policy would differ from price and output policy for a profit maximiser.

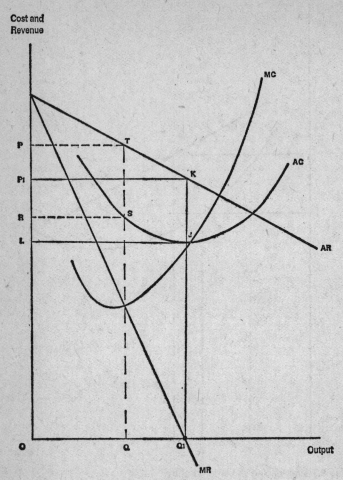

Figure 9.8 Price and output under sales revenue maximisation

In Diagram 9.8, let us suppose the firm faces a downward-sloping demand curve and has the appropriate cost and revenue curves as shown. What output should the firm produce in order to maximise sales revenue? This question can be easily answered by remembering that the firm is looking for that output level at which total revenue is at a maximum, which, under conditions of a downward-sloping demand curve, is that output level at which marginal revenue is zero. (Since if MR = +ve or −ve, TR cannot be at a maximum.) This output level is OQ_1, where the marginal revenue curve cuts the output axis. The corresponding price is found by extending a vertical line from Q_1 to the demand curve (point K) to fix a price of OP_1 per unit.

It is interesting to compare price and output under the assumption of sales revenue maximisation compared with profit maximisation. The profit-maximising price and output in Diagram 9.8 would be OP and OQ, which are higher and lower than OP_1 and OQ_1 respectively. We can easily understand this point by noting that at OQ_1, marginal cost is greater than marginal revenue, and so OQ_1 must be greater than the profit-maximising output. The actual level of profits earned under sales-revenue maximisation is denoted by P_1LJK which is a smaller area than the maximum profit area PRST. But as long as P_1LJK is at least equal to the minimum level of profits required by the firm to pay shareholders in dividends, etc., P_1LJK is acceptable. If the minimum profit constraint was higher than P_1LJK then it can be seen that the firm would cut back on output from OQ_1, thereby giving larger areas of profit than P_1LJK until a level of output just consistent with the profit constraint was reached.

Maximisation of Growth

The separation of ownership from control in large firms led the Cambridge economist Robin Marris[10] to hypothesise that the discretion enjoyed by managers will be directed towards maximising the **growth rate** of the firm. Marris's hypothesis places the theory of the firm into a more dynamic setting, where policies are shaped towards the expansion of the size of the firm. We can see how the growth-maximisation assumption involves behaviour which departs from the behaviour patterns associated with profit-maximisation in Diagram 9.9.

In Diagram 9.9 let us suppose a firm is faced with the cost and revenue curves as shown. What price and output policy might be adopted if the firm's managers intended to achieve the maximum expansion in the size of the firm? One answer might be to produce

[10] Marris, R. L., *The Economic Theory of Managerial Capitalism* (London, Macmillan, 1964).

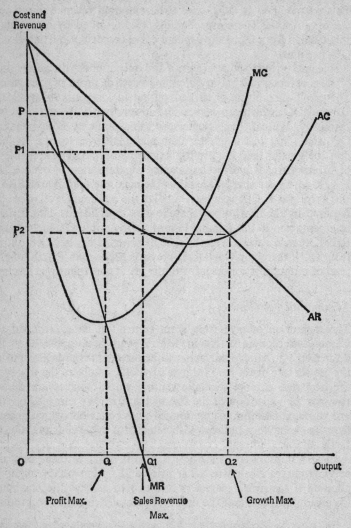

Figure 9.9. Price and output under growth maximisation

the maximum output technically possible, but Marris argued that even growth maximisers would operate under some constraints. The constraints he envisaged were avoiding the extremes of the firm being taken over or becoming bankrupt (either of which might radically reduce the power of the firm's managers by making them unemployed!). Accordingly, firms might go for rapid expansion, Marris argued, subject to earning a rate of profit which did not cause either bankruptcy or the possibility of being taken over by other firms.

It might be argued, then, that the firm represented in Diagram 9.9 should expand output to OQ_2, corresponding to the point of equality between price and average cost, thus yielding a normal profit. To expand output beyond OQ_2 would involve the firm in making losses and so increase the possibility of the firm closing down altogether. The interesting point to notice about the growth-maximisation objective is that the level of output produced by the firm (and hence the firm's size) is greater than would be the case under the objective of profit maximisation. As a consequence, price would be lower under the growth-maximisation hypothesis than under the profit-maximisation hypothesis. It might be the case, however, that the sales-revenue maximisation hypothesis of Baumol and the growth-maximisation hypothesis of Marris would yield the same result in cases where the possibility of a takeover or bankruptcy was avoided by the firm explicitly recognising a minimum profit constraint. The larger the element of supernormal profits within the constraint the more the growth-maximising output would be reduced from OQ_2 towards the profit-maximising output.

Managerial Utility Maximisation

A slightly more ambitious alternative to the profit-maximisation assumption has been developed by the American economist, Oliver Williamson.[11] It is ambitious in the sense that Williamson puts forward several variables which the management of a firm might attempt to maximise. Briefly, Williamson's argument runs as follows. Managers in large firms have sufficient discretion to pursue those policies which give them personally most satisfaction. We can call this **managerial utility.** Williamson then specifies four main factors which may be uppermost in the managerial calculations:

[11] O. R. Williamson, *The Economics of Discretionary Behaviour: Managerial Objectives in a Theory of the Firm* (Prentice-Hall Englewood Cliffs N.J. 1964).

(*i*) *Managerial Salaries* – Managers will attempt to obtain large salaries for themselves partly as a result of their desire for financial security and partly because their status is directly related to their salary level. When we speak of managerial salaries, we also include other forms of monetary income such as bonuses, or income from the shareholding owned by some managers in the assets of the firm.

(*ii*) *Number and Quality of Staff* – Managerial utility can be affected by the number and the ability of employees within the organisation. The greater the quantity and the higher the skills of subordinate staff, the more management enjoys feelings of power and status.

(*iii*) *Discretionary Investment* – Managers attach great importance to their ability to control discretionary investment – by which is meant new investments which are not essential to survival or to profits, but which may nevertheless influence the general development of the firm. Firms in many industries invest heavily in the research and development of new techniques and products. There is a debate about how much has to be spent on such activities for any firm to remain competitive. Investment above this level in a firm might be regarded as discretionary since the money might well be used to sponsor the 'pet project' of the management, whereas it might have been put to alternative uses.

(*iv*) *Fringe-Benefits* – Management will tend to strive for a range of fringe-benefits, or added luxuries, which allow them to conduct their jobs in a certain style. For example, satisfaction will be derived when management move into offices with mahogany desks and thick-pile carpets, receive expense accounts which allow them to charge activities such as entertaining important customers to the firm, and drive executive-class cars supplied by the firm. Such items were regarded by Williamson as **slack,** a term which denotes expenditures which are non-necessary but which nevertheless form part of a firm's cost schedule.

By combining (i) and (ii) (because Williamson believes there is a close association between the level of managerial salaries and the number and quality of subordinate staff), Williamson reduced the managerial utility function to the form

$$U = f(S, Id, M)$$

where U denotes managerial utility, S denotes expenditure on staff (combining (i) and (ii)), Id denotes discretionary investment and M represents spending on managerial fringe-benefits. Williamson puts forward the hypothesis that managers attempt to maximise U, subject to earning a minimum required level of profits, partly to distribute to shareholders in dividends and partly to finance those investments necessary to the development of the firm.

The three hypotheses about firms' objectives mentioned above share one common feature – they specify that firms aim to *maximise* some variable, whether it is sales revenue, growth or managerial utility. The hypotheses of Baumol, Marris and Williamson thus replace the assumption of profit maximisation with some other objective but the hypotheses still assume maximising behaviour on the part of firms. In contrast, a rival approach to the theory of firm's behaviour called the **Behavioural Theory of the Firm** stresses that firms do not attempt to maximise the value of some objective, but rather to achieve a **target** level which may be less than the maximum available.

Behavioural Theories of the Firm

The interest of the behavioural approach lies in explaining entre-preneurial decision-making; it is less concerned with the outcome of decisions and their economic significance. Behavioural theories, as their name implies, consist of hypotheses about actual managerial actions. Their aim is to define more clearly the motivation governing major objectives and to study methods of evaluating objectives. They are also concerned with analysing the way in which organisa-tions respond when the chosen policies either fail to meet objectives or over-fulfil them.

The behavioural approach starts by recognising that those in control of large organisations may have a variety of objectives to consider – e.g. a production objective, a profits objective and a sales objective. Conflicts in objectives may exist, which have to be settled by bar-gaining amongst managers in different areas of the organisation.

In formulating objectives, it is believed that target (or satisfactory, or acceptable) levels of attainment are aimed for, i.e. the aim of the firms' managers is to **satisfice** rather than maximise. The be-havioural approach has been influenced by the work of psychologists who maintain that people's actions are influenced by their levels of aspiration – i.e. their perception of how well they ought to be doing in the light of their experience. In terms of the theory of the firm, managers' aspiration levels initially define the target level of pro-duction, sales, profits, etc., which they attempt to satisfy. If the target levels are not reached two processes take place within the organisation. First, managers begin what the behavioural theorists call **search procedures,** which basically amount to a series of investigations into the reasons why the target levels of performance were not met and the evaluation of alternative courses of action for improving performance. The second process involves a change in the aspiration levels of managers themselves, perhaps as they realise that the initial objectives might have been over-ambitious. The consequence is that the firm adapts its policies to the changes in levels of managers' aspiration over time.

The behavioural approach, then, really involves going outside the boundaries of economics and into the disciplines of psychology and organisation theory since the approach is basically concerned with explaining how people actually behave in coming to certain decisions, and how the organisation of the firm changes and adapts to these decisions. Perhaps the most notable difference between the assumptions made in the behavioural approach and the assumptions made in the approaches discussed previously lies in the notion of satisficing rather than maximising.

Conclusion

Given this diversity of opinion about the theory of the firm, what can we say about the validity of the alternative approaches? Since so little empirical work has in fact been done, we are at the moment in the unsatisfactory position of saying that a little evidence can be gained to support each of the hypotheses outlined above. But none of the hypotheses has yet emerged as unequivocally superior as a general theory of the firm. Perhaps we should not be too surprised about this. One of the reasons why economists became interested in specifying alternative assumptions was because of the alleged lack of reality about the profit-maximisation assumption. But striving for more reality often has an opportunity cost, which is the sacrifice of some generality. The assumption of profit maximisation does yield powerful predictions about the level of price and output in industries operating under different competitive conditions – predictions which as we shall see in the chapter on Economic Welfare indicate how efficiently an economy working under conditions of perfect competition would allocate its resources between alternative uses. Because of the nature of oligopoly, however, it must be admitted that the assumption of profit maximisation yields only limited guidance as to the type of behaviour expected and the alternative assumptions do inject more realism into oligopolistic situations.

Industrial Structure, Behaviour and Performance: Some Empirical Evidence

The theory of the firm which we have developed gives some indication of how we would expect firms to behave and perform in different market situations. For example, we might expect that in industries consisting of a large number of price-taking firms a lower level of profits would be earned than in those exhibiting significant elements of monopoly or oligopoly, including barriers to entry. Our next task is that of outlining some methods of measuring market structure and examining some of the available evidence about industrial performance and behaviour. Our aim is to see to what extent the evidence confirms the predictions made by the theory.

Concentration Ratios

How can we measure **market structure?** It all depends on what features we want to measure. The basic idea of market structure relates to the number of firms operating in a market and the proportion of sales accounted for by each firm. In other words, the theory of the firm was built round assumptions about the number of firms and the size distribution of firms in different types of market structure, so ideally we need some index which quantifies the number of firms in a market and their size distribution. A method widely used by economists for this purpose is a **ratio of concentration,** which is nothing more than a measure of the proportion of output[12] accounted for by a number of the largest firms in an industry. In the UK relevant information is contained in the periodic Census of Production and the ratios are calculated on the basis of the percentage of output accounted for by the largest three firms in the industry (although in the USA the ratios are calculated for the largest four, eight and twenty firms). We can understand the ideas involved by looking at Diagram 9.10.

In Diagram 9.10, we have measured the output percentage on the vertical axis and the number of firms in the industry beginning with the largest (i.e. corresponding to number one) on the horizontal axis. **Concentration curves,** showing the cumulative percentage of output accounted for by the largest firms in the industry, are drawn for three hypothetical industries. Naturally they rise from left to

[12] Or some other variable such as employment.

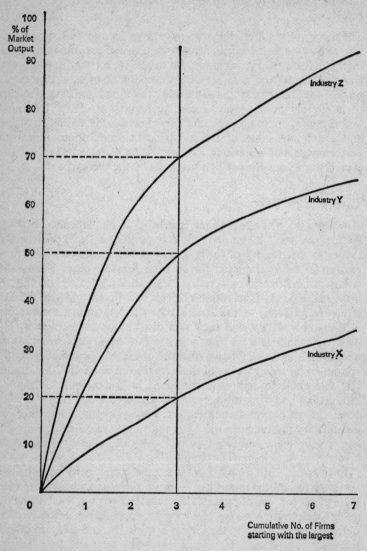

Figure 9.10 Concentration curves

right since two firms will account for more output than one, and three firms for more than two, and so on.

The concentration ratio is obtained from the curve by reading off on the vertical axis the output corresponding to the three-firm point on the horizontal axis. The ratios for industries X, Y and Z would thus be 20, 50 and 70 per cent respectively. Measurement, of course, takes place at one particular point on the curve. Clearly therefore the steeper the slope from the origin to the three-firm point, the higher the reading will be.

In a major study of British industry, Evely and Little[13] attempted to measure the level of concentration in a sample of 220 industries. They devised three categories into which the industries might be classified according to the degree of concentration observed: **high** for industries with ratios of 67 per cent or more; **medium** for industries in which the ratios ranged from 34 per cent to 66 per cent; and **low** where the ratio was below 34 per cent. The results of Evely and Little's survey showed that 50 of the 220 industries (i.e. 23 per cent) fell into the high category; 69 (i.e. 31 per cent) were defined as medium and 101(i.e. 46 per cent) showed low concentration.

Such measures, however, should be interpreted with care, because they give only partial information about market structure for the following reasons:

(a) The published statistics simply provide information about *one point* on the concentration curve. No information is available from which the market shares of the larger firms in the industry can be calculated. The lack of such information could be a problem if we were to consider two industries with exactly the same concentration ratio but with considerably different market shares amongst the largest three firms. For example, a ratio of 75 per cent could be found if each of the three largest firms accounted for 25 per cent of market output. In another industry, however, a similar ratio is quite compatible with the largest firm accounting for 50 per cent of market output, the second largest firm 15 per cent and the third largest firm 10 per cent. Indeed, to push the example further one firm could itself supply almost 75 per cent of the market! Apart from saying that the industries showed signs of high concentration (according to Evely and Little's definition), we could not go further and state that we would expect the pattern of behaviour and performance to be

[13] R. Evely and I. M. D. Little, *Concentration in British Industry* (London, Cambridge University Press, 1960).

much the same in each of them, since in our third example we are much nearer to a monopoly situation than in the first.

(b) The previous point really amounts to saying that the concentration ratio tells us nothing about the shape of the curve to the left of the three-firm mark. Similarly the ratio does not indicate how many firms share the market output unaccounted for by the largest three firms. Consider, for example, two other possible cases. In each case we will assume a concentration ratio of 75 per cent with the largest three firms each producing 25 per cent of market output. However the remaining 25 per cent of output could be accounted for by one other firm, or shared by twenty-five firms. Both industries might be correctly classified as oligopolies with high concentration; but again we would expect somewhat different behaviour patterns in the industry consisting of only four firms of equal size compared with that where three large firms of equal size existed side-by-side with twenty-five much smaller ones.[14] In the former case we might suspect that high barriers to entry (in one of the forms suggested earlier) were present, and there would be good opportunities for the four firms to adopt policies towards maximising the joint profits of the group with the effect of maintaining supernormal levels of profit. In the other industry, the existence of so many small firms would tend to suggest that barriers to entry were low and so it would be more difficult for the three large firms in this industry to behave in exactly the same way as the four large firms in the other case.

Despite these objections, however, concentration ratios do convey at least an outline impression of the structure of the market, and enable us to place industries roughly on the spectrum from perfect competition to monopoly. If we use such measures as broad indicators of market structure we should expect (from the predictions of the theory of the firm) that industries with high ratios would exhibit higher levels of profit, partly due to the existence of barriers to entry, than industries with low ratios.

Structure and Performance

Economists have conducted some studies which attempt to discover relationships between industrial structure and performance. The majority of evidence comes from America, and only a very few studies have been done in Britain. One of the latter, undertaken by

[14] There exist *other* measures of concentration which try to meet this objection. *See* M. A. Utton, *Industrial Concentration*, pp. 34–51.

Professor P. E. Hart,[15] was interesting in that it was found that profit rates in thirty-seven different industries did not vary with the level of concentration. Hart compared industries with high concentration on the one hand, with industries having medium or low concentration on the other. No significant difference in average profitability was found.

However, there is some evidence to show that above a certain critical level of concentration profit rates are significantly higher than in less concentrated industries. This is particularly true when high concentration is accompanied by high barriers to entry.

An investigation of American industries by H. M. Mann[16] produced the following interesting relationships between concentration, barriers to entry and profit levels. Mann worked with concentration ratios calculated on the basis of the market share accounted for by the largest eight firms, and divided thirty industries into two categories – those with ratios above and below 70 per cent. The results of his tests showed that the mean rate of profit earned in industries with the higher ratios was distinctly above that earned in the others. Another major conclusion of Mann's study concerned the relationship between barriers to entry and profit levels. Grading the thirty industries according to the height of barriers to entry, Mann found that high barriers were associated with higher profit levels. The highest average profit ratios of all were found in industries having both the highest concentration ratios and the highest entry barriers.

Mann's study, of course, does not *prove* that the existence of higher average profit rates in some industries can be explained purely by the existence of higher concentration ratios and barriers to entry. Indeed, in some research conducted by Collins and Preston,[17] it was found that the differences in profit rates between American industries in certain major product groups could only partly be explained by differences in concentration ratios. In foodstuffs, for example, 40 per cent of the difference in profit levels between the industries studied could be accounted for in this way, but in some product groups, notably chemicals and textiles, Collins and Preston found that only 3 to 4 per cent of the difference was explainable by differences in concentration. The work of Collins and Preston does

[15] P. E. Hart (ed.), *Studies in Profit, Business Saving and Investment in the U.K., 1920–62,* Vol. 2 (1968, Allen and Unwin).

[16] H. M. Mann, 'Seller Concentration, barriers to entry and rates of return in thirty-six industries, 1950–60'. *Review of Economics and Statistics,* August 1966.

[17] N. R. Collins and L. E. Preston, *Concentration and Cost-Price Margins in Manufacturing Industries* (Berkeley, University of California Press, 1968).

not deny that there is a relationship between concentration and profit levels; it simply states that the strength of the relationship does vary from industry to industry.

One further piece of evidence about the relationships between concentration, barriers to entry and profits is found in some work done by Samuels and Smyth.[18] Although their enquiries were mainly directed towards the relationship between size and profitability, they looked at the variation in profit levels to be found in firms in industries with high and low concentration. Such evidence would be a useful addition to the general conclusions thrown up by the work of people like Mann, Collins and Preston who considered average profit levels in an industry. The use of any average always contains the possibility that some values will lie above it and some below it. Samuels and Smyth found that there was less *variation* in profit rates earned by firms in highly concentrated industries than in industries with low concentration.

Conclusion

We have now analysed structure – behaviour – performance relationships in four types of competition. Before proceeding to the final stage in our analysis we leave the issue of competition in the market for goods and examine the operation of markets for factors of production.

---

[18] J. S. Samuels and D. Smyth, 'Profits, Variability of Profits and Size of Firm' *Economica*, May 1968.

Chapter 10

Factor Markets

We will now analyse the markets for factors of production and in particular the market for labour. In previous chapters we specified the conditions under which firms would achieve the least-cost combination of inputs to achieve certain levels of output, assuming given levels of factor prices. We will now examine the forces determining those prices.

Our interest in factor markets stems from many sources. In part, the outcome of market forces may determine the total value of rewards accruing to each category of factor – labour, capital and land – and consequently the share of each factor in the total income generated in an economy.

Table 10.1 **UK Distribution of Incomes, 1972**

Income Category	£m.	% Share in Total
Wages and Salaries	37,138	68
Income from Self-Employment	4,764	9
Profits of Companies (inc. nationalised industries)	8,374	15
Rent	4,182	8
Total Domestic Income	55,088	100

Table 10.1 illustrates the way in which income was distributed between the major classes of resources in the United Kingdom in 1972. By far the largest single category of reward was earned by people offering their services for a wage or salary, and much lower shares went to the other factors. A whole branch of economics called Distribution Theory has developed around the central question of 'what determines the distribution of incomes between factors?', in order to provide an explanation of the relative shares as shown in Diagram 10.1.

We may also wish to enquire about the forces influencing the earnings obtained by resources in particular markets. Taking labour as a specific example, controversy about the earnings of different categories of people – from unskilled manual workers to directors of large companies – is an ever-present ingredient in current economic and political debate. Some people argue that it is disgraceful for many highly-educated and qualified schoolteachers to earn less than some semi-skilled people working on an assembly line in a car factory. The opinion is often put forward that it is scandalous for nurses and ambulancemen, whose efforts contribute to the saving of human lives, or coal miners whose work supplies part of our vital energy needs, to be paid less in a whole year than pop music stars earn for a single concert.

Debates such as these usually focus on the central issue of what a person's labour is *worth* and how it is determined. Why is it, we can ask, that the chairman of the National Coal Board and the Chairman of the London Transport Authority each earn about ten times as much as the average coal miner and bus conductor?

Glaring differences between the payments made to certain individuals, of course, always catch the public's attention. But we should also be interested in explaining why large groups of workers in certain industries earn more than those in others. For example, why is it that workers in the engineering industry earn over 25 per cent more than agricultural workers? Also, how do we explain the phenomenon of low pay for women, amounting to little more than half the earnings of males, except in a few professions such as teaching?

From the static comparisons mentioned above we may go further and attempt to explain the causes and pace of changes in wage rates and employment levels in different industries. We know, for example, that in the one year interval between September 1972 and September 1973 coal miners' weekly earnings rose by about 8 per cent whereas workers in the construction industry enjoyed an earnings increase of over 26 per cent. In addition, the number employed in coal mining fell over that period from 373,000 to 358,400 whereas the labour force in the construction industry rose from 1,246,600 to 1,317,400.

Another source of interest in factor markets is the extent to which resources have common characteristics or possess unique differences. Our stance on this issue will largely determine whether the analysis we develop is applicable to all factor markets or whether (and in what ways) we must introduce changes in our analysis of each type of resource. Labour has traditionally been regarded as having special

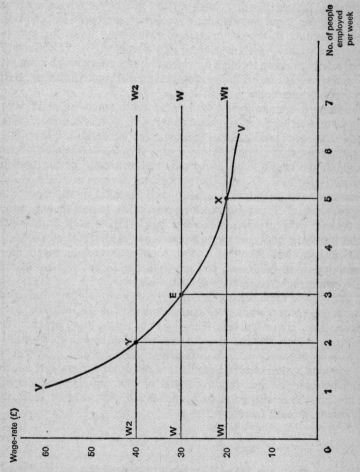

Figure 10.1 Demand for labour – value of marginal product curve

distinguishing characteristics as a factor of production for two broad sets of reasons. First, we know that wages and employment are determined not only by economic forces but by a host of social and institutional ones as well. For example, a person's educational achievements, in terms of 'O' and 'A' levels, professional qualifications or university degrees, may limit the range of occupational choice and earnings. Also, wage levels may be affected by the activities of organisations both on the side of employees, such as trades unions, and employers in the form of employers' associations. Also, because of the importance of rising wage levels for macroeconomic policy,[1] the government may participate in the process of wage determination through the operation of a policy which attempts to influence the rate of change of wages in general and the differentials between occupational groups.

Secondly, human beings must inevitably stand in a different social and technical relationship towards employers compared with other factors of production. The famous economist, Alfred Marshall, pointed out that employers could only buy the services of labour and, unlike capital, did not retain the ownership of the person himself. He also stressed the importance of human feelings and emotion, which endowed labour with definite views about the adequacy of their pay and working conditions. Indeed thanks to the work not only of economists, but psychologists such as Maslow and Herzberg, we know that a whole range of human needs, such as physical survival, financial reward, social relationships with fellow employees, self-fulfilment, and the challenge and excitement of the job, can be affected by the work situation.

Because of these distinguishing features and their importance in the economy as a whole, we shall devote most of this chapter to an analysis of labour markets. This does not mean, however, that the returns to the other factors of production will be left unexplained. The body of theory we shall consider – marginal productivity theory – contains hypotheses and predictions about labour markets which can be easily applied in the context of rent, profits and interest, although the institutional background will obviously be radically different for each factor.

The Demand for Labour

Economists call the demand for labour a **derived demand.** Employers

[1] *See* A. G. Ford, *Income, Spending and the Price Level.*

wish to hire labour not to obtain satisfaction in the same way that a consumer obtains satisfaction when purchasing goods or services. Rather labour is hired to help satisfy the demand that exists for products. The demand exerted by firms in the labour market is therefore determined by the demand for the product in the goods market. Hence the demand for construction workers depends on the demand for buildings such as schools, hospitals and houses: the demand for many specialised trades in the shipbuilding industry is determined by the demand for ships; and so on.

Perfect Competition in the Product Market

Let us first of all explain the demand for labour exerted by a firm operating under perfect competition in the product market. It will also be helpful to assume initially that the firm faces a perfect market for labour, by which we mean a market with a large number of firms wishing to hire labour and a large number of people seeking employment, where no single employer, or group of employers or employees can affect wage or employment levels.

Assuming that the firm will attempt to maximise profits, it will employ more labour if the revenue received from the incremental output produced and sold as a result of employing one more person exceeds the extra cost of hiring him. The extra revenue is called the **value of the marginal product**. Moreover, since in perfect competition the firm takes the price of the good as given (i.e. it faces a perfectly elastic demand curve), the value of the marginal product is equal to a factor's marginal physical productivity multiplied by the price of the good. For example, if the firm can produce and sell twenty extra units of a product priced at £2 each by employing one more worker at a wage rate of £30, the firm should hire him. The value of the marginal product (20 × £2 = £40) exceeds the extra cost of the worker (£30).

Assuming that the firm is able to employ additional workers at the same wage of £30 (this follows from our assumption of a perfect labour market) and that the price of the good is £2 per unit, Table 10.2 shows values for total product, marginal product and the value of marginal product as the firm's level of employment increases. To maximise profits the firm would hire three workers. In order to verify this statement let us compare the value of marginal product and the extra wage cost for different numbers of workers.

We have already shown that it would pay the firm to hire two

Table 10.2

No. of People Employed	Total Product	Marginal Product	Value of Marginal Product (£)
0	0	0	0
1	30	30	60
2	50	20	40
3	65	15	30
4	77	12	24
5	87	10	20
6	96	9	18

workers. There would, however, be a decrease in profits if the firm extended its employment level beyond three because the fourth person would add more to costs (£30) than the value of his marginal product (£24). If the wage rate fell from £30 to £20 then, of course, the firm would take on the fourth worker because the value of his marginal product would then exceed the extra wages paid.

The example above suggests that under perfect competition the firm's demand for labour is based on the value of a factor's marginal product. In Diagram 10.1, for example, where wage rates are measured on the vertical axis and numbers employed on the horizontal axis, the curve representing value of marginal product (VV) slopes downwards from left to right as extra workers are employed.

Since, under conditions of perfect competition in the labour market, the firm is able to purchase all the labour it wishes at a wage rate of £30, the horizontal line WW is the supply curve of labour to the firm. When the size of the firm's labour force is less than three (i.e. where VV and WW intersect) the value of marginal product exceeds the wage rate, and so the firm has the opportunity of increasing profits by taking on more workers. Conversely, if the number employed by the firm exceeds three the cost of hiring additional labour is greater than the value of their marginal product and so the firm's profits cannot be at a maximum. A profit-maximising firm will therefore hire extra workers until the value of the marginal product of the last person employed is exactly equal to the wage paid. In Diagram 10.1, profits are maximised at point E where three workers are employed at a wage rate of £30.

The value of marginal product curve is the firm's demand curve for labour under perfect competition because it enables us to say how much labour would be employed at a series of wage rates. If, for example, the wage rate fell to £20 (denoted by the supply curve W_1W_1) the firm would expand its labour force to five as indicated at point X in Diagram 10.1. A rise in the wage rate to, say, £40 (illustrated by W_2W_2) would force the firm to cut back its employment level to two, as denoted by point Y.

Imperfect Competition in the Product Market

When a firm is operating in an imperfectly competitive product market (but still a perfect labour market) the general principle outlined in the previous section still holds. The firm will continue to employ more labour until the last person adds just as much to revenue as he does to cost.

The major difference, however, lies in the fact that the value of marginal product (marginal product × price) is greater than the extra revenue gained by selling the marginal product of an additional worker because under imperfect competition price exceeds marginal revenue. We can analyse the implications of this difference for wage and employment determination as follows.

The firm will face a downward-sloping demand curve for its product because price must be lowered to sell additional units. If, for example, the firm was employing one worker and was considering hiring a second it can be seen from Table 10.3 that total product would rise from 30 units to 50 units per day, i.e. the marginal product of the second worker would be 20 units. But in order to sell the extra 20 units price falls from £2 to £1.90. Total revenue would increase from £60 to £95, which means that increased revenue of £35 can be attributed solely to his productivity.

The additional revenue from the output of an extra unit of labour is called **marginal revenue product,** and the example above shows that marginal revenue product (£35) is less than the value of marginal product (20 × £1.90 = £38). When the firm's employment of workers increases from one to two the total additional revenue is the value of the marginal product, i.e. £38. But in expanding output from 30 to 50 units the firm has to accept a fall in price of 10p on each of the 30 units it was previously selling at £2 each, i.e. a fall in revenue of £3. Hence the net addition to revenue from employing the second worker, or the marginal revenue product as we have called it, is £38 − £3 = £35. Indeed as shown in Table 10.3, marginal

No. of People Employed	Total Product	Marginal Product	Product Price (£)	Value of Marginal Product (£)	Total Revenue (£)	Marginal Revenue Product (£)
0	0	0	0	0	0	0
1	30	30	2	60	60	60
2	50	20	1.90	38	95	35
3	65	15	1.80	27	117	22
4	77	12	1.70	20.4	130.9	13.9
5	87	10	1.60	16.0	139.2	8.3
6	96	9	1.50	13.5	144	4.8

Table 10.3

revenue product is always less than the value of marginal product after the first worker has been employed.

At the margin, it would pay the firm to hire the second worker if the wage rate was £30 (as was the case in the previous section) because his marginal revenue product would be greater than the marginal cost of employing him, thereby increasing profits. The firm should not, however, expand its labour further because the marginal revenue product contributed by a third employee (£22) would be less than the wage paid. In general, the profit-maximising firm will employ labour until the cost of an additional worker just equals marginal revenue product, which will be less than the value of the marginal product attributable to the last unit of labour hired.

The Supply of Labour

In this section we examine some determinants of the supply of labour. It will be useful to distinguish between three levels of supply – to the economy as a whole, from the individual, and to the firm.

(i) **Supply of Labour to the Economy** The limit to the size of the potential labour supply in the economy is set by the size of the population, which is affected in turn by birth rates, death rates and migration. The age distribution of the population at any point in time is also important. Compulsory school education means that full-time employment opportunities can only be considered when people have reached the age of sixteen, and it is customary to retire from work sometime after the age of sixty (or in some occupations sixty-five).

As we already noted in Chapter 1, the potential labour supply to the United Kingdom economy in 1971 (excluding full-time housewives) was about twenty-three million people. The majority of this number can be regarded as permanent members of the labour force in the sense that from the date they become available for employment until the date they retire, their services are constantly offered on a full-time basis. This is certainly true for most male members of the working population since the decision to work is primarily based on the need to earn a stream of income to support families and dependants.

(ii) **Individual Supply of Labour** Assuming a given number of people in the labour force, the second general feature of labour supply is the number of hours worked by each individual. The problem is often regarded by economists as a choice between time which is paid for (i.e. working time) and time which is unpaid (i.e. non-working time). How will any individual allocate his time between the two categories?

We can analyse this choice by relating the supply of hours worked by an individual to the wage rate offered by employers and predicting what effect a rise in wage rates would have on the number of hours worked. As hourly wages rise, the opportunity cost of enjoying leisure time (i.e. not working) increases. Hence an individual's labour supply curve is thought to slope upwards from left to right, indicating that a person will forego leisure time for working time as the hourly wage rate rises. For example in Diagram 10.2(a), where the hourly wage rate is measured on the vertical axis and the number of hours worked per day is shown on the horizontal axis, the individual will increase his working time until wages reach the level OW_2 (where ten hours per day are worked). However, it may be argued that any further increase in wages, say to OW_3, actually reduces the amount of time the individual is prepared to work (e.g. to nine hours in Diagram 10.2(a)). The rationale behind the backward-bending supply curve, as it is called, is that as higher income levels are reached workers wish to spend more money on leisure-time activities. Once a certain standard of income has been reached people respond to any further wage rise by cutting down the number of working hours in order to have more time available for other pursuits.

We can understand this argument more clearly by using indifference curve analysis. In Diagram 10.2(b), income is measured on the vertical axis and the number of leisure hours enjoyed by the individual on the horizontal axis. Indifference curves I_1, I_2, I_3 and I_4 have been drawn in, representing successively higher levels of utility derived from different combinations of income and leisure. ON measures the maximum number of leisure hours possible (twenty-four daily). Notice that the slope of any indifference curve at any point will measure the individual's marginal rate of substitution between income and leisure, i.e. it shows the rate at which he is willing to exchange leisure for an extra unit of income.

Also drawn in are some budget lines, NW, NW_1, NW_2 and NW_3. For example, if the budget line was NW and he chose to work all day he would earn OW in income. The slope of each budget line

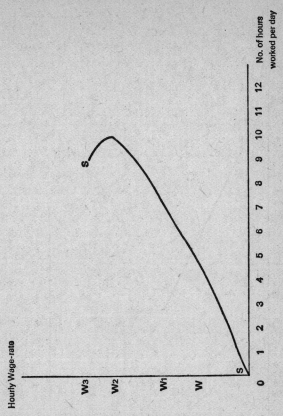

Figure 10.2 (*a*) 'Backward-bending' supply curve for labour

measures the wage rate, or the rate at which leisure can be exchanged for income.

Given a certain wage rate the individual's highest level of utility will be denoted by the point of tangency between the budget line and an indifference curve. Hence if his budget line was NW, he would choose that combination of income and leisure shown at point A where NW just touches indifference curve I_1. Since he would

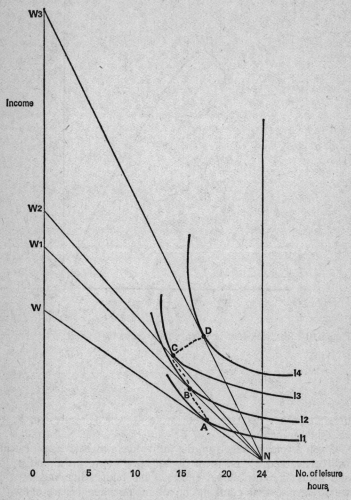

Figure 10.2 (b) Individual Supply of Labour

take eighteen hours of leisure, that means he is prepared to work for six hours at a wage rate measured by OW/ON.

Now let us see what would happen as the wage rate increased to OW_1/ON (shown by the budget line NW_1) and OW_2/ON (line NW_2). The successive tangency points B and C on indifference curves I_2 and I_3 trace out the individual's response. As the wage rate rises, he substitutes income for leisure and so increases the number of hours worked. Points B and C illustrate the further fall in his leisure hours from sixteen to fourteen hours per day. But when the wage rate increases beyond OW_2/ON (which corresponds to OW_2 in Diagram 10.2(a)), the individual can enjoy even higher income while also cutting back on his working time and increasing his leisure hours. The budget line NW_3, for example, is a tangent to indifference curve I_4 at D, indicating a decrease in working time from ten to six hours per day.

The reason why we should expect a person to behave in this fashion lies in our assumption about substitution and income effects. The rise in wage rates motivates him to substitute working time for leisure time. Higher wage rates, however, also allow him to maintain his consumption standards because the same level of income could be earned by cutting down his working time. The substitution and income effects are opposing forces and his reaction to a specific wage-rate increase will depend on the direction of the outcome. The rationale behind the backward-bending supply curve for labour is that when wage rates for individuals reach a certain level the strength of the income effect will be sufficient to outweigh the substitution effect.

Whether the supply curve in Diagram 10.2(a) is an accurate description of the choice facing the individual worker depends to a large extent on the flexibility in the length of the working day. It is often argued, for example, that the analysis is inapplicable in many situations because employees are not able to make adjustments to their working hours in response to wage-rate changes. In many industries the number of hours people work is fixed by agreement with employers and is expected to be observed.

Against this argument however, it is common to find in occupations where an hourly wage rate is paid that workers are offered **overtime** – a payment normally greater than the hourly wage for work undertaken outside the agreed times. These overtime rates can be taken as evidence of the need to pay more in order to induce people to supply more working hours, thus supporting the positively-sloped section of the supply curve. Indeed a body called the National Board for Prices and Incomes reported that over 80 per cent of industrial manual workers in Great Britain had a large degree of choice about whether or not to work overtime and how many overtime hours they desired.

As always, however, we can find plausible exceptions and the experience of absenteeism in some industries (notably coalmining) suggests that we can find some examples of people who, having earned a certain level of income, decrease their working time and undertake extra leisure activities. Commenting on the report mentioned in the previous paragraph, Dr Ralph Turvey, who was Joint Deputy Chairman of the National Board for Prices and Incomes, noted that the proportion of industrial manual workers who were prepared to sacrifice income through absenteeism, sickness, late arrival or early departure from work, was higher for those doing a standard working week than those working more than two hours' overtime.

(*iii*) **The Supply of Labour to the Firm** In analysing the supply of labour to the firm, we shall make the assumption that labour is homogeneous (i.e. all workers have the same level of skill) and so we can concentrate our attention purely on the determinants of the number of workers and the number of hours worked. The most important explanation of the supply of labour to the firm lies in the degree of competition in the market for labour. In our earlier discussion of marginal productivity we referred to a perfect market for labour and it is now necessary to show in more detail how such an assumption affects the supply curve of labour to the firm.

(*iv*) **Supply of Labour in a Perfect Labour Market** For conditions of perfect competition to prevail in the labour market there must exist a large number of workers and firms wishing to employ them so that no individual firm or worker can influence wage rates. Workers must have access to complete information about job opportunities in different firms and in different areas, and no barriers to movement into or out of the labour force or between areas must exist. Under these conditions, the supply curve of labour would be perfectly elastic as shown in Diagram 10.3.

The supply curve SS indicates that at a wage rate of OW any firm can employ all the labour it requires to produce any planned output level. There would be no need for a firm to offer a wage rate

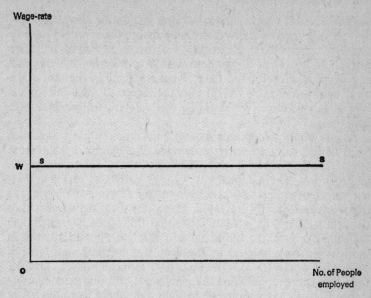

Figure 10.3 Labour supply curve in perfect competition

above OW to acquire more labour, and to do so would mean earning less than maximum profit. Also, if a firm attempted to cut wages below OW, its workers could easily (according to the assumptions of perfect competition) find similar employment elsewhere.

(*v*) **Supply of Labour in an Imperfect Labour Market** If we assume a break in one or more of the conditions outlined in the previous section, the labour market can no longer be described as perfect. One important source of imperfection may derive from the power of individual firms to influence the wage rate. This situation will most clearly arise when, instead of a large number of firms purchasing labour, only one firm – called a **monopsonist** – hires workers.

Such a firm would face an upward-sloping labour supply curve. To increase output by hiring one more person, the firm would have to raise the wage rate to attract workers from elsewhere. Further, the extra cost of each additional worker will not be measured solely by the wage paid to that person. The monopsonist would have to pay the higher rate to all existing employees as well as the extra worker. Hence when the monopsonist is considering the marginal cost of hiring more labour, the relevant costs will be the sum of the wage paid to the extra worker plus the increased wage bill for the current labour force. We shall call this amount the **marginal wage cost**.

As an example, suppose a monopsonist employs five people at a wage of £30 each. In order to increase employment by one more person the firm has to increase the wage rate to £31 to attract the extra worker. The marginal cost of that particular person is £31, but the monopsonist will also have to pay £1 more to each of the five workers currently employed. Hence the marginal wage cost to the firm is £31 + £5 = £36. Notice that this figure is greater than the supply price of the additional unit of labour. Indeed apart from the first person employed by the firm, the marginal wage cost of each extra worker exceeds the wage paid to those workers. Graphically, the curve representing marginal wage cost under monopsony would slope upwards from left to right and would lie to the left of the labour supply curve.

The Market for Labour – Demand and Supply Together

We have so far considered the determinants of the demand for labour and supply of labour independently. In order to analyse the market for labour and the determination of wage and employment levels we need only to consider demand and supply together. Competitive conditions in both the output and input markets are important and hence the analysis we use depends on whether the firm is perfectly competitive or has monopolistic power in the goods market, and whether it is perfectly competitive or a monopsonist in the factor market. We shall examine different combinations of conditions in turn.

(*i*) **Perfect Competition in Product and Labour Markets** It was established earlier that a firm operating in perfect competition in the product market would face a demand curve for labour represented by the value of marginal product curve. The labour supply curve in a perfectly competitive labour market would be a horizontal straight line. The demand and supply curves for labour could thus be as shown in Diagram 10.1. In equilibrium (i.e. in order to maximise profits) the firm would employ three workers at a wage rate of £30 as indicated at the point where the curves intersect.

Notice also that each worker would be paid the value of his marginal product. More generally, if labour markets were perfectly competitive throughout the economy each unit of labour would earn exactly the same wage and this wage would be equivalent to the value of each worker's marginal product. In other words,

$MP_L \times P_L$ in industry $A = MP_L \times P_L$ in industry $B \dots =$ $MP_L \times P_L$ in industry n.

This conclusion is extremely important and we shall recall it in the next chapter when we consider the conditions for efficiency in the economy as a whole.

(*ii*) **Imperfect Competition in the Product Market, Perfect Competition in the Labour Market** Let us now consider the case of a firm operating as a monopolist in the product market but purchasing labour in a perfectly competitive market. We have already established that the monopolists' demand curve for labour is represented by the marginal revenue product curve which lies to the left of the value of marginal product curve. The firm's labour supply curve will still be a horizontal straight line.

In Diagram 10.4, the monopolist will employ ON workers at a wage of OW, as denoted by point E where the labour supply curve intersects the marginal revenue product curve. Compared to the perfectly competitive firm which would employ ON_1 people, the monopolist hires fewer workers. Because of this lower level of employment, each worker's value of marginal product is higher under monopoly than perfect competition, but of course each unit of labour is paid a wage rate lower than the value of its marginal product.

(*iii*) **Perfect Competition in the Product Market, Imperfect Competition in the Labour Market** The third case involves a firm operating under perfect competition in the product market, but purchasing labour monopsonistically. The firm's labour demand curve will be its value of marginal product curve, denoted by VV in Diagram 10.5. The supply curve of labour to the firm is labelled SS and the curve representing the marginal wage cost is MM which (as we established previously) lies upwards and to the left of SS.

Using the familiar conditions for profit maximisation, the firm

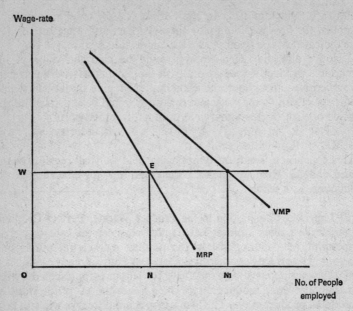

Figure 10.4 Perfectly competitive labour market and monopolistic
goods market

will increase its labour force until the value of the marginal product
of the last person employed just equals the marginal wage cost of
employing him. This condition is satisfied at point E where VV
intersects MM. The firm will therefore employ OQ workers and pay
them a wage rate of OW which, according to the labour supply
curve, is the price which would induce OQ workers to offer their
services.

It is interesting to compare this outcome with the equilibrium
position for a firm in a perfect labour market, where the supply
curve of labour to the firm might be given by S_1S_1 as shown in
Diagram 10.5. The firm would now employ OQ_1 workers at a rate
of OW_1 because of the intersection of VV and S_1S_1 at E_1. Wage and
employment levels would be higher in a perfect compared to an
imperfect labour market.

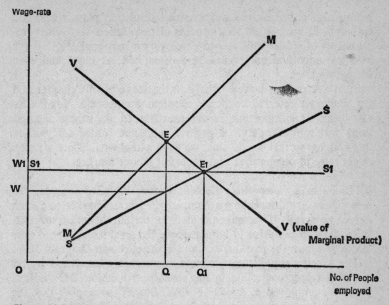

Figure 10.5 Imperfect competition in the labour market, and competitive product market

(iv) Imperfect Competition in both Product and Labour Markets

When imperfectly competitive conditions exist in both product and labour markets we can analyse wage and employment determination simply by combining the conclusions of (ii) and (iii) above. The firm will face a marginal revenue product curve with a steeper slope than the value of marginal product curve. In addition, the marginal wage cost curve will slope more steeply upwards than the labour supply curve. The firm, in equilibrium, will employ even fewer people at a lower wage rate than a firm operating under perfectly competitive conditions in both markets.

Labour Market Institutions

No analysis of labour markets is really complete without a survey of labour market institutions and the roles which they play. Wages and employment are subject to a process of negotiation between representatives of trades unions and employers at national level, at the level of individual companies, and often, too, at plant and even shop-floor level.

Such a survey, however, is beyond the scope of this chapter and the reader is referred to some excellent and concise summaries elsewhere.[2] It is important, however, at least to place these negotiations within the context of general economic forces analysed in this chapter so far. To do this, we shall assess what effect a union might have in competitive and imperfect labour markets.

(i) **Union in a Competitive Labour Market** First we consider the case where a union enters a competitive labour market to fix an agreed wage rate. If we make the assumption that the union succeeds in bidding up the price of labour above the level which would normally obtain in the market, we can see the effects in Diagram 10.6.

The market supply and demand curves are represented by SS and DD respectively, and in the absence of a union ON workers would be employed at a wage of OW. But let us suppose that the union can fix wages at the higher rate of OW_1. The effect of this, diagrammatically, is to make the supply curve of labour W_1aS, i.e. ON_2 workers would offer their services at a wage of OW_1 and after that the supply curve would become upward-sloping. We can therefore say that the power of a union to fix wage rates is realised through a change in supply conditions in the labour market.

Demand conditions, however, are still determined by employers, and at a higher wage of OW_1 they will wish to hire only ON_1 workers. The cost, therefore, of raising wages is a reduction in employment from ON to ON_1. At the agreed wage of OW_1 there exists an excess supply of labour (ba or N_1N_2) and, according to the supply curve SS, these workers would be prepared to accept a lower wage than OW_1 in order to secure employment. Whether in fact they are eventually employed at lower rates depends on the union's ability to enforce strictly the agreement with employers to pay each person OW_1 and prevent employers attempting to cut wages.

Although the fixing of a wage above the market level reduces the volume of employment, it may still lead to a larger total wage bill being paid by firms to the reduced numbers of workers employed. For this to happen, the relevant section of the market demand curve

[2] *See* 'Suggestions for Further Reading'.

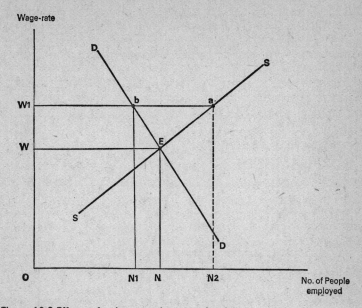

Wage-rate

D

S

W1   b   a

W   E

S

D

O   N1   N   N2   No. of People
employed

Figure 10.6 Effects of union entry into a perfect labour market

must be relatively inelastic. In Diagram 10.6, for example, area OW_1bN_1 is greater than area $OWEN$. If, however, the demand curve was relatively elastic, the enforcement of a higher wage rate could only be achieved at the expense of both lower employment and a smaller total wage bill.

(*ii*) **Union in a Monopsonistic Labour Market** The effects of the entry of a union into an imperfectly competitive labour market are slightly more complicated to analyse, so we shall simplify matters by assuming the most extreme case of imperfection where labour is employed by a single firm – a monopsony.

In Diagram 10.7 the wage and employment levels without unions would be OW and ON respectively, since the marginal wage cost curve (MW) and the demand curve intersect at e. A union entering

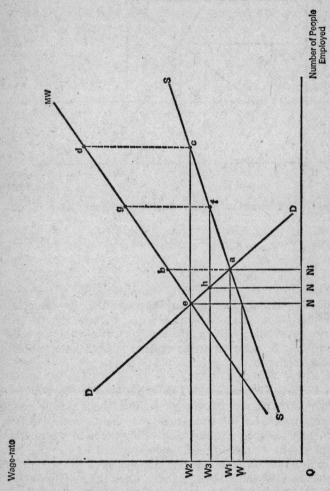

Figure 10.7 Effects of union entry into an imperfect labour market

this type of market has a number of strategies open to it, each of which will affect wage rates and numbers employed in different ways. Let us first look at two extreme strategies, namely maximising employment and, alternatively, maximising the wage level for the number of people already working before the entry of the union.

To obtain maximum employment the union would try to fix a rate of OW_1 which would create a supply curve represented by W_1aS. This curve is horizontal until it intersects the demand curve at point a. The range W_1a also represents the marginal wage cost curve to the monopsonist since each additional person can be hired for the same rate. After point a, extra labour can only be obtained by raising the wage rate for all workers and so the marginal wage cost curve and the labour supply curve will diverge. When a union fixes the wage rate at OW_1 the marginal wage cost curve is represented by W_1abMW, i.e. the curve is discontinuous at point a where it 'jumps' to point b and thereafter takes the shape of the MW curve. The overall effect of an agreed rate of OW_1 is to achieve the same result obtainable in a perfect labour market since equilibrium is established at the intersection of the market supply and demand curves. Compared to the position before the existence of the union both wage rates and employment levels have risen, from OW to OW_1 and from ON to ON_1 respectively.

Alternatively, the union might attempt to negotiate the maximum wage consistent with at least maintaining the existing workforce, i.e. ON people. To achieve this, the union would try to establish a wage rate of OW_2, thereby setting up a supply curve W_2cS, and a marginal wage cost curve W_2cdMW. The supply and demand curves intersect at e, meaning that the monopsonist would hire ON workers at a rate of OW_2.

The above strategies have been called 'extremes' only in the sense that it would not have been possible for the union to raise wages above the level of OW_2 without lowering the number of people employed below ON, nor could the union, by wage bargaining, increase employment beyond ON_1. For the monopsonist to employ more people than ON_1 an upward shift in the demand curve or a downward shift in the supply curve, or both, would be required.

Between these two strategies lies a range of possible adjustments to wage and employment levels. For example, if the union fixed a rate of OW_3, the supply curve would become W_3fS and the marginal wage cost curve W_3fgMW. Equilibrium is achieved at point h, where the monopsonist is prepared to employ ON_2 people at the negotiated wage of OW_3. Such a strategy is a compromise between the two extremes mentioned above. The agreed rate of OW_3 is not as high as the union could achieve but it is still higher than the market rate which would exist in the union's absence. Also, ON_2 is less than the maximum employment obtainable, but it represents an increase in the number of people who would otherwise be employed by the monopsonist (i.e. ON).

Conclusions

Even the analysis in the preceding section may seem slightly unrealistic to the reader who is practically involved in wage negotiations either on the employer or union side. Certainly unions have power not only to affect wage levels directly but also to control the supply of workers by a variety of devices, including the regulation of the duration of apprenticeships and the **closed shop** – a system which requires an employer to hire only members of a union and employees who belong to that union. Also, when negotiations take place between a union with a virtual monopoly of workers in a profession or trade and a large employer (or a combination of employers of similar types of labour, known as an **Employers' Association**), it often seems as if the outcome depends as much on the intricacies of the bargaining process and the skills of the participants and sanctions which they hold, as on pure economic influences. It may be that meetings between the Engineering Employers' Federation and the Amalgamated Union of Engineering Workers, or between the National Coal Board and the National Union of Mineworkers, or between the Department of Education and Science and the National Union of Teachers cannot be neatly analysed using the tools developed in this chapter.

In the widest sense, however, markets for labour set up a system of relative wages which perform the same function as prices do for goods and services. They act as rationing devices, allocating labour between different uses, and as a signalling device to employers and employees for reallocating labour in response to changes in demand and supply conditions in different markets. We shall see in the following chapter how labour markets would have to operate in order for the economy to perform with maximum efficiency.

Chapter 11

Welfare and Efficiency

This chapter will develop criteria designed to assist us in judging how efficiently the economic system operates. To do this we will define what we mean by **efficiency**, find out under what conditions an economic system would operate with maximum efficiency, and then see to what extent these conditions are met in real life.

The derivation of a satisfactory definition of efficiency is a tricky business which has caused much debate amongst economists. Clearly the efficiency of an economic system must have something to do with its ability to satisfy human wants, for as we saw in Chapter 1, the central problem in any economic system is the allocation of limited resources to meet unlimited needs. What we therefore require is some way of measuring the extent to which human wants are best satisfied; in other words we need a measure of people's general level of satisfaction with life or **welfare**. To say, however, that an economy is operating at maximum efficiency when it maximises the welfare of its citizens is rather unsatisfactory, because the concept of welfare is itself capable of very wide interpretation. Most people, for example, would certainly agree that to raise the level of welfare in an economy would involve increasing people's satisfaction with life. But this kind of definition is too vague and abstract to be adequate as a basis for developing criteria.

How can we measure satisfaction? Satisfaction is really a state of mind; a subjective experience which can only properly be understood by each single individual. To make the definition of welfare more concrete we could postulate that welfare is related to an individual's consumption of goods and services. At its simplest level, then, the argument could be that since an individual's welfare is dependent on his consumption, the greater the quantity of goods and services available to him the higher his level of welfare, and vice versa.

In defining welfare in this way, however, we immediately run into two problems. First we obviously lay ourselves open to the charge that our definition of welfare is materialistic in the extreme. Surely individual welfare depends upon many sources of satisfaction and well-being other than those gained from the consumption of goods and services? It is arguable that people derive welfare from a great variety of factors – the enjoyment of a walk in the country, the freedom to practise religion, the companionship of family and friends and so on. Indeed the current increased emphasis on the importance of the environment in which we live has revived an often-quoted argument that an increase in consumers' welfare gained through increased consumption of goods and services can be offset by a decrease in their welfare due to a decline in the *quality* of life through increased congestion on roads, increased levels of noise experienced near motorways and airports or increased levels of pollution of the atmosphere.

Our second problem in defining welfare is that an individual's consumption of goods and services can only be a rough indicator of the level of satisfaction which he enjoys. Because satisfaction is subjective, we cannot simply measure the volume of goods and services which an individual can buy and take this as an exact quantitative indicator of his level of welfare. It follows that we cannot say that if a person's consumption of goods and services were to rise by 50 per cent that his welfare would increase by 50 per cent. This problem is really a facet of the debate about the relative merits of cardinal versus ordinal measurement of utility, first outlined in Chapter 4. If we accept the ordinalist view, what we are implying is that our theory can most appropriately be based on indifference curve techniques.

In the following analysis we shall use a definition of welfare which is based on a consumer's satisfaction derived from consumption of goods and services. By measuring whether a consumer moves on to higher or lower indifference curves we can talk of his welfare increasing or decreasing, and say whether he is better off or worse off. But we cannot derive exact values for quantities of welfare enjoyed nor can we quantify the exact difference in welfare which is experienced when a person changes his consumption pattern.

Now that we have defined the concept of welfare we can say that the higher the level of welfare enjoyed by people the more efficiently an economic system is operating. But how do we know when an economic system is operating with maximum efficiency?

The Pareto Criterion and Aspects of Efficiency

One of the most influential writers on the subject of the economics of welfare was an Italian economist, Vilfredo Pareto, whose original formulation of the definition of maximum efficiency and the conditions of achieving it provide the starting point for discussions of welfare. The **Pareto criterion** states that the welfare experienced by people in an economy is maximised (i.e. maximum efficiency will be attained) once it is impossible to increase the satisfaction of one person (in his own estimation) without decreasing the satisfaction of anyone else. To rephrase the Pareto criterion in a negative sense, an economy cannot be operating at maximum efficiency if it is possible to make at least one person better off without adversely affecting the welfare of any other person. To analyse the way in which economic welfare is maximised according to this criterion, it is convenient to divide the concept of efficiency into three distinct but related aspects which are themselves related to the basic questions asked about allocation decisions in Chapter 1, i.e. questions concerning the manner in which goods and services will be produced, their relative quantities and distribution among the population.

(*i*) **Productive Efficiency** In analysing productive efficiency we are interested in the way in which resources are combined to produce goods and services. It was suggested in Chapter 1 that choices have to be made relating to quantities of labour, capital and materials to be used in the production of each type of commodity. Efficiency clearly requires that limited resources should be used to obtain the maximum possible output or, more strictly, that they should be deployed in such a way that the economic system operates at the limits of the production frontier.

(*ii*) **Allocative Efficiency** Allocative efficiency depends upon the relative quantities of different goods and services which are produced. The attainment of productive efficiency is consistent with the actual production of many possible combinations of goods and services. Allocative efficiency, however, is a matter of achieving the best possible allocation of resources between different types of output so that the combination of goods and services produced will maximise the welfare of consumers.

(*iii*) **Distributive Efficiency** Distributive efficiency is concerned with the way in which the actual combination of goods and services produced in an economy is shared among consumers. This aspect of efficiency corresponds to the question 'for whom?' discussed in

Chapter 1, since it attempts to provide a guide to who should receive the total output produced.

(*i*) **Productive Efficiency** In Chapter 1, the production possibility curve was defined as a boundary which showed the combinations of two goods which an economy was capable of producing when all its resources were being used as efficiently as possible. We did not specify in detail what 'as efficiently as possible' meant, apart from suggesting that the output combinations lying on the production possibility curve represent the limits of the feasible range of operation. We can now say explicitly that if an economy reaches a point on the production possibility curve it has achieved productive efficiency. To specify the conditions under which this will occur we shall simplify the analysis by assuming that the economy has two kinds of inputs, labour and capital, which can be used to produce two goods, cigarettes and books, which can then be allocated to two consumers.

First let us consider the implications of the system being at a point such as S, in Diagram 11.1, where output amounts to 4,000 cigarettes and 1,000 books. Since S lies inside the production possibility curve, the economy is not operating efficiently. But why should this occur? Two answers are possible. Either some resources in the economy are lying idle,[1] or the way in which resources are used in the production of cigarettes and books means that the economy is producing a lower output combination of the two goods than it is capable of. Let us assume that all resources are in fact being used so that we can narrow the problem down to one of resources being used inefficiently. To understand the reason which could be responsible for this state of affairs let us imagine that the economy was initially at point T using all of its resources in the production of 5,000 cigarettes. If, however, a smaller quantity of cigarettes was to be made it would be possible to use a range of different input combinations to produce them – as we have already seen from the analysis of isoquants in Chapter 6. Diagrams 11.2(*a*) and (*b*) illustrate the argument.

The isoquants for 5,000 cigarettes and 4,000 cigarettes are shown in Diagram 11.2(*a*). We have noted above that the production of 5,000 cigarettes requires the use of the total labour and capital stock, denoted by O_cL and O_cK respectively. As soon as the economy

---

[1] Perhaps because unemployment exists generally throughout the economy. *See* A. G. Ford, *Income, Spending and the Price Level.*

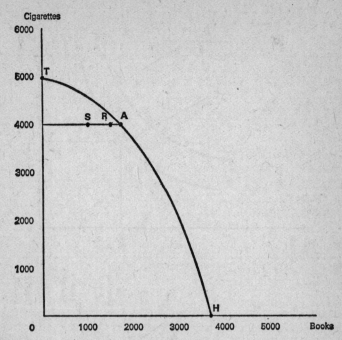

Figure 11.1 Productive efficiency achieved at any point (such as A) on the production possibility curve

begins book production, resources must leave the cigarette industry to allow the manufacture of books to proceed. The exact relative quantities of labour and capital moving into book production must obviously depend on the factor combination used to produce the lower cigarette output.

Let us assume that it is decided to produce 1,000 books (the iso-quant for this quantity is shown in Diagram 11.2(b)), and as a result cigarette output falls to 4,000 using O_cL_1 units of labour and O_cK_1 units of capital. This factor combination is represented by point S on the 4,000 cigarettes isoquant. The quantities of labour and capital left over to produce 1,000 books are thus [$O_cL - O_cL_1$, i.e. LL_1] and [$O_cK - O_cK_1$, i.e. KK_1] respectively, and we may assume that these relative factor proportions are represented by point P on the 1,000-book isoquant.

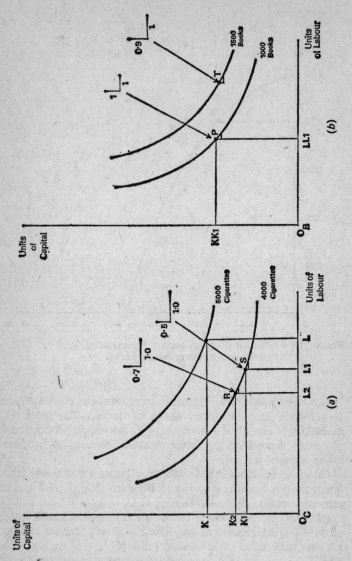

Figure 11.2 Cigarette and book isoquants
(a) Cigarette production
(b) Book production

Let us further suppose that at point S the marginal rate of substitution of labour for capital is 0.5, meaning that one unit of labour substitutes for 0.5 units of capital. Also, the marginal rate of substitution of labour for capital at P may be presumed to be equal to one, meaning that one unit of labour substitutes for one unit of capital.

Therefore we have a situation where, using the specified factor combinations to produce 4,000 cigarettes and 1,000 books: (*a*) **In cigarette production,** one unit of labour substitutes for 0.5 units of capital; (*b*) **In book production,** one unit of labour substitutes for one unit of capital, as a result of which the economy lies on a point inside the production possibility curve (point S in Diagram 11.1). The economy is not achieving productive efficiency because by reallocating inputs between the industries it would be possible to produce more of one of the goods without decreasing the output of the other.

If, for example, one unit of labour was transferred from cigarette production to books, notice what would happen. By using an extra unit of labour, the books industry can release one unit of capital and still produce 1,000 books (since one unit of labour substitutes for one unit of capital). However, only 0.5 units of capital need to be reabsorbed into the cigarette industry to maintain output at 4,000 (since one unit of labour substitutes for 0.5 units of capital in cigarette production). Hence the economy is left with 0.5 units of capital which can be put into either industry thereby increasing the output of one of the goods (i.e. making it possible to reach a higher isoquant for either industry). By reallocating inputs, the economy is capable of producing, say, 500 more books without lowering the output of cigarettes and so the economy would move closer to the production possibility curve, reaching point R in Diagram 11.1.

Point R, of course, is still not quite on the production possibility curve and so full productive efficiency has not yet been achieved. From the analysis in the above paragraphs we can see that a further reallocation of inputs between the two types of good would lead to even more books being made without any fall in cigarette production. Why should this be? First, let us trace the effects of the new input combination in cigarette production which is now using relatively more capital and relatively less labour than before. This changed input combination would be represented by a point such as R on the isoquant in Diagram 11.2(*a*), and we know from the analysis of isoquants in Chapter 6 that because of the principle of diminishing marginal substitution, the marginal rate of substitution of labour for capital will be higher at point R than at point S. By using now only OL_2 units of labour and OK_2 units of capital, let us suppose that the marginal rate of substitution of labour for capital at point R is 0.7. Of course, production of books is now represented by the higher isoquant (1,500 books) in Diagram 11.2(b), and the factor combination is more labour-intensive than it was initially. This means that at point T the marginal rate of substitution of labour for capital in book production will have fallen to, say, 0.9. Therefore we now have the situation where (a) **In cigarette production,** one unit of labour substitutes for 0.7 units of capital; (b) **In book production,** one unit of labour substitutes for 0.9 units of capital.

It would still be worthwhile to reallocate resources. By shifting one unit of labour from cigarette production to books, 0.9 units of capital can be released from the books industry without affecting the total quantity of books produced; but only 0.7 units of capital are required to make up for the loss of one unit of labour in cigarette production in order to keep the same quantity being made, and so 0.2 units of capital are still left over which can be put back into book production, thereby increasing the number of books made. This further reallocation of inputs has taken the economy even nearer the production possibility curve.

Under what conditions will the economy be operating when the production possibility curve is reached, say at point A? As extra units of labour are reallocated from cigarette production to the book industry, we have seen that the MRS of labour for capital in cigarette production gradually rises, and the MRS of labour for capital in book production gradually falls.

Once the marginal rates of substitution between labour and capital are exactly the same in both industries it will be impossible by reallocating resources to produce more books without decreasing the output of cigarettes or vice versa. When the marginal rates of substitution between the two inputs are equal in the production of both goods the economy will thus achieve productive efficiency. When this condition is satisfied, the economy will reach the production possibility curve at A.

One way of getting an overall picture of the above analysis is by using a device known as an **Edgeworth Box,** shown in Diagram 11.3(a) and (b).

In Diagram 11.3(a), the axis O_cL measures the total quantity of labour available in the economy and O_cK measures the total quantity of capital available. Because the box is a rectangle,

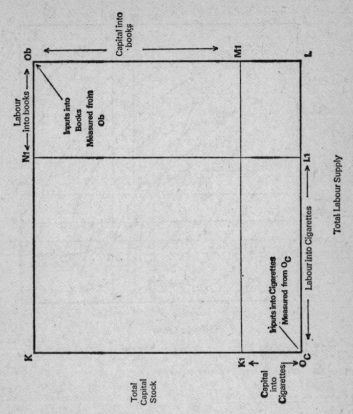

Figure 11.3 (a) The Edgeworth Box diagram

$O_cL = O_bK$ and $O_cK = O_bL$. Quantities of capital and labour in the production of cigarettes are measured from the origin O_c, and quantities of capital and labour in the production of books are measured from the origin O_b. We started the analysis of productive efficiency by assuming that O_cL_1 units of labour and O_cK_1 units of capital were used in cigarette production. Therefore LL_1 units of labour and KK_1 units of capital can be used in book production. Measured from the

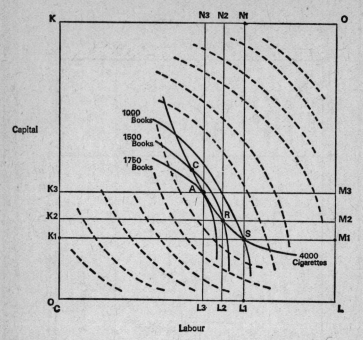

Figure 11.3 (*b*) Point A denotes a position of productive efficiency

origin O_b, this means that O_bN_1 denotes the amount of labour and O_bM_1 the amount of capital used in producing books.

We can now look at the box from point O_c using O_cL and O_cK as the axes for labour and capital respectively and draw in a series of isoquants for cigarette production. Similarly, we can look at the box from point O_b (it might be easier to turn the box round at first just to make sure the point is understood!) and, using the axes O_bL and O_bK to represent quantities of labour and capital, draw in isoquants for book production. The isoquants are shown in Diagram 11.3(*b*).

Point S represents the initial point on the cigarette isoquant where

4,000 cigarettes are produced using O_cL_1 units of labour and O_cK_1 units of capital. Point S is also on the isoquant for 1,000 books, using O_bN_1 units of labour and O_bM_1 units of capital. By reallocating inputs between the two types of production it is possible to use more capital and less labour in cigarette production (e.g. point R representing O_cL_2 units of labour and O_cK_2 units of capital), remain on the same isoquant for cigarette production (i.e. for 4,000 cigarettes) and move to a higher isoquant for books (point R lies on an isoquant representing 1,500 books) using a different input combination for book production (at point R, O_bN_2 units of labour and O_bM_2 units of capital).

The process of reallocation of inputs can go on until point A is reached, where the isoquant for 4,000 cigarettes just touches (i.e. is a tangent to) the isoquant for 1,750 books. The quantities of labour and capital used in cigarette production are O_cL_3 and O_cK_3 respectively, and the quantities of labour and capital in book production are O_bN_3 and O_bM_3. It can easily be seen from the Edgeworth Box that the isoquant for 1,750 books is the highest which can be reached if the rate of cigarette production is to be maintained at 4,000. To go further up the cigarette isoquant for 4,000 cigarettes by transferring more labour from cigarette production to book production would mean going back to a lower books isoquant than that representing 1,750 books (e.g. to point C).

When point A is reached, inputs have been allocated between the two types of production in such a way that the isoquants have the same slope. The slope of isoquants, of course, denotes the marginal rate of substitution between two inputs. The Edgeworth Box thus illustrates the general condition that for productive efficiency to be achieved, inputs must be allocated to the production of different goods and services so that the marginal rate of substitution between the inputs is the same in the production of each good. More generally we can say that for productive efficiency in an economy,

MRS x for y (A) = MRS x for y (B) . . . MRS x for y (n)

where x and y represent different inputs, and A and B represent two of the n goods produced.

It was also established in Chapter 6 that the marginal rate of substitution between two inputs is equal to the ratio of their marginal products, i.e. MRS x for y = MPx/MPy.

Hence we can extend our condition for productive efficiency in an economy by saying that the ratio of the marginal products of any two inputs must be the same in the production of all goods and services produced, i.e.

$$\frac{MPx\,(A)}{MPy} = \frac{MPx\,(B)}{MPy} = \frac{MPx\,(n)}{MPy}$$

Point A in Diagram 11.3(*b*) represents, of course, only one point on the production possibility curve TH in Diagram 11.1. If we drew in all the isoquants for cigarettes and books we would find many points of productive efficiency, corresponding to all the other points on the production possibility curve.

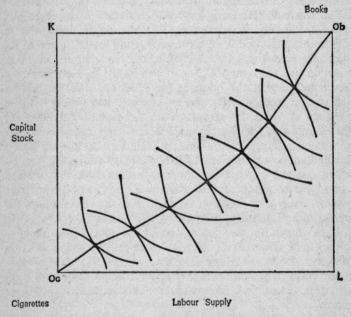

Figure 11.4 Points of tangency between isoquants form the production possibility curve

In Diagram 11.4, for example, a large number of isoquants for both cigarette and book production have been drawn in. By joining up all the points of tangency between cigarette and book isoquants, we trace out a curve which represents the maximum quantities of cigarettes and books which can be produced when the conditions for productive efficiency are achieved. In other words, the line O_cO_b represents all those combinations of the two goods which lie on the production possibility curve. What started off as an intuitively plausible proposition in Chapter 1 can now be seen to be based on some relatively sophisticated economic reasoning.

(ii) **Allocative Efficiency** The conditions for allocative efficiency are concerned with identifying one particular combination of output as defined by the production possibility curve; one which yields maximum welfare to consumers in the sense that by reallocating resources and so producing a different combination, no one could be made better off without making someone else worse off.

We need two analytical concepts to derive the rule for allocative efficiency. First, let us suppose that the economy has a production possibility frontier as shown in Diagram 11.5. For convenience we can use the curve derived from our analysis of the conditions for productive efficiency in the case of cigarettes and books. In Chapter 1, we introduced the notion of opportunity cost as a measure of how many units of one good had to be sacrificed to obtain an extra unit of another good by moving along the production possibility curve. In the context of our production frontier, opportunity cost is often called the **marginal rate of transformation** (MRT) of one good into another because it represents the marginal cost of one good in terms of another good. It can be measured by slope of the production possibility curve at different points along it. If we consider marginal changes in units of 100, it can be seen from Diagram 11.5 that the marginal rate of transformation of cigarettes into books at point R is one, since 100 cigarettes have to be given up to obtain an extra 100 books; at point E the MRT of cigarettes into books is two, since 200 cigarettes must be given up to obtain an extra 100 books; and at point P the MRT of cigarettes into books is three, since 300 cigarettes would be sacrificed to obtain an extra 100 books.

Secondly, let us add to the production possibility curve in Diagram 11.5 some indifference curves which show those combinations of cigarettes and books yielding the same level of satisfaction to a representative consumer in the economy. Points lying on each indifference curve (I_1, I_2) therefore show the consumer's marginal rate of substitution between the two goods. Which point on the production possibility curve will maximise the consumer's welfare?

Let us first consider point P, at which the economy produces

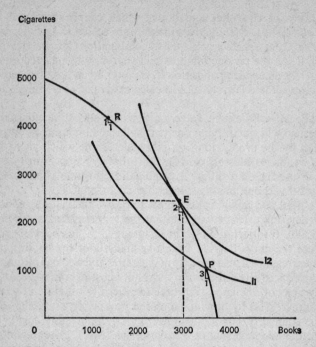

Figure 11.5 The Pareto criterion is met where the production
possibility curve is a tangent to the consumers'
indifference curve

1,000 cigarettes and 3,500 books. The marginal rate of transformation between cigarettes and books is greater than the consumer's marginal rate of substitution at point P since the slope of the production possibility curve is greater than the slope of the indifference curve at P. The output combination denoted by P does not achieve allocative efficiency because by producing more cigarettes and fewer books it would be possible to make the consumer better off. Since the MRT between cigarettes and books at P equals three it is technically possible for the economy to produce thirty extra cigarettes by decreasing the output of books by ten. Since the MRS between cigarettes and books is less than three (in our diagram it is, in fact, unity) the consumer is in fact willing to exchange ten cigarettes for ten books at point P. Therefore by shifting resources out of book production and into cigarette manufacture it would be possible to compensate him for the loss of ten books by having an additional ten cigarettes, but there would still be twenty cigarettes left over. Hence by moving up the production possibility curve from P, it would be possible to increase the welfare of the consumer by locating him on a higher indifference curve.

We can infer from the example in the above paragraph that allocative efficiency can only be achieved when the marginal rate of transformation between two goods is exactly equal to the consumer's marginal rate of substitution; only when the rate at which he is prepared to exchange one good for another good is equal to the rate at which that good is technically capable of being transformed into the other good would it be impossible for any reallocation of resources between the two goods to make him better off. Any other point on the production possibility curve would take him on to a lower indifference curve. We can therefore state the condition for allocative efficiency as:

MRT x for y = MRS x for y

Graphically, this condition is met where the slopes of the production possibility curve and the indifference curve are exactly the same, i.e. at point E in Diagram 11.5 where one curve is a tangent to the other. When the rule for allocative efficiency is met, the economy would produce 2,300 cigarettes and 3,000 books.

(*iii*) **Distributive Efficiency** The concept of distributive efficiency concerns the conditions required for sharing out the total combination of goods and services produced in an economy among consumers so that their welfare is maximised. Using the Pareto criterion, maximising consumers' welfare means allocating output amongst them so that it is impossible, by making any reallocation of the output between individuals, to increase one person's level of satisfaction without decreasing that of someone else. Finding the conditions for distributive efficiency involves an analysis which is in a sense rather similar to that discussed in the section on productive efficiency, though we now use consumer indifference curve analysis as the basis of our treatment.

Let us suppose that, at any point in time, certain quantities of cigarettes and books were allocated in some arbitrary fashion to two consumers in the economy. It is very likely of course that each individual has different relative evaluations of the goods. Consumer A could be a very heavy smoker who does not care for reading. Consumer B could be a bookworm who only likes the occasional cigarette. We can show that unless each consumer's marginal rate of substitution between the two goods is exactly the same, it would be possible for the consumers to 'swap' some cigarettes and books and make at least one of them better off without decreasing the welfare of the other. To show this condition it is convenient to use the Edgeworth Box diagram again, but this time putting quantities of cigarettes and books on the axes and drawing in a set of each consumer's indifference curves. Quantities of cigarettes and books for consumer A are measured from the origin O_A, and for consumer B are measured from the origin O_B.

In Diagram 11.6 output of cigarettes is shown on axes O_AC and O_BB, and output of books is measured along axes O_AB and O_BC. Looking at the box from point O_A, we could draw in a series of indifference curves to represent consumer A's relative evaluation of cigarettes and books. Similarly, starting from the other corner of the box at point O_B a set of indifference curves representing consumer B's relative preference for the two goods could be drawn in. Any point inside the box will denote the relative quantities of cigarettes and books which A and B actually have.

Let us suppose, for example, that point X represents the existing distribution of cigarettes between A and B so that consumer A has O_AC_1 cigarettes and O_AB_1 books. Consumer B therefore has O_BS_1 cigarettes and O_BT_1 books. Does point X represent an efficient distribution of cigarettes and books between the two consumers? Not really, because if consumer B gives consumer A some cigarettes in exchange for some books, it would be possible to keep consumer A on the same indifference curve but move consumer B on to a higher one. For example, let us suppose that B gives A a quantity of cigarettes measured by S_1S_2. For consumer A to receive an extra quantity of cigarettes measured (on his cigarette axis) by C_1C_1, and retain the same level of satisfaction (i.e. remain on the same indifference curve) he is just prepared to give up B_1B_2 books. Consumer A would thus move to point Y in the box diagram. Meanwhile, the extra books received by consumer B (measured by T_1T_2 on his book axis) in exchange for S_1S_2 cigarettes means that he has now moved to a higher level of welfare since point Y lies on a higher indifference curve than point X.

From Diagram 11.6 it can be seen that it would make consumer

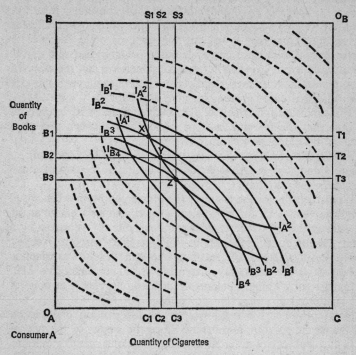

Figure 11.6 Distributive efficiency achieved at a point of tangency between two consumers' indifference curves

B continuously better off, and consumer A no worse off, if consumer B kept giving cigarettes to consumer A until the distribution of cigarettes and books was denoted by point Z. At this point, consumer A would have $O_A B_3$ books and $O_A C_3$ cigarettes while consumer B would have $O_B T_3$ books and $O_B S_3$ cigarettes. If consumer B gave up any more cigarettes he would move back on to a lower indifference curve again. The indifference curve labelled $I_B 4$ is the highest indifference curve which consumer B can reach consistent with consumer A remaining on indifference curve $I_A 2$. There is something special about point Z because it denotes a point of tangency between an indifference curve of consumer A and an indifference curve of consumer B. The slopes of the two indifference curves must therefore be exactly the same at point Z. Since the slope of an indifference curve measures the marginal rate of substitution between two goods for a consumer, we can therefore say that at point Z, consumer A and consumer B have the same marginal rate of substitution between cigarettes and books.

The condition for achieving distributive efficiency in an economy is thus that the marginal rate of substitution between two goods must be the same for consumers, i.e.

MRS x for y (A) = MRS x for y (B) = ... MRS x for y (n)
where x and y refer to two goods, and A and B are two of n consumers in the economy.

We can easily see the sense of the above condition when we remember what is meant by concept of a consumer's marginal rate of substitution. Consumer A's marginal rate of substitution of cigarettes for books is the rate at which he is prepared to exchange books for cigarettes while retaining the same level of satisfaction. For example we might say that at point X, consumer A's MRS between cigarettes and books is 2, i.e. for consumer A at point X, one cigarette substitutes for two books.

Now consumer B's marginal rate of substitution of cigarettes for books at point X is different (since the slopes of the two indifference curves are different at point X). Consumer B's marginal rate of substitution of cigarettes for books is lower than A's at point X; let us say it is equal to one, i.e. for consumer B at point X, one cigarette substitutes for one book.

If consumer B gives consumer A one cigarette, consumer A can give up two books and still retain the same level of satisfaction. But, of course, consumer B needs only one more book to compensate him for the sacrifice of one cigarette and so by receiving two books B can reach a higher level of welfare than before. This process of redistribution of cigarettes can continue until the marginal rates of substitution between the two goods are equal. Only then is it impossible to make one consumer better off without making the other consumer worse off.

It was shown in Chapter 4 that a consumer's marginal rate of substitution between two products was equal to the ratio of the marginal utilities of the two products, i.e.

$$\text{MRS x for y} = \frac{MU(x)}{MU(y)}$$

Hence we can extend our definition of distributive efficiency by saying that consumers' welfare from the consumption of two goods will be maximised when the goods are distributed between consumers so that the ratio of the marginal utilities of the two products is the same for all consumers, i.e.

$$\frac{MU(x)\,(A)}{MU(y)} = \frac{MU(x)\,(B)}{MU(y)} = \frac{MU(x)\,(n)}{MU(y)}$$

Diagram 11.6 shows on its own, of course, that there is no unique point of distributive efficiency. Since there is a very large number of indifference curves for consumer A and consumer B, there will be a series of tangency points between the indifference curves, each one representing a point of distributive efficiency of which point Z was only one.

In Diagram 11.7, for example, a series of tangency points between the two consumers' indifference curves have been joined up to give a curve which looks very like that in Diagram 11.4. Indeed the mode of analysis has been much the same. The curve in Diagram 11.7 is often called a **contract curve**. Point Z therefore represents *one* position of distributive efficiency on the contract curve, since the two consumers' relative valuations of cigarettes and books are the same. But points E, F, G and H are *also* points of distributive efficiency, at which the two consumers' marginal rates of valuation of cigarettes and books are the same. Unfortunately, however, there is a snag. If we look again at Diagram 11.6 it can be seen that point Z is more efficient, in the distributive sense, than points X or Y. The implied distribution of goods at Z raises B's satisfaction without diminishing that of A. But compare this with an alternative, illustrated in Diagram 11.7, in which a movement from point X (which is off the contract curve) is made not to Z, but to G. Now consumer B's satisfaction is unaltered (X and G lie on the same indifference curve), while that of A is raised – G, for him, is on a higher indifference curve than Z.

Thus while we have clearly shown that a point off the contract curve (X, say) represents an inefficient distribution of the two goods between consumers in that one of them could be made better off without affecting the welfare of the other *we cannot say which of the two* should have his lot improved! Similarly when we look at our contract curve in Diagram 11.7 we can find a range of points (E,

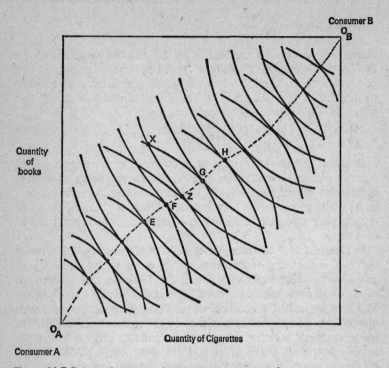

Figure 11.7 Points of tangency between two consumers'
indifference curves form a contract curve

F, Z, G, H) which satisfy the condition that the marginal rates of
substitution should be equal for each consumer. But we have no
means of saying that any one of these points is the best. For example,
while G or Z are better than X – unequivocally since A *or* B could be
made better off – we cannot choose between G and Z for this would
require us to make an interpersonal comparison. Our general rule
is that at any point of intersection of indifference curves like X
(and there can be as many points as we like to make since we can
fill the diagram with indifference curves) an improvement can

potentially be made. But this still does not help us to solve the problem completely.

It is often said that each point on the contract curve represents a particular **distribution of income** in the economy between consumers. For example, if the economy was operating at point E the rule for distributive efficiency would be satisfied, but the distribution of income in the economy would be very heavily biased in favour of consumer B because of the relatively larger quantities of both goods which he has compared with consumer A. Alternatively, a point such as H, although again satisfying the rule for distributive efficiency, would mean that income was distributed very much towards consumer A because of the relatively higher quantities of cigarettes and books which he has at that point.

Conclusions

The three types of efficiency just discussed are necessary for an economy to conform to the criterion of Pareto optimality. Productive efficiency ensures that the production possibility curve is actually reached by specifying that the marginal rates of substitution between inputs is the same in the production of different goods; allocative efficiency ensures that the actual point chosen on the production possibility curve will result in maximum consumer welfare; and distributive efficiency ensures that the combination of goods and services is distributed amongst consumers so that their subjective evaluation of the two goods – as measured by the marginal rate of substitution – is equal.

For many years economists have accepted the logic of the three aspects of efficiency. There is, however, one widely agreed drawback in the analysis of efficiency. If a point such as E in Diagram 11.8 is regarded as satisfying the Pareto criterion, then this implies we are content about the way in which income is distributed in the economy. To understand this argument, it should be remembered that point E specifies an output combination where consumers' marginal rates of substitution between cigarettes and books were equal. In other words, a point such as E on the indifference curve I_2 in Diagram 11.8 can be imagined as corresponding to some point in an Edgeworth Box diagram where the slopes of the indifference curves for two consumers were the same. Such a situation would satisfy the rule for distributive efficiency, but it was already mentioned that there are many points of distributive efficiency contained

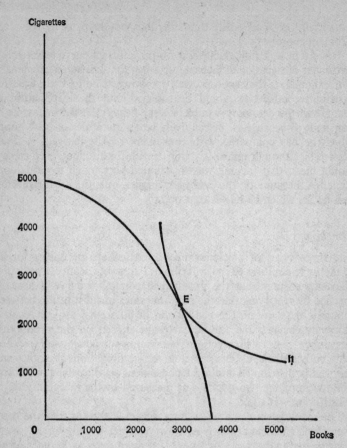

Figure 11.8 Maximum welfare point E depends on distribution of income

in an Edgeworth Box. Thus to call a point such as E the maximum welfare position for the economy is really to accept E as the best output combination consistent with a specific distribution of incomes between consumers. If the distribution of income was considerably different, for example being very much biased in favour of book-lovers, there would be a relative change in consumers' preferences; a different indifference curve (touching the production possibility curve further down towards the books axis) would be set up, and a point other than E would then be defined as the maximum welfare point for that particular distribution of income. In other words, there is no uniquely optimal point on the production possibility curve; instead, different points can satisfy the Pareto conditions depending on the way in which income is distributed in the economy. We shall return to the problem of income distribution in Chapter 12.

Methods of Achieving the Pareto Conditions

Now we turn to the important question, 'How can the conditions for achieving the three aspects of efficiency be met?' This question really asks us to specify the type of economic arrangements in society which is likely to bring the economy to the production possibility curve at a point where the marginal rate of substitution between two goods is equal to the marginal rate of transformation between them.

One of the traditional postulates of welfare economies is that these conditions could be achieved if goods and services were produced, and resources bought and sold, under conditions of perfect competition. The price mechanism established by the competitive forces of supply and demand in all markets in the economy is, in principle, capable of bringing the economic system to a point on the production possibility curve where the marginal rate of substitution between goods is equal to the marginal rate of transformation between them. To see why this should be so we need to recall the conditions for productive, allocative and distributive efficiency and see how the operation of perfect competition would lead to the conditions for each of these aspects of efficiency being achieved.

(*i*) **Productive Efficiency** For the economy actually to reach the production possibility curve, i.e. achieve productive efficiency, we have seen that marginal rate of substitution between any two inputs in the production of two goods must be the same; in other words

MRS x for y (A) = MRS x for y (B)

i.e. $\left(\dfrac{MP(x)}{MP(y)} = \dfrac{P(x)\,(A)}{P(y)} \right)$ $\left(\dfrac{MP(x)}{P(x)} = \dfrac{MP(y)\,(A)}{P(y)} \right)$

$$or$$

$= \left(\dfrac{MP(x)}{MP(y)} = \dfrac{P(x)\,(B)}{P(y)} \right) = \left(\dfrac{MP(x)}{P(x)} = \dfrac{MP(y)\,(B)}{P(y)} \right)$

In order that the marginal rate of substitution between the two inputs is the same in the production of both goods, the price of both inputs to both producers would have to be the same. Such a condition, of course, is achieved under conditions of perfect competition; the price of input x would be the same everywhere in the economy, and so too would be the price of input y. Therefore under conditions of perfect competition,

$$\text{MRS x for y (A)} = \frac{P(x)}{P(y)} = \text{MRS x for y (B)}$$

Hence in perfect competition the prices of inputs would be the same to all producers and the input combinations automatically chosen will ensure that the marginal product of each input is the same in every productive activity. The economy would thus reach a point on the production possibility curve and productive efficiency would be achieved.

(*ii*) **Allocative Efficiency** How does perfect competition satisfy the condition for allocative efficiency, which states that the marginal rate of transformation between two products should be equal to consumers' marginal rate of substitution between the two products? The explanation is that under conditions of perfect competition each producer manufactures his output at a price which equals marginal cost; and when price equals marginal cost, consumers' relative evaluation of any two products is exactly the same as the rate at which one good can be technically transformed into the other. We can best explain this as follows.

Since perfect competition ensures that price equals marginal cost the economy will reach equilibrium at that point on the production possibility curve which has the same slope as the highest attainable consumer's indifference curve.

In Diagram 11.9 the line PB has the same slope as the production possibility curve and the consumers' indifference curve at point E, and so can be taken to represent the relative prices of cigarettes and books in the economy, as set up under conditions of perfect competition. Notice the significance of these relative prices. In the example the marginal rate of transformation of cigarettes into books is equal to the ratio of the prices of the two goods, so that the relative prices in the economy measure the opportunity cost of gaining an extra unit of either good. Prices also reflect consumers' marginal rates of substitution between the two goods. It may seem to the reader that we have come a long way since the general suggestion in Chapter 1

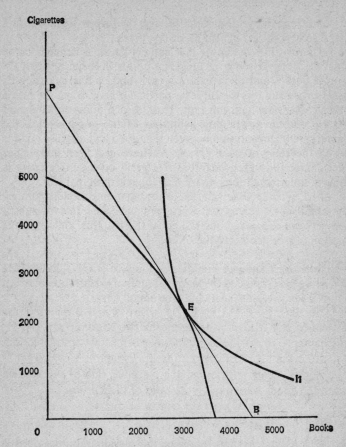

Figure 11.9 Relative prices (PB) reflect both opportunity costs
and consumers' preferences between two goods

that prices act as an allocative device, and, in Chapter 2, that the
tools of supply and demand analysis could broadly illustrate the
process at work. But the information contained in Diagram 11.9
really only provides the theoretical base for the general statements
made in the first two chapters, and helps to explain why and under

what conditions the price mechanism and the forces of competition can lead to an optimal allocation of resources.

For example, it was shown in Chapter 4 how a demand curve was derived from a series of tangency points between a set of indifference curves and budget lines – each budget line changing its slope as a result of a price fall for a particular good when the prices of other goods were held constant. Thus at each point on a demand curve the consumer will buy quantities of the good so that the marginal rate of substitution between that good and another good is equal to the ratio of their prices. We have also seen that under perfect competition each quantity of a good on a supply curve is produced under conditions where price equals marginal cost.

So when a competitive market is brought into equilibrium by the mechanism of price, the consumers' marginal rate of substitution between the two goods will equal the marginal rate of transformation of one good into the other.

(*iii*) **Distributive Efficiency** For the economy to achieve distributive efficiency we have seen that the marginal rates of substitution between two goods for two consumers must be equal, i.e.

^{MRS}A for B $(^C{}_1) = {}^{MRS}A$ for B $(^C{}_2)$, where A and B represent the two goods, and $^C{}_1$ and $^C{}_2$ represent the two consumers.

In Chapter 4, the analysis of consumer behaviour postulated that in order to maximise satisfaction from the consumption of two goods any consumer would ensure that the marginal rate of substitution between the goods was equal to the ratio of their prices, i.e.

$$^{MRS}A \text{ for } B = \frac{P(A)}{P(B)} \text{ or } \frac{MU(A)}{MU(B)} = \frac{P(A)}{P(B)}$$

where MU(A) and MU(B) represent the marginal utilities derived from the two goods.

If we now supposed that goods A and B were produced under conditions of perfect competition in the economy, the prices of A and B would be the same for all consumers. Hence, for any two consumers the ratio of the prices of the two goods would be the same and so would the ratio of marginal utilities. By ensuring that any good is sold at the same price throughout the economy, perfect competition ensures that

$$^{MRS}A \text{ for } B (^C{}_1) = {}^{MRS}A \text{ for } B (^C{}_2)$$

and so places consumers at one point on the contract curve, thereby ensuring distributive efficiency in the sense in which we have defined it.

Conclusions

The analysis outlined in this chapter leads to the conclusion that an economy organised on the basis of perfect competition provides a means of allocating resources according to consumers' preferences in a way that satisfies the Pareto criterion. This conclusion has profound implications. It suggests that as long as consumers maximise utility and interact with profit-maximising producers operating in a perfectly competitive environment, the economy at large would perform as efficiently as possible. As a consequence, the economic role of the elected government would be negligible.

Yet can we trust the price system in practice to allocate resources in the manner suggested by the theory? While there remain genuine philosophical disagreements between major political parties about the precise extent of government intervention in the economy, there is no doubt about the trend towards increasing government involvement. In 1900 only 8 per cent of the United Kingdom's Gross Domestic Product[2] was accounted for by government activities, whereas in 1973 this proportion had risen to 46 per cent. Hence in practice there has been a very marked departure from the 'laissez-faire' standpoint since the beginning of the century. To understand the economic forces behind this trend and the arguments for the government to undertake corrective action in the economy, we will examine in the next chapter the causes of market failure.

[2] A measure of the value of all goods and services produced in the economy over a period of one year.

Chapter 12

Causes of Market Failure

There are some important reasons why an actual economy does not operate in a perfectly competitive fashion. These reasons may cause prices, operating through the market mechanism, to fail to locate the economy at that point on the production possibility curve which satisfies the Pareto criterion. Let us see why.

Monopoly

It has been a long-standing argument in economic theory that the monopolisation of the market for any good causes a misallocation of resources in the economy. Indeed there are several reasons why monopoly conditions may prevent the Pareto criterion from being satisfied.

(*i*) **Allocative Inefficiency** The first is that a monopolist who aims to maximise profits will produce a level of output where price exceeds marginal cost, as shown in Chapter 8.

At its simplest level, we have shown that price measures consumers' valuation of the marginal unit of consumption of a good, while marginal cost measures the real resource costs involved in its production. However, if price exceeds marginal cost, we can infer immediately that consumers will place relatively high value on extra units of a good, whereas the costs of production will be relatively low. This means that consumers' welfare would be increased if the monopolist would expand output to the point where price and marginal cost were equal. But if the monopolist wished to maximise profits he would not do so; output would be maintained at a lower level, and consumers' welfare would not be maximised.

Basically the argument is that too little of the monopolists' output is produced (and hence too few resources are allocated to monopolistic industries) relative to other sorts of output. Hence resources are misallocated, taking the economy on to a point on the production possibility curve which does not have the same slope as the consumers' indifference curve. Existence of monopoly thus means that it would be possible to make at least one person better off without making anyone else worse off.

(*ii*) The Concept of 'X-Efficiency' Apart from allocative inefficiency, monopolies may cause **X-inefficiency** – a term coined by the American economist, Harvey Liebenstein. In a well-known article, Liebenstein attempted to show that the exact quantitative losses to the economy expressed in money terms due to X-inefficiency were considerably greater than the losses due to other forms of inefficiency. Liebenstein defined X-inefficiency as a situation in which costs are higher for any level of input than they need to be. Hence X-inefficiency represents a misuse of resources *within* firms rather than between them. We can illustrate this concept by examining again the relationships between isoquants and iso-cost lines, as shown in Diagram 12.1.

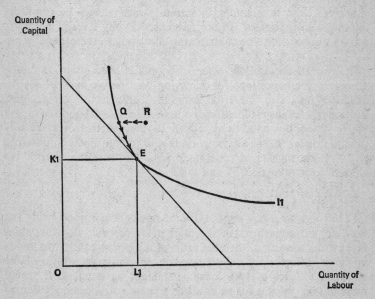

Figure 12.1 X-inefficiency present when a firm uses more resources than necessary to produce a given ouput

Given the relative prices of labour and capital, the least-cost combination of inputs required to produce the output level denoted by isoquant I_1 is OL_1 units of labour and OK_1 units of capital. In practice, however, a firm may be using a combination of inputs denoted by points such as Q or R. At Q, there would be some allocative inefficiency in the economy which would be removed by moving along the isoquant from Q to E. At R, however, the firm would not even be operating on the relevant isoquant, and therefore could achieve an improvement in its use of resources simply by moving from R to Q.

Such a move, which might be brought about by the reorganisation of the firm and the introduction of better management techniques, is broadly what is meant by improving X-efficiency. The corner-stone of Liebenstein's argument was that the gains to an economy by removing X-inefficiency (i.e. by firms moving on to an isoquant from a point off the isoquant) outweigh the gains by removing allocative inefficiency (i.e. by moving along an isoquant to the point of tangency with the iso-cost curve, as in a shift from Q to E).

Here, then, is another issue of concern resulting from monopoly situations. If a dominant firm seriously mismanages its resources internally so that costs are not minimised at any level of output it can hardly be said to be contributing effectively to the general good.

(*iii*) **Price Discrimination** Where monopolies practise price discrimination, the conditions for achieving distributive and productive efficiency may also fail to be achieved. Consider the implications, for example, of the production of one good in our two-good economy under monopoly conditions, added to the practice of price discrimination so that the same good is sold to consumers in different parts of the market at different prices. The rule for distributive efficiency for two goods A and B is

$$\frac{MU(A)}{MU(B)} = \frac{P(A)}{P(B)}$$

for each consumer and depends on the price of each good being the same for all consumers in the market. Since price discrimination breaks this condition, then the ratio of the prices of the two goods might be different for different consumers and so the ratio of the marginal utilities of two consumers might be unequal. It would therefore be possible for at least one consumer to become better off without a reduction of welfare for the other consumer by reallocating the total output of the two goods between them.

Apart from price discrimination to consumers, there might also be cases where a monopolist practises price discrimination towards other producers in situations where the good made by the monopolist is used as an input in the production of other goods. If this was so, price discrimination would break the rule for productive efficiency with the result that the economy might fail even to reach the production possibility curve. Since the rule for productive efficiency rests on the condition that the marginal rate of substitution between two inputs is equal to the ratio of their prices, the achievement of the rule depends on the price of any input being the same in all lines of production. Now if price discrimination exists, the same input would be sold at different prices to different producers and the price ratio between that particular input and any other input would be different for different producers. It would be possible, therefore, for more of one type of good to be produced without reducing the output of any other type of good.

Indeed in one of its reports, the Monopolies Commission in Britain specifically criticised the price discrimination practice of Courtaulds, whereby fibre inputs were sold to their subsidiaries and other companies at different prices. Such a practice, it was argued, led to productive inefficiency in the economy. We shall be looking in the next chapter at policies introduced by governments to try to prevent allocative inefficiency in the economy through the existence of monopoly and monopolistic practices.

External Costs and Benefits

One of the most influential writers in the field of welfare economics, A. C. Pigou, stressed the importance of **external costs and benefits** which can occur in production and consumption decisions.

The growing interest in the quality of the environment within which people live gives some clear examples of such **externalities.** One time-hallowed example is the case of the firm which decides to dispose of its industrial waste by dumping it into a nearby river. The firm may regard the dumping facilities offered by the river as free, but there may be external costs imposed on other people who have nothing to do with the firm's activities at all. Pollution of the river may reach such an extent that the people who live further downstream could face health problems unless resources were used to carry out purification of the river. The costs of purification might not necessarily be borne by the firm because it is required, in judging the profitability of its actions, to account only for the costs that are incurred within its organisation (sometimes called **private costs**). But part of the firm's activities impose an external cost, in the sense of a cost on 'third-parties', and so a divergence between private costs and the additional wider social costs of the firm's actions may exist.

As a further example of externalities, let us consider the operation of an underground line running through the middle of a major city. In calculating how many journeys would be made we might take into account those private costs and revenues such as the costs of building the system and its operating costs, and the revenue earned from the fares paid by passengers. But such an activity might also engender external benefits, i.e. benefits occurring due to the existence of the new system but received by people who do not use the system. External benefits might best be seen in the reduction of time taken by cars to make journeys through the city, simply because many people have been diverted from using cars to using the underground system thereby making the city roads less congested and so speeding up journeys. Of course, there may be even further external benefits imposed in the form of reduced accident rates in the city centre because the roads are less congested.[1]

External effects like these can occur in many ways, sometimes even between consumers. For example, if a music-loving family decide to install a hi-fi system in their flat which is in the middle of a large block, there is no doubt that some of their neighbours could suffer such noise levels that expenditure on sound-proofing (or large quantities of cotton wool) was needed. The existence of external costs and benefits does change the pattern of resource allocation in the economy from the form that would occur if either they were absent or if organisations which imposed them took them into account in evaluating their activities. For example, the resources diverted into river purification would be available for other uses if the river pollution did not occur. Equally, if organisations were required to bear the full social costs imposed by their activities, then the output which was produced would either be reduced or take a different form.

As long as private costs do diverge from social costs it is unlikely that the resulting pattern of resource allocation will satisfy the Pareto criterion. Indeed, a fully correct interpretation of the Pareto criterion would be that for optimal resource allocation production

[1] For a fuller treatment, *see* G. H. Peters, *Private and Public Finance.*

of each good must take place under conditions where price equals marginal social cost, where marginal social cost measures the true value of the opportunity cost of resources used in any productive activity to society as a whole. If private and social costs diverge, then this condition will not be satisfied.

Public Goods

While a very large range of goods and services in our economy is produced and distributed by private businesses there are some goods which instead are provided centrally by the government, often at no direct charge to the people who benefit from them. The resources are provided largely by receipts from taxation. Goods of this type are normally called **public goods**. Many economists in recent years have spent a good deal of energy specifying the reasons why public goods are not bought and sold in markets, and isolating those characteristics which make a good public. The best way of working towards a definition of a public good is to take one of the best-known examples, namely defence.

What would be the implications of defence being bought and sold in markets? If defence goods and services were allocated by price, the result would be the unthinkable situation (at least in modern states) where each individual chose to buy his own army, his own aircraft carriers, his own nuclear submarines, etc. So what are the characteristics which make defence so different from TV sets, food, books, cigarettes and other goods bought and sold in markets? One reason why we could not envisage defence provided by the market to individuals is that virtually no one could afford to pay for the amount of the good that would be necessary to fulfil its function. Indeed it is certainly true that one reason for governments providing certain goods is that the market mechanism would either fail to provide them at all, or would provide them on an undesirably low scale.

To get to the root of the characteristics of public goods, we need to focus on the two concepts of **excludability** and **rivalry**. A good is excludable if the use of it can be confined to particular persons or households – if one uses what one pays for and no more or no less. All private property (houses, cars, clothing, food, etc.) falls into this category. By contrast defence services can be defined as non-excludable in the sense that as soon as a certain amount of defence is provided, its benefits cannot be limited to just a few people in the country, but rather are available to everyone. Notice that the widespread availability of the benefits of defence occurs despite differences in individuals' feeling towards the good. Although certain individuals may object deeply to the provision of defence at all, and would not buy any defence even if it could be allocated by the mechanism of price, they still benefit, however, from whatever provision is made. The concept of rivalry concerns the extent to which individual consumers are rivals for the supply of any good, in the sense that a unit of any good bought by one consumer is a unit which is unavailable to another consumer. Where the principle of rivalry can operate, goods and services can be allocated by price. If one consumer buys a set of golf clubs, then that action reduces the amount of golf clubs available for other people to buy and enjoy.

A public good like defence, however, exhibits the characteristic of non-rivalry in the sense that if one person derives a measure of protection from the existence of armed forces that in no way reduces the amount available to others. Individuals are not really rivals in consumption.[2] Where goods combine the characteristics of being both non-excludable and non-rival they are really unsuitable for provision by individual producers to individual consumers through a system of markets because of the impossibility of arranging the supply of such goods only to those individuals who are prepared to pay, and the impossibility of ensuring that only those who pay actually benefit from the quantities produced. Rather they are pure public goods in the sense that their supply must be organised, if at all, by the government.

In Britain, not all goods and services provided by the government fit the definition of public goods as we have framed it. In the case of roads, for example, the conditions of non-rivalry and non-excludability are not fully met. We know that in some other countries motorists cannot use motorways or turnpikes unless they pay a toll. This amounts to excludability because if a motorist would not pay, he could not enjoy the benefit of that stretch of road. But charging for roads in this way, although possible in practice, is limited to those stretches of motorway whose physical characteristics make payment possible and not excessively expensive to collect. For example, if there is a stretch of motorway which has the same features as the Forth Road Bridge – namely a well-defined entrance and exit at both ends with no possibility of using just a part of the stretch by entering and leaving on unsupervised slip-roads – then excludability is

[2] This assumes, of course, that all defence services are not located in a particular geographical area.

possible. But charging in this way is usually limited to a few well-defined routes and the major part of the road system can be looked upon as non-excludable.

Also, the principle of non-rivalry only fits the example of roads when roads are not crowded. If roads are generally quiet and relatively free from traffic, the consumption of road space by one individual in a car does not seriously reduce the amount of road space available for other drivers. Once any stretch of road becomes congested, however, it is certainly the case that individuals face much more rivalry for the limited road space (and rivalry can literally be seen in the way many people drive in rush-hour traffic!). The above example poses the interesting question of whether we should attempt to devise a method of pricing goods which are non-excludable but rival. Some economists, for example, advocate a system of road pricing in city areas in order to reduce demand for road space and so ease the congestion problem, although others are sceptical about whether such a scheme could be implemented.

There are close linkages between the concepts of public goods and externalities. The pure public good provides an example of nothing more than an extreme form of externality, since if it is non-rival the benefits can be received by everyone; and if it is non-excludable people may enjoy the benefits without payment. Even in cases of government-provided goods which conform to a diluted definition of public goods (such as roads, and also education and health services which are largely excludable and rival), part of the case for not having them provided and allocated by the market rests on the extent of external costs and benefits which they engender.

What methods can a government use to determine how many of these goods should be provided in the absence of the price mechanism? A technique called **cost-benefit analysis**[3] has been developed to tackle this problem. Basically, cost-benefit analysis attempts to estimate all the economic (i.e. opportunity) costs involved in providing some good or service so that they can be compared to an estimate of the total economic benefits which accrue to everybody affected by the good or service. For example, cost-benefit analysis was used to evaluate the desirability of building the Victoria Underground Line in London. Estimates were made of the construction costs, maintenance costs, fare levels and the expected number of journeys, and also the wider economic benefit of time saving to travellers not only on the Victoria Line itself but on the London transport system as a whole.

[3] For a further discussion *see* G. H. Peters, *Private and Public Finance*.

For comparative purposes such benefits should be calculated in monetary terms, and a good deal of research has been done into methods of imputing monetary values to factors like travelling time which are not directly bought and sold in markets. The interesting conclusion brought out by the Victoria Line study was that while the line was unprofitable in purely financial terms (i.e. considering only *internal* costs and revenues such as construction, maintenance and fares on the Victoria Line itself) it was very profitable in the wider economic sense once external benefits such as time savings had been included.

Adjustments to Changes in Demand and Supply

A further reason for expecting that the market system may fail to maximise consumers' welfare is the fact that markets may be very slow to adjust to changes in demand and supply conditions. Consequently, disequilibrium may exist for a substantial period of time. Consider, for example, the problem often faced by the Central Electricity Generating Board. A rise in demand for electricity takes place which cannot be met by the existing stock of capital equipment. Market theory predicts that eventually more resources will be used by the industry, output will expand and price will rise. But how long is 'eventually'? A new generating station takes on average five or six years to construct before it comes into operation, so that the adjustment process is not immediate. Nor is it necessarily smooth, because the new level of capacity after the station has been installed may be more than is needed to meet the new level of demand. The extra demand may be able to be met by an extra station working at one-fifth of full capacity, but because of the problem of indivisibilities it is not possible to construct one-fifth of a power station. Thus in industries where the type of capital equipment used is very large, indivisible, and takes a long time to install, the adjustment process to changes in market conditions may not work as smoothly or as quickly as the theory suggests.

The markets for certain resources may also exhibit the same lack of adjustment to change for other reasons. First, the theory assumes that following a fall in demand for a good output will decrease, firms will leave the industry and the resources thereby released will be available for use in industries for whose goods demand has risen. It may be the case, however, that the skills needed to perform jobs in the expanding industries are not possessed by people who are released from those in decline. The most vivid example of this problem is seen in the plight of people made redundant in industries such as coal mining and shipbuilding. Their skills are often very specialised; while there may be vacancies for precision work in, say, the microelectronics industries, the skills required would not often be found in mining or shipbuilding. Indeed people working in certain trades are often said to be 'locked in' to an industry because of the extremely specialised nature of the work which they do. This is not to say, of course, that labour in declining industries cannot be reabsorbed into expanding industries. It simply underlines the fact that some kind of retraining of workers may well be required before the readjustment process takes place.

Secondly, certain resources may be relatively immobile geographically. For example, an economy like the United Kingdom's may have a pattern of industrial activity such that many expanding industries are concentrated in certain areas (e.g. the South-East of England and some parts of the Midlands) while the declining industries are located in other regions (e.g. the North-East of England, West Central Scotland, South Wales, etc.). Because labour may be unable or unwilling to move from one area to the other, an economy suffering from what is often called **regional imbalance** may experience chronic unemployment in some areas and severe shortages of labour in other areas. Even if, however, resources were perfectly mobile, it has been argued that the effect of a continual movement of labour out of some parts of the country into others would impose external social costs – congestion and overcrowding in the heavily populated areas, and the under-utilisation of social capital (roads, schools, hospitals, etc.) in the depressed areas. Hence successive governments for over forty years have pursued policies to persuade firms to set up in depressed areas, and made it impossible for firms over a certain size to set up in areas of very low unemployment.

Income Distribution

It was shown during the analysis of welfare criteria that the condition for Pareto optimality can be met despite possible wide variation in the distribution of income between consumers. Hence to say that the attainment of some point on the production possibility curve maximises consumers' welfare is to imply that the distribution of income at that point is satisfactory. Many economists argue that it is not possible to distinguish between various points on the production possibility curve which can satisfy the Pareto criterion because of the implied value-judgement about income distribution which is involved. Moreover, a change in any existing income distribution will make some people better off and other people worse off. Again, most economists have maintained that trying to assess whether a change in income distribution increases or decreases total welfare is the Achilles' heel of welfare economics, since it involves making interpersonal comparisons of utility. And if, as was outlined in Chapter 4, utility is not measurable in any cardinal way, how can anyone judge whether an increase in the welfare level of one consumer more than offsets the decrease in the welfare level of another consumer?

A good way of seeing the problem of interpersonal comparisons of utility is by putting it into the context of a problem often faced in the application of cost-benefit analysis, which was referred to in the previous section. Let us suppose that a decision has to be made about whether or not to build five miles of motorway in a particular part of the country. Estimates might be made initially of the costs of constructing the motorway and maintaining it year by year. In addition, let us suppose that two other items which are to be taken into account are the value of increased time savings to motorway travellers and the value of increased noise and pollution affecting residents in the vicinity of the motorway. How do we judge whether this stretch of motorway increases total welfare? Using cost-benefit analysis, if the aggregate value of the benefits of time savings exceeds the aggregate value of construction, maintenance, noise and pollution, there is a net surplus of benefits over costs. However, the fact remains that some people will have their welfare increased (mainly travellers) and some people will have their welfare decreased (mainly local residents). If the motorway was built, it is assumed that the increase in welfare for one group is more than enough in quantitative terms to make up for the loss in welfare to another group and still leave the community as a whole better off. In other words, an interpersonal comparison of utility is being made. And the assumed increase in total welfare derived from the motorway might be consistent with a direct effect on the distribution of income between the two groups if, for example, the local residents were mainly drawn from low income groups whereas the motorway travellers were mainly drawn from the middle and higher income groups.

Conclusion

This section has shown that the attainment of the most efficient allocation of resources is likely to be limited by the existence of monopoly; by divergences between private and social costs and benefits; by the need to face the problem posed in handling the provision of public goods; by the fact that markets adjust slowly to changes in demand and supply; and finally because of the difficulty in judging what the *correct* distribution of income ought to be. Such factors provide the rationale for government policies designed to improve the performance of the market system and we shall analyse one major strand of policy in the next chapter. The remaining section of this chapter illustrates the way in which some principles of welfare economics can be applied to the operation of nationalised industries.

Welfare Economics and Policy towards the Nationalised Industries

The sheer size of the nationalised sector of industry in the United Kingdom ensures that the policies which guide their behaviour will have a significant effect on resource allocation in the economy at large. The output of the nationalised industries accounts for about 10 per cent of Gross National Product. These industries make considerable demands on resources since they collectively employ about 8 per cent of the working population and their investment programmes amount to roughly one-fifth of all capital formation.

The industries' strategic position in the economy is based on the importance of their output as inputs to the production processes of many other industries, as well as final goods and services sold to consumers. For example, the energy sources of coal, gas and electricity are critical for the operation of most privately-owned companies (and indeed one nationalised industry's output is often the input of another – coal is used in the production of electricity), and the nationalised British Steel Corporation produces most of the steel which is vital to industries such as cars and shipbuilding.

The very fact that industries operate under government control suggests that governments ought to have something to say about their behaviour if the general aim of efficient resource allocation is to be achieved. In the early years of nationalisation just after World War II the industries were simply required to break even, taking one year with another, but no specific policies for achieving such a target were suggested.

The White Paper of 1961[4] on the Financial and Economic Obligations of the Nationalised Industries represented a major step forward in official thinking, and several important recommendations were made. These included a requirement of the nationalised industries to break even over a five-year period (since an annual horizon represents too short a planning period), to make sure that enough money was put aside to replace capital equipment when it wore out and to finance more of their growing expenditure on capital equipment from their own reserves of profits rather than borrowing money from the government. Yet although the 1961 White Paper had much to say about the general results expected from the nationalised industries, it was not nearly so explicit about the type of policies which would lead to the achievement of those results. In this context one particular aspect of behaviour is crucial, namely pricing policy. On what basis should prices be set for the output of the nationalised industries? The answer to this question, both in theory and practice, will have a profound effect on resource allocation in the economy.

Marginal Cost Pricing

It was not until 1967 that specific guidelines were laid down for pricing policies in the nationalised industries. A White Paper entitled *Nationalised Industries: A Review of Economic and Financial Objectives*[5] made the suggestion that '... prices need to be reasonably related to costs[6] at the margin and to be designed to promote the efficient use of resources within industry'. The proposition that prices should be based[7] on marginal costs is, as we have seen, well rooted in welfare economics as a precondition for efficient resource use. The argument was developed in the context of the nationalised industries by a committee of Members of Parliament whose task it was to look closely at the way the nationalised industries were run: 'There is ... the requirement that prices should reflect costs so that a transfer of resources from one activity to another can raise economic welfare. If consumers are willing to pay more for some extra output than it costs to produce, welfare will *prima facie* rise if that expansion of output and sales takes place. In the reverse case, if consumers are unwilling to pay a price that covers the costs of

[4] Cmnd 1337 (1961).
[5] Cmnd 3437 (HMSO).
[6] Notice that this does not necessarily imply prices should be *equal to* marginal costs.
[7] *See* footnote 6.

producing marginal output, welfare will rise if a contraction of output and sales takes place. This is the rationale behind a policy of marginal cost pricing. It suggests that if any industry can use certain resources to produce output of greater value than another industry, those resources should be transferred from the latter to the former.' The rationale, then, behind marginal cost pricing seems, on the surface, straightforward. Translating it into practice requires knowledge of two factors. We need to know first how much consumers would value (i.e. would be willing to pay for) some extra (marginal) units of electricity, or provision of public transport, etc. Secondly we have to establish how much would be added to the total costs of electricity supply or public transport provision (i.e. the marginal costs) if this extra output were to be provided. If the former exceeds the latter, then there is an economic case for producing the extra output.

One example of marginal cost pricing in practice (although not in its purest form) is the Bulk Supply Tariff arranged between the Central Electricity Generating Board and the Area Boards in the Electricity industry in England and Wales. The CEGB is responsible (through building and operating power stations) for the production and supply of electricity to the Area Boards which then market the electricity to final consumers. The Bulk Supply Tariff concerns the price at which electricity is charged to the Area Boards from the CEGB. Before explaining this in a little detail, it is worth outlining some features of the way in which electricity is produced and the nature of the demand for electricity.

Electricity Demand and Supply

Demand for electricity varies considerably between winter and summer, and also at different times during the day. The time of day and year at which demand reaches a peak is around 5.30–6.00 p.m. in the winter, so that when a cold spell does occur the electricity industry must be technically capable of supplying this peak level. Such an occurrence is rare and so the best method in principle of dealing with it would involve storing electricity generated from existing capital equipment which could then be used whenever peaks occurred. However, a generally satisfactory method of storing electricity has not been found, and so the problem for the electricity industry is ensuring that enough productive capacity is installed to cope with the occasional periods when demand is greatest, even though some of that productive capacity which operates only when demand is highest remains unused for the rest of the year.

Electricity supply can be seen as an interconnected system produced by power stations located in different areas of the country. The nature of the power stations is different in a number of respects. A large number produce electricity by using coal as a fuel, but some are now based on nuclear power (and a few on other methods, e.g. gas turbines). Also, the vintage of plants at any point in time will vary, some being relatively new and others having been in use for a long time. Stations also vary in capacity, some small ones with a low potential output and some large ones (especially the nuclear ones) with a very high capacity. The result of these differences in sources of supply throughout the system is that the average cost of producing electricity from different sources can vary considerably. Costs per unit tend to be lowest in the largest and newest nuclear stations, and highest in the very old and smallest stations.

In order to achieve production at least unit cost it would obviously pay the CEGB to avoid as far as possible using the highest cost sources of supply. The extent to which the most expensive sources are needed depends on the level of demand at any point in time. When demand is relatively low at off-peak periods the required quantity of electricity can be generated using relatively low-cost power stations. But as demand rises, electricity can only be supplied by bringing the higher-cost stations into the generating system, and the peak demand levels require the use of the smallest and most costly stations which have only a small capacity and are maintained purely for the purpose of satisfying such demand levels.

The Bulk Supply Tariff represents an attempt to price electricity according to the different costs of generation from the different supply sources. Basically, the Bulk Supply Tariff has two major components – a charge for running costs and a charge for capacity costs. The first component is intended to give the CEGB enough revenue to cover the running costs of the stations.

Since, as was mentioned in the previous paragraph, the cost of supplying electricity varies according to the level of demand and hence the type of station used, the running costs charge has three levels. There is, first, a night charge for electricity supplied by the CEGB to each Area Board at the off-peak times of day when demand is lowest and can be satisfied from the lowest-cost source. Secondly, there is a slightly higher daytime charge which reflects the running costs as a result of bringing more expensive stations into the generating system. And thirdly, there is the peak period running charge for electricity supplied from the highest-cost sources. The second major component of the Bulk Supply Tariff is a capacity charge, designed to cover the fixed capital costs of the stations in operation at any time. This capacity charge, in turn, has two components called a basic capacity charge and a peak capacity charge. The basic capacity charge is intended to cover the fixed costs of virtually all the power stations except the ones reserved for peak demand periods, and the peak capacity charge reflects the extra costs incurred by bringing the costliest sources into operation. The overall charge, therefore, made by the CEGB to each of the Area Boards depends on the cost of the sources used to supply electricity to each Board.

Problems in Marginal Cost Pricing

The subject of marginal cost pricing has generated much debate amongst economists, and it is difficult to understand many of the arguments unless a good deal of sophisticated microeconomic theory (well beyond the scope of this book) has been absorbed. It must be stressed, however, that there are important drawbacks, both theoretical and practical, to the notion of marginal cost pricing and some of the most important (and most easily understood) are outlined below.

(i) There may be great difficulty in identifying marginal costs in practice. Often this is due to the presence of **indivisibilities,** where large unit sizes of capital are associated with the provision of a certain good or service. The classic example is where the addition of a single passenger to a train filled to capacity is impossible so that the marginal cost of railway transport for that particular individual would include the cost of a new train. But if the same fare is charged to all passengers journeying between two stations it is clear that some averaging of costs must take place.

(ii) There may be a conflict between the objectives of efficient resource allocation (via marginal cost pricing) and breaking even (i.e. covering costs in the financial sense). This point is most easily seen in Diagram 12.2.

Unless a nationalised industry is producing a level of output corresponding to the minimum point on the average cost curve, it is likely that losses or supernormal profits will appear by adopting a policy of marginal cost pricing. If for example, demand was such

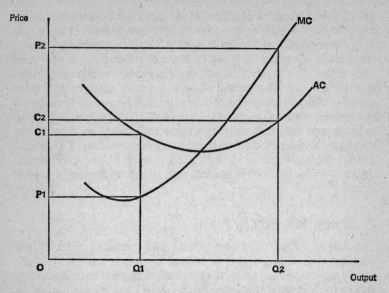

Figure 12.2 Marginal cost pricing in a nationalised industry

that an industry would produce OQ_1 units per week, and if price was set equal to marginal cost, the price charged would be OP_1 per unit. But this price level lies below the average cost per unit (OC_1) of producing OQ_1 units and so a loss would be incurred. Alternatively, let us suppose that OQ_2 units were supplied. On a marginal cost basis, price would be OP_2 which would be above the average cost (OC_2) for this level of output and so the industry would be earning supernormal profits.

Since it is believed that many nationalised industries operate under conditions of decreasing average costs, some economists have argued that marginal cost pricing condemns the nationalised industries to run at a loss which can only be recovered by funds from general taxation. More realistically, each nationalised industry operates a whole system of production activities or services (e.g. power stations, railway services, etc.) with quite different individual cost structures, and it is sometimes argued that, in general, price should be set equal to the aggregated average cost for the provision of the good or service so that the industry as a whole can break even. Such a policy is known as **cross-subsidisation** since the price being charged ensures that the losses made in some parts of the system are just balanced by the profits made on other parts.

The principle of cross-subsidisation has often been criticised, usually on the grounds that it causes a misallocation of resources (and possibly has damaging effects on the distribution of income) by charging consumers a price which may be well out of line with the marginal cost of producing the good or service they purchase. However, this merely serves to underline the conflict between the duty imposed on nationalised industries to cover their accounting costs and the objective of contributing towards efficient resource allocation. In any event, within the highly complex interdependent set of production activities which nationalised industries run, it may very often be difficult to appraise the costs and revenues associated with particular activities. Indeed the principle of externalities often works *within* the organisation of nationalised industries where some activities impose external costs or benefits on other activities.

Let us consider, for example, the following hypothetical situation quoted by one author in this field.[8] The three major cities in a country are served by two independent airline companies, one flying people from city A to city B and vice versa and the other flying people from city B to city C and vice versa. Let us further suppose it is not possible to fly direct between cities A and C, so that anyone wishing to fly between A and C must use the services of both airlines by changing at city B. If the airline flying from A to B runs at a profit and the airline flying from B to C runs at a loss and is considering closing down, what should the former airline do? At least it would be sensible to contemplate taking over the loss-making airline simply because part of the former airline's profits must be due to passengers travelling between C and A. If the latter airline closed down, this traffic would be lost.

So if the contribution to the first airline's profits made by the existence of the second airline was at least equal to the costs of keeping the second airline in existence, the first airline should take over the second airline. Now the second airline would be running at a loss when analysed in isolation, but because of the external benefits it imposes on the first airline the two airline services really have to be judged as an interdependent system. Although it might look as if

---

[8] A. Nove, 'Internal Economies', *Economic Journal* (December 1969), and *Efficiency Criteria for the Nationalised Industries*.

cross-subsidisation is taking place, there is obviously a sound economic argument for doing it in this context.

If we could imagine the same situation occurring *within* the organisational framework of a nationalised industry, the same argument still holds. For example, a small suburban railway line may run at a loss when analysed in isolation and in strict accounting terms. But the line may provide important feeder traffic to a main line whose profitability may be affected if the suburban line were to be closed down. The whole of the above argument shows how difficult it can sometimes be to define the nature of the product or service which is to be costed. In other words, difficulties can arise, as we have mentioned, in estimating what costs are marginal. Further difficulty can be encountered in attempting to answer the question, 'Marginal cost of what?'

(*iii*) There is a debate also about whether the relevant definition of marginal costs relates to the short-run or the long-run. This debate hinges on some complicated theoretical arguments, so it is sufficient for our purposes simply to present the broad nature of the dispute. To base price on short-run marginal cost first of all implies that extra output can be coaxed out of existing capacity, so that making the assumption that fixed costs of installing the present capital equipment are bygones, consumers should only be charged for the short-run variable costs associated with extra output, e.g. running costs, fuel, etc. Short-run marginal cost pricing is therefore primarily concerned with the output produced from an existing stock of capital equipment such as power stations, railway rolling stock, etc. The proposal to base price on long-run marginal costs is obviously concerned with the costs of installing new capacity in the future and replacing obsolete plant, since the concept of the long-run in economics refers to a period when all factors of production are variable. Consumers should, according to this latter proposal, be charged a price based on costs which partly reflect the costs of new capacity needed to satisfy demand in the future. At the moment, official policy towards the nationalised industries by the government is founded on the proposition that prices should be based on long-run marginal costs.

Chapter 13

Competition and Economic Policy

It was seen in the previous chapter that the existence of monopoly in an industry is one of the causes of market failure, resulting in the economy failing to achieve maximum consumers' welfare. In this final chapter, we shall examine the policies introduced by governments in Britain to modify the influence of monopoly and anticompetitive practices.

Policy towards Monopolies, Mergers and Restrictive Practices

Governments can influence resource allocation in the economy by attempting to reduce the degree of monopoly power in markets and by prohibiting agreements between firms which are designed to lessen competition. There are also cases where the merging of two independent firms into a unified company might lead to a monopoly or uncompetitive situation in a particular market, and these cases are also a concern for government policy.

Why should governments worry about monopolies? Let us recap first of all on the relationships between structure, behaviour and performance. A monopolist was defined as the only seller of a particular product in a market which, by definition, has virtually complete barriers to entry. In order to maximise profits, the output level chosen would be that where marginal cost was equal to marginal revenue, and because average revenue was greater than marginal revenue price would be above marginal cost. The monopolist would probably earn supernormal profits in the short-run if price was above average cost, and supernormal profits could also be earned in the long-run because of barriers to entry into the industry. As we saw in Chapter 11, if price is greater than marginal cost, resources are misallocated because too few resources are diverted into the production of the monopolist's output and too many resources go into the output of competitive industries. The major charge against monopoly, then, is that it causes allocative inefficiency in the economy. In considering policy towards monopolies, restrictive practices and mergers there are a number of important themes to be looked at closely. First we must enquire carefully into the relevance of the theoretical model of monopoly as a guide for anti-monopoly policy. Secondly, we must consider the question of how intensive anti-monopoly policy should be. Should governments wage an all-out assault on all monopoly situations in order to move the economy nearer to an optimum point on the production possibility curve? Alternatively, should governments simply attempt to remove the most extreme examples of monopoly in the economy? If the latter stance is adopted, the policy might be likened to the tip of an iceberg – by removing the tip the rest becomes invisible from the surface, but it nevertheless remains. Our third theme relates to the overall objectives of anti-monopoly policy. Traditional microeconomic theory has been concerned with the misallocation of resources due to monopoly, i.e. to allocative inefficiency. But there may well be other objectives pursued by governments which conflict with their concern for competitiveness, and we shall see to what extent policy has been influenced by such conflicts.

Monopolies

How far does the basic theory of monopoly as outlined in Chapter 8 provide a basis for policy-making?

First, in order to define a monopoly, the theory tells us to look for a market where only one producer supplies the total market output. Secondly, the theory assumes that the monopolist's behaviour is guided by the objective of maximising profits. Thirdly, as a result of profit-maximising behaviour, we should look for the existence of supernormal profits. Fourthly, we should see where supernormal profits have been earned in the long-run. Finally, we should ascertain whether such supernormal profits in the long-run have been caused by the existence of barriers to entry.

Such a model gives broadly useful guidelines for investigating a monopoly situation, but it does come up against many practical problems:

(i) If governments defined a monopoly situation as a market containing only one producer, there would be virtually no need for policy at all since there are extremely few examples of a firm supplying 100 per cent of a market. The nearest we find to 'pure' monopoly in practice are oligopolies with perhaps one or two of the few firms in the market supplying a relatively large proportion of market output.

The last point really shows up the first problem of translating monopoly theory into monopoly policy. How large is a 'relatively large' proportion of the market? Given that governments have to define a monopoly in the context of an oligopolistic market structure, some proportion of the market supply supplied by one firm must be defined as the lower threshold level of a monopoly. But is it to be 80 per cent, or 70 per cent, or 60 per cent or what? In other words, some degree of monopoly power has to be defined.

The first major piece of UK legislation was passed in 1948. The Act defined a monopoly as occuring when one-third of the market supply of a good was accounted for by one firm, or more than one firm acting as a group. At first glance, a one-third market share does seem substantially different from the 100 per cent share assumed in the theory. But the 'one-third market share' only shows up the difficulties of defining a degree of monopoly power for policy purposes. Any definition of market share has to be high enough to isolate those markets where one firm dominates, but low enough to be operationally useful. And all such definitions must be arbitrary to some extent. It would be, for example, very difficult to defend $33\frac{1}{3}$ per cent of the market compared with 30 per cent or 35 per cent as an acceptable definition of the minimum quantity of the market supply accounted for by one firm to constitute a monopoly. All such definitions will also probably change over time; in the Fair Trading Act of 1973 the minimum market share constituting a monopoly was reduced to 25 per cent.

(*ii*) Monopoly theory predicts that a profit-maximising monopolist will probably earn supernormal profits in the long-run. But does this mean that if a firm of monopoly size was found to be earning more than some *average* rate of profit, we could take this to be evidence of misallocation of resources, just as the theory predicts? To do so would imply that the supernormal profits are owed purely to the monopoly structure (e.g. via barriers to entry) and behaviour (via producing profit-maximising outputs). Supernormal profits may exist, however, at a specific point in time for a number of reasons.

First, the industry itself may not be in equilibrium. For example, the firm which is charged with earning supernormal profits may be doing so simply because it has pioneered some new method of production involving the very latest design in capital equipment. In time competition might be effective. Again there may be differences in the quality of management between firms which show up in a variation in profit rates between them. High profits by themselves are not a sufficient indication of monopoly. Rather it is necessary to show the causal links between structure–behaviour–performance, i.e. that high profits occur only because a firm is protected by the market structure through features like high barriers to entry, and is able to pursue profit-maximising price and output policies which give rise to a level of supernormal profits in the long-run. The trouble, of course, with the use of terms like the *long-run* (as pointed out in Chapter 5) is that they are not used in economic theory to refer to specific time periods. For policy purposes, however, some definition of what constitutes the long-run is needed.

(*iii*) In attempting to discover whether barriers to entry have been an important explanation of a firm's ability to earn supernormal profits in the long-run, we should be careful to distinguish between the various forms which barriers to entry can take. As suggested in Chapter 9, it may be the case that barriers to entry into a particular industry are very high because of significant economies of scale. Hence there may be a built-in conflict, as we shall see later in the chapter, between the existence of a degree of monopoly power in an industry and having the output of that industry produced at the lowest possible unit cost. Alternatively, it may be the case that barriers to entry are erected in an industry by a firm's policies towards product differentiation and advertising. In order to establish whether this is the case, the problem for monopoly policy becomes one of deciding to what extent the advertising and promotional expenditure incurred by a firm is consistent with behaviour we would normally expect from a firm with a minor degree of monopoly power, and to what extent it is excessive and intended largely to keep out possible new entrants.

The above examples illustrate just some of the problems involved in attempting to apply the concepts used in monopoly theory to monopoly policy. Let us now examine the way in which monopoly policy has tackled these problems in practice.

The Approach of Monopoly Policy

Turning now to the second issue posed by monopoly policy, we take up the question of what the approach of monopoly policy ought to be. There are essentially two broad approaches which governments might take – one we shall call the **structural approach** and the other the **behavioural approach.** Put at its simplest level the issue is this. At what point in the structure–behaviour–performance relationship should policy be directed? Should monopoly policy simply be aimed at proving that a monopolistic market structure in fact exists, on the basis of which some action can be taken? Or is such proof not sufficient? Should governments go further and establish that the behaviour of the monopolist is liable to lead to resource misallocation in the economy? Let us consider each of these approaches in turn.

The structural approach would be run along the following lines. We must begin by investigating the important structural features in a market. So estimates are made of the share of the market accounted for by one firm, the extent and height of entry barriers into the market, and so on. Having established some threshold level of market share which is taken to constitute a minimum degree of monopoly power (notwithstanding the difficulties mentioned above), if a firm is found to be above this threshold level then action of some type should be taken against it. The assumption lying behind the structural approach is that a straight causal line linking structure –behaviour–performance can be drawn as soon as a monopolistic market structure is declared to exist. It is assumed that a firm in a monopoly situation will behave in such a way that resource misallocation is bound to occur. The interesting feature about the structural approach is that a monopoly situation is defined to be undesirable *per se*. It is this kind of approach to monopoly policy which has been largely practised in the USA since 1945. As soon as a firm in the USA is defined as having a monopoly, it becomes liable to examination by governmental agencies. Such an approach, however, lays even more stress on getting an appropriate definition of what share of market output is needed before a monopoly exists.

There are further potential drawbacks to this approach. First, since we are really talking about degrees of monopoly power rather than pure monopoly, is it really correct to assume such a deterministic relationship between market structure, behaviour and performance? The section on oligopoly in the previous chapter showed how difficult it was to predict how an oligopolist would behave. A firm with 40 per cent of the market faced by three rivals each with 20 per cent of the market is liable to behave differently from a firm with 40 per cent of the market surrounded by twenty firms each with 3 per cent of the market. Secondly, using the structural approach, what kind of action can effectively be taken against a monopolist? The most direct possibility would be to lessen the degree of concentration in the market by breaking up the monopolist into a number of smaller units. Such a policy is some-what extreme, however, and has been largely resisted in the USA. Besides, breaking up a monopolistic firm would entail the further practical problem of making sure that the divided units really were separate and independent, and not linked in some undercover way by formal or informal agreement (see later section on restrictive practices).

The alternative approach – called the behavioural approach – rejects the assumption that as soon as a monopolistic market structure is identified, a predictable mode of behaviour and level of performance leading to a misallocation of resources will occur. The behavioural approach starts from the supposition that a mono-polistic market structure by itself is neither good nor bad; what matters is how monopolists actually behave. Do they use (or, really, abuse) their market position to pursue policies likely to lead to a misallocation of resources? Or does their behaviour give no cause for concern? Thus the onus on the behavioural approach lies in establishing whether the level of performance achieved in an industry has come about purely by the misconduct of the monopolist.

This approach would lead to a different style of policy. Each situation would have to be considered on its individual merits; the existence of a monopoly, in itself, would not be judged to be a bad thing. It is the monopolist's behaviour which must give cause for concern. If, for example, a firm is discovered to have been making very high profits consistently over a long time period, the be-havioural approach would argue that these high profits are not in them selves *prima facie* evidence of a monopolist misallocating the economy's resources. There would instead be an attempt to see to what extent the high profits were really due to the deliberate be-haviour of the monopolist taking advantage of the structural conditions in the market. If policy towards monopoly was to be based on the behavioural approach, it is likely that only some proportion of monopolies would be investigated, and some of these might be acquitted of bad behaviour.

Monopoly policy in the UK

The first major anti-monopoly legislation (referred to previously) in the UK came in 1948 with the passing of the Monopolies and Restrictive Practices Act. The Act established a Monopolies and

Restrictive Practices Commission to look both at monopoly situations and any restrictive agreements between firms (such as market sharing, price-fixing, exclusive dealing with certain customers) which would tend to lessen competition. The 1948 Act was interesting in two respects. First it defined monopoly in terms of a market where at least one-third of total output was supplied by one firm or a group of firms acting together. Secondly, it set the style of intervention that was to characterise UK monopoly policy by adopting the behavioural approach. The Monopolies and Restrictive Practices Commission was required, on a reference from the appropriate Government Department,[1] to investigate and report on a monopolist whose behaviour was suspected of being against a loosely-defined **public interest.**

In the 1948 Act, there was no presumption that monopoly as such was against the public interest. The Monopolies and Restrictive Practices Commission would investigate first to see if the firm or group of firms really did constitute a monopoly as defined in the Act and secondly to assess whether it was using its monopoly situation to behave in a way which was harmful to the public interest. If the case was proven the Commission could recommend what action, if any, might be taken against an offending monopolist. The position of the Monopolies and Restrictive Practices Commission was purely investigatory and advisory; its power only that of recommendation. The final decision as to whether the Commission's advice would be taken lay with the government.

Monopolies Commission Reports

We have already suggested that a behavioural approach to monopoly policy would lead to each case being examined on its individual merits. Such an *ad hoc* approach has certainly formed the basis of the Monopolies Commission's reports since 1948. In a situation where the onus has been on the Commission to establish that a firm has abused its monopoly power, we might normally expect that a number of firms whose activities were examined would be found innocent. In the cases of those firms actually found to have abused a monopoly position we might also expect that an *ad hoc* approach might lead to different types of remedy and recommenda-

[1] For over twenty years this was the Board of Trade. Since 1968 responsibility has been held, for shorter periods, by the Department of Employment and Productivity, the Department of Trade and Industry, and the Ministry for Prices and Consumer Affairs.

tion being made by the Commission in individual cases. Such expectations have certainly been borne out in practice.

There have been several monopolies which have been cleared by the Commission of behaviour which had been or was likely to be against the public interest. Perhaps the most famous of such investigations were concerned with the supply of chemical fertilizers where Imperial Chemical Industries held a monopoly; and with the supply of flat glass where the dominant producer was Pilkingtons. In each case the Monopolies Commission found nothing in the behaviour of either company to suggest that their monopoly position was being exploited, and no recommendation for action was made.

There have been other cases where the Monopolies Commission has, in general, cleared firms of operating against the public interest but still made some minor reservations about certain practices. In the investigation into the supply of asbestos and certain asbestos products, for example, the Commission found that the degree of monopoly power held by Turner and Newall did not harm the public interest. Nevertheless, the Commission still recommended that certain agreements between Turner and Newall and other firms were uncompetitive and recommended that these agreements be abandoned. The Commission found that the Kellogg company had not abused its monopoly position in the supply of breakfast cereals, but thought that in the future Kellogg's level of profits might be high enough to cause concern. The Commission recommended that Kellogg's profits be reviewed periodically and that any proposed increase in the price of Kellogg's cereals be approved by the government first of all.

In cases where the Monopolies Commission found that a firm has used its monopoly power to act against the public interest, a number of different remedies have been proposed. These have either been aimed at changing some structural characteristic in the market in order to influence a firm's behaviour and performance, or they have been designed to change a firm's behaviour directly.

Of the structural recommendations made by the Commission, those proposed after investigations into cellulosic fibres, colour film and tobacco are of interest. Two of the Commission's proposals in the cellulosic fibres case were intended to modify the structural features of the market in which Courtaulds maintained a monopoly position. First, the Commission recommended that import duty on fibres be reduced, thereby lowering the barriers on foreign competition in the British market . Secondly, the Commission thought that Courtaulds should be prevented from taking over any other firm in the textile or clothing industries if the effect would be to lessen competition in those industries. A similar recommendation about import duties was made in the Commission's report on the supply of colour film, in order to reduce Kodak's monopoly position in this market. But perhaps the most extreme structural policy of all is an attempted break-up of one large firm into a number of smaller independent units. The nearest the Commission came to recommending such a course of action was in its report on the supply of tobacco.

The tobacco industry is a very extreme form of oligopoly, with over 90 per cent of market output being accounted for by two firms, namely the Imperial Tobacco Company and Gallahers. When the Monopolies Commission made its investigation in 1961, Imperial Tobacco had about 63 per cent of the market and Gallahers about 29 per cent. The Commission was concerned predominantly with Imperial Tobacco's monopoly position. Though the company's behaviour was not challenged, it was found, however, that Imperial Tobacco owned 42 per cent of the shares in Gallahers, and such a bond of ownership between the two companies aroused the Commission's suspicion. The Commission argued that Imperial Tobacco's shareholding in Gallahers might be used to strengthen Imperial Tobacco's position and ultimately operate against the public interest. Hence the recommendation was that Imperial Tobacco should divest itself of its shareholding in Gallahers.

On the occasions when the Monopolies Commission has produced behavioural recommendations the target has usually been some aspect of a firm's pricing behaviour or advertising policy. In its report on the supply of industrial and medical gases, the Commission established that the dominant supplier – the British Oxygen Company – had acted against the public interest. But the Commission simply recommended that the Board of Trade periodically review British Oxygen's level of prices, costs and profits. In another case the high level of advertising and promotional expenditure in the supply of household detergents was thought by the Commission to be excessive. It was argued that it provided a classic example of the creation of barriers to entry into the industry, thereby maintaining the position of the two dominant firms – Proctor and Gamble, and Unilever. The Commission reasoned that the way to modify this structural characteristic was by changing the behaviour of the firms towards advertising and promotional activities. The Commission recommended that both companies should cut their advertising and sales expenditure by 40 per cent, and the prices of their detergents by 20 per cent. In their report on the supply of certain drugs the Commission also recommended price cuts. The dominant firm, Roche Products Ltd., was charged with overpricing in the supply of two drugs – Librium and Valium – and the Commission recommended that the prices of these drugs be cut by 40 per cent and 25 per cent respectively. Perhaps the most interesting aspect of monopoly policy in Britain is the way in which it was administered by the Board of Trade. Since the Monopolies Commission's powers were only those of recommendation, it was always open to the Board of Trade to accept or reject their findings. In quite a number of cases, the Board of Trade has been unwilling to implement the conclusions of the Commission and has preferred instead to rely on assurances from the firms themselves that they would stop abusing their monopoly power in the future. This *voluntary* approach of the Board is best seen in their reaction to some of the cases mentioned above.

Thus the Board of Trade rejected the Commission's plea for a periodic review of prices, costs and profits in the British Oxygen Company, and accepted promises from the company not to 'misbehave' in the future. Assurances were also accepted from the management of Imperial Tobacco not to interfere in the running of Gallahers and so the Board of Trade refused to implement the recommendation that Imperial Tobacco should divest itself of its shareholding in Gallahers. The tariff-cut recommendations in the cases of Courtaulds and Kodak were also unacceptable to the Board of Trade, and an alternative policy suggested by Proctor and Gamble and Unilever to market a different range of detergents with relatively low advertising expenses and at a lower price than existing brands was accepted by the Board instead of the straightforward general 40 per cent cut in sales expenditure and 20 per cent price cut on existing brands advocated by the Commission. The Board of Trade, however, did seem very anxious to implement the recommendation of the Commission in the case of Roche Products Ltd, and since Roche refused to implement the directives from the Board, the whole case had to go to the courts for a settlement.

Conflict of Objectives in Monopoly Policy

Given the *ad hoc* approach of the Monopolies Commission, it is not surprising that some commentators[2] have levied charges of inconsistency against the work of the Commission. In a sense, however, scope for inconsistency was built into the 1948 Act because the concept of the public interest was defined so loosely. The recurring problem in monopoly policy has been to clarify in some meaningful way the factors which affect the public interest, and, moreover, to assess the extent to which they may conflict, i.e. to set up some objective criteria against which individual firms' behaviour can be measured.

We have seen, for example, that the theory of monopoly and the theories of welfare economics have much to say about consumers' welfare defined in terms of allocative efficiency in the economic system. The theory predicts that the public interest will be harmed because that combination of goods and services most desired by consumers will not be produced when there is a profit-maximising monopolist in an industry. Monopoly leads to the 'wrong' mix of goods and services being produced at a particular time.

But within the definition of the public interest there may be other aspects of efficiency which should be of concern to policy makers. There is, for example, the possibility of conflict between the level of concentration needed in an industry for a firm to enjoy economies of scale and the extent to which that level of concentration implies a monopoly position. We have seen in Chapter 6, for example, that in some industries the market share accounted for by a single plant has to be fairly large for the point of minimum efficient size on the average cost curve to be reached. If such a market share is, say, 50 per cent, where does the balance of interest lie? Of course there is a danger of allocative inefficiency, but there are also advantages to consumers in having a product made as cheaply as possible. Is the public interest best served by a highly-fragmented industry of relatively small firms each operating at a considerably lower output point than the minimum efficient size, or by a much more monopolistic structure where the dominant firm or firms are able to produce the product at lower unit cost? This is precisely the kind of conflict which the Monopolies Commission often has to resolve when making its investigations.

There is also an argument which places emphasis on the dynamic, rather than the static, aspects of efficiency. Sometimes these aspects are defined as **innovative efficiency,** because they are primarily con-

[2] Notably A. Sutherland, *The Monopolies Commission in Action* (Cambridge University Press, September 1969).

cerned with the introduction of new products and new methods of production, usually at a lower unit cost. The effect of innovative efficiency is best seen by imagining a downward shift in a firm's average cost curve over time. One method of ensuring the introduction of such innovations is for firms to spend money on research and development. It is often claimed by firms who are investigated by the Monopolies Commission that large size is a prerequisite of the ability to spend sufficient money on R and D for the activity to be worthwhile at all. Again we have a potential source of conflict, which we will discuss further in the section on policy towards mergers.

Policy towards Mergers

In this section we shall first of all define the characteristics of different types of merger. We shall see whether there are any features inherent in them which might lead to a reduction in consumers' welfare. Finally we shall look at the policies which have been introduced to influence mergers, and the problems which such policies face.

A merger is a term describing a process by which two (usually) independent firms come together under the same ownership. Sometimes this process can occur as a result of agreement to join forces. But often it is precipitated by one firm making what is known as a **takeover bid.** This involves an approach to another firm with an offer to buy its shares. Where the firm which is approached is a joint-stock company, the management would normally announce the bid to its own shareholders and recommend either that they accept or reject the takeover bid. For example, the Glaxo Company, the largest of the British drug manufacturers, was approached in 1971 by both the Beecham Group and the Boots Company with separate takeover offers. The management of Glaxo recommended to its shareholders that they should not accept the offer from Beecham but that they should accept the proposed merger with Boots.

Mergers can be classified into three broad categories – **horizontal, vertical,** and **conglomerate.**

(*i*) **Horizontal Mergers** When two firms which make virtually identical or easily substitutable products join forces the process is called a horizontal merger. This type of merger, then, takes place when firms operating in the same market join together as a single company.

The most obvious motive behind the proposal of one firm to take over another in this way would be a wish to increase market power at a stroke; indeed a horizontal merger can be seen as a direct alternative to the internal expansion of the firm. The main advantage to the economy in general of having one relatively large firm replace two relatively smaller ones would be the gain of economies of scale – usually technical economies but sometimes also managerial, financial and marketing economies. More recently, firms proposing horizontal mergers have referred to the proposed economies of scale in research and development expenditure, especially in markets characterised by the constant introduction of new products and new techniques of production. Both Beecham and Boots made such claims for R and D economies in the proposed merger bids for Glaxo.

Against this possible advantage, however, has to be set the obvious danger of increased market concentration and monopoly power. Very many horizontal mergers occur between small firms as part of the normal process of industrial change in the economy with no serious effects on market concentration. But in cases where two firms, each supplying a substantial share of the market for a particular good, propose to merge there may be the danger that the degree of competition in that market is seriously reduced, and that the new monopolist position held by the merged firms might operate against the public interest.

(*ii*) **Vertical Mergers** A vertical merger occurs when two firms operating at different stages in the supply of a certain good are combined together. In many industries, production involves a number of stages each carried out by quite separate firms. For example, one firm may fabricate an article which is sold directly to consumers. However, the firm may find it convenient to purchase raw materials from others. Once the product is actually made, another company might take on the business of distribution to retail outlets. Thus if the assembler merged with a component manufacturer or with a distributor, or even took over all the retail outlets, the process would be called a vertical merger.

A notable example of a vertical merger was that between the British Motor Corporation (BMC) and Pressed Steel. When the merger was proposed in 1965, BMC was the larger British car manufacturer and Pressed Steel was the largest remaining independent manufacturer of car bodies. Pressed Steel supplied about 40 per cent of the bodies for BMC's car output, but it also supplied

the bodies for nearly all the cars produced by other car manufacturers, including Rootes (which was eventually taken over by the
American firm Chrysler). This particular merger serves to illustrate
both the potential benefits and potential dangers of vertical
mergers. BMC argued strongly that the merger would result in
substantial production economies and would match the trend in
other countries towards larger manufacturing units in car production.
Such a merger might possibly, however, be against the public
interest if BMC were to use its control over production so as to
affect the supply of car bodies to other manufacturers operating in
direct competition with BMC itself.

(*iii*) **Conglomerate Mergers** The union of two firms making entirely
different products which do not form part of the same chain of
production and supply, is termed a conglomerate merger. The
phenomenon is a relatively recent one and is not easy to explain
in conventional economic terms. Indeed one author has described
the process of forming conglomerates as having 'little industrial
logic'. Why should a firm like the Rank Organisation, whose products
include the Xerox copying machine and entertainment activities,
desire to merge with the De la Rue Company which is a manufacturer of Formica, boilers and banknotes?

A general motive underlying conglomerate mergers is a wish for
diversification. A company may, for example, be operating in a
market where the expansion of demand is slowing down, and it
may consider it a prudent move to spread its risks by diversifying
into different activities. In this way, a sudden slump in the market
for one of the products manufactured by the company need not
threaten its corporate existence. Firms engaging in conglomerate
mergers have also very often stressed the benefits to be gained in
terms of managerial and financial economies. They argue that their
purchase of seemingly unrelated companies produces benefits to the
economy by replacing poor and ineffective managers with persons of
greater dynamism and efficiency and by providing financial resources
for development which the 'victim' would be unable to obtain alone.
It is also claimed that a conglomerate merger may help to achieve
substantial marketing economies, especially overseas, since the same
distribution outlets can be used for a variety of products. Such
benefits may be difficult to identify and quantify but they can still be
significant.

It may, however, also be worthwhile to acquire a company purely for the sake of its profits or its assets, even though there may be no long-term plan for improving its use of resources. For example, one academic observer has noted that of the twenty-nine largest mergers which took place in 1968, the company proposing a take-over had a lower profit rate than the company being taken over in about half the cases.[3] Though these were not all the conglomerate type there was increasing concern in the early 1970s about a process nicknamed **asset-stripping,** where one company took over an apparently unrelated business simply to obtain control of its most profitable activities and then sold off or closed the rest.

Conglomerate mergers would not appear at first sight to have a direct influence on competition and concentration in certain markets. But some indirect competitive effects might be felt – some advantageous, others less so. Where a market has had no new entrants for some time and quality of management in existing firms is poor, the entry of a new company into the market by acquisition might invigorate an inefficient company and make it more capable and active. Alternatively, if a small firm in a competitive market was taken over by a large 'outside' company, the merged firm might succeed in getting itself accepted as price leader in the market and use its leadership to promote less competitive price policies.

UK Policy towards Mergers

Until the 1965 Monopolies and Mergers Act, there was no law in the United Kingdom which could prevent a merger taking place. However, the upsurge in the number of mergers, especially horizontal mergers, which began to take place in the late 1950s and the early 1960s began to turn people's attention to the possible dangers to the public interest. Perhaps a key case was the attempted bid by the Imperial Chemical Industries for Courtaulds in 1961. The possible merger between two such industrial giants (involving horizontal as well as conglomerate aspects) shocked many observers, and questions were asked in the House of Commons about whether the two companies should not demonstrate the arguments about the benefits of the merger (or at least give assurances against possible detriments to the public interest) before it was allowed to proceed. The official answer from the Board of Trade was that no powers were available to stop such a merger, and that arguments relating to the public

[3] A. Sutherland, 'The Management of Mergers Policy' in *The Managed Economy* ed. A. Cairncross, (Basil Blackwell, Oxford, 1970).

interest could only be heard if, as a result of the merger, the unified company was referred to the Monopolies Commission under the 1948 Act.

This lack of power to deal with mergers-in-prospect which might lead to a monopoly situation or result in some possible detriment to the public interest stimulated both the governing Conservative Party and the Labour Party to think out a strategy for dealing with mergers, and the 1965 Act spelled out the following provisions. There was no change in the definition of or attitude towards existing single-firm monopolies as outlined in the 1948 Act. But a merger which would involve at least one-third of the supply of a good being accounted for by one company or where the value of the assets being taken over exceed £5 million could be referred by the Board of Trade to the Monopolies Commission for investigation.

The 1965 Act thus empowered the government to stop a monopoly coming about as a result of a merger, or simply to outlaw a merger on the grounds that the sheer size of the unified company might present concern for the public interest. But in one important way the 1965 Act exhibited no change from the 1948 Act; there was still no presumption that any merger which came under the provisions of the 1965 Act was necessarily against the public interest. Hence a merger falling within the provision of the Act would not automatically be referred to the Monopolies Commission. Even when a referral was made, the onus would still be on the Commission to establish from an ex-ante position that, on balance, the merger would be likely to operate against the public interest. And even if the Commission recommended that a merger be prohibited, the Board of Trade was under no obligation to accept the recommendation.

Merger policy in practice seems to have followed the 'tip of the iceberg' fashion set by monopoly policy. Between 1965 and 1973, over 700 mergers which qualified under the 1965 Act were officially considered. Of these 700, approximately 80 per cent were horizontal, 10 per cent were vertical and 10 per cent conglomerate. Only a few cases, however, were referred to the Monopolies Commission which in turn recommended that six should not be allowed to proceed. These were the proposed mergers between the Ross Group and Associated Fisheries; United Drapery Stores and Montague Burton; the Rank Organisation and De la Rue; British Sidac and Transparent Paper; and Beecham and Glaxo and Boots and Glaxo (both mergers being considered in the same report).

The verdicts of the Monopolies Commission show quite clearly how each example was treated on its merits, without reference to any case which had been considered before – no matter how similar the arguments might have been. The recommendation of the Commission not to allow Rank to merge with De la Rue was interesting since this was the first major conglomerate merger to be examined, and was thus considered by many academics and businessmen to be something of a test case. Despite many arguments about possible technical economies of scale, and marketing and financial economies which Rank claimed would flow from the merger, the Commission in their report seemed to be heavily influenced by the threat of the De la Rue management to leave the company if the merger went through, and the possible effects this 'walk-out' would have on De la Rue's business. In the case of the Beecham-Boots-Glaxo triangle, there were arguments about the effects of increased concentration in the market for drugs; and also the very close vertical integration in drug supply which would occur if Boots, in particular, was allowed to merge with Glaxo – this was because Glaxo also owned the main drug distribution company in Great Britain, Vestric Ltd, and so a Boots-Glaxo merger would have given Boots a high degree of control at the manufacturing, distribution and retailing levels. But the main argument used by the Commission against both proposed mergers was the adverse effect they might have on the type of research and development work done on drug discovery and manufacture. In both cases, the Commission thought that a merger would remove the incentive on Boots and Beecham to widen the scope of their research, and might jeopardise the flow of new discoveries in the British pharmaceutical industry.

In the late 1960s, dissatisfaction was being expressed in many quarters about the basis and conduct of merger policy. Some industrialists, for example, complained that they were unsure of the reasons for the Board of Trade referring some qualifying mergers under the 1965 Act to the Monopolies Commission, but not others. And in view of the increasing number of conglomerate mergers taking place, there were charges that the Commission was inconsistent in its decisions over the first two conglomerate mergers which it examined. The merger between Unilever and Allied Breweries[4] was allowed to proceed mainly on the strength of the arguments about possible contributions to exports, while, as we have noted, the Rank-De la Rue merger was turned down. Some aca-

[4] In fact, despite getting the all-clear from the Commission, the merger did not eventually take place.

demic economists further complained that merger policy – on the evidence of the number actually stopped compared with the total number falling within the scope of the 1965 Act – was far too passive.

Despite these criticisms, official statements from the Board of Trade made it clear that the basis of monopoly and merger policy was at least consistent since the 1948 Act. It was stated that most mergers were regarded as acceptable; and, significantly, the suggestion was rejected that there ought to be set rules to show when certain mergers would be referred to the Monopolies Commission, since this would go against the philosophy of all post-war legislation which does not start from the assumption that certain types of market structure are undesirable in themselves.

Some further clues to official government thinking on the subject of mergers came with the publication by the Board of Trade of a 'Guide to Mergers' which set out to show the factors which the Board believed important in assessing the effect of any merger on the public interest. The factors specified were (a) market power (b) efficiency (c) balance of payments (d) regional policy (e) redundancy. But apart from stating that these were the criteria used in examining proposed mergers which fell under the 1965 Act, the Guide did not really examine the factors in specific detail nor did it give any clues as to the relative weighting to be given to each of the factors in an examination of any merger.

At present, there are two broad and distinct lines which merger policy could follow in the future. Either the approach adopted since 1965 (and based on the voluntary attitude towards monopolies since 1948) could be continued, or policy could be based on some stricter rules about what types of merger would be automatically referred to the Commission, or even outlawed altogether. Such a policy would begin to mirror the practice in America of taking quite different official attitudes to different types of mergers – almost prohibitive in the case of horizontal mergers, slightly less strict over vertical mergers and reasonably tolerant over conglomerates. But the logical outcome of such an approach would be to move towards the philosophy that certain types of market structure, are, in themselves, undesirable; and that for mergers falling into such categories to proceed, the firms would have to demonstrate that the merger would positively benefit the public. This would reverse present procedure – where the Monopolies Commission must prove a possible detriment to the public interest arising from the merger. The Fair Trading Act of 1973, however made no radical changes in the approach of government towards merger situations.

Policy towards Restrictive Practices

By 1956 many of the reports of the Monopolies Commission had highlighted the extent of restrictive practices in many sectors of British industry. Such action often took the form of market sharing agreements whereby each firm agreed to supply a certain percentage of market output; or discriminatory dealing whereby producers would agree to supply their product only to certain retailers or consumers. As an example of such restrictive practices, the Chemists' Federation had an agreement to supply medicines only to licensed chemists' shops. One practice – **collective discrimination** – was examined by the Monopolies Commission in 1955 and caused such public concern that follow-up legislation to deal specifically with restrictive practices was inevitable. Briefly, collective discrimination is a practice whereby a retailer or wholesaler who did not comply with the terms of sale (for example the fixed retail price of the good) set down by the manufacturer could have his supplies stopped not only by that particular manufacturer but also by all other manufacturers, according to a general agreement existing between manufacturers. For example, tyre manufacturers used to conduct checks on tyre sellers to ensure that tyres were being sold at the price agreed by all the manufacturers. Any dealer found to be cutting prices was liable to be put on a 'stop list' which meant that no manufacturer would sell to him. As a direct result of this report, the government introduced the Restrictive Practices Act of 1956. As an indication of the importance of this strand of competition policy, the responsibility for investigating restrictive practices which had previously been held by the Monopolies Commission was given over to a new judicial body invested with High Court status called the Restrictive Practices Court. The 1956 Act proposed to deal with restrictive practices on two fronts:

(i) Certain practices were prohibited outright, notably the practice of collective resale price maintenance as outlined above. No exceptions were to be made to this general prohibition. It is interesting to note that a practice called **individual resale price maintenance** (a practice which allowed the manufacturer to dictate to the wholesaler or retailer the price at which his product should be sold) was not included in the 1956 Act, and indeed was not to be dealt with until a further Act of 1964.

(*ii*) Certain other practices (including price fixing between manufacturers, market sharing, exclusive dealing, etc.) had to be registered with the Restrictive Practices Court, and were to be regarded as being against the public interest and abandoned unless they could be defended successfully before the Court under one or more of seven **gateways** which are exceptional reasons for allowing the practice to be continued. These are as follows:

(*a*) That the practice was necessary to protect the public against injury which might arise from the purchase of the product;

(*b*) That the removal of the practice would deny the public specific and substantial benefits;

(*c*) That the practice was necessary to counteract measures taken by others to prevent competition;

(*d*) That the restriction was needed to counterbalance the power of a monopolist at the wholesale or retail stage;

(*e*) That the removal of the practice would lead to serious and persistent unemployment in the areas where the trade is located;

(*f*) That the removal of the practice would lead to a substantial loss of exports either in relation to Britain's exports as a whole or to the exports of the particular industry in which the trade took place;

(*g*) That the practice was needed to maintain a restrictive practice already permitted by the Court.

Even if, however, a restriction passed one of the seven gateways, it had still to surmount a final obstacle known as 'the tail-piece' of the 1956 Act, by which the Court had to be satisfied that, on balance, the detriment caused to the public interest by having the restriction maintained would be outweighed by the positive benefits flowing from it.

There were two interesting features about the 1956 Act which had great significance for the way in which it was to affect restrictive agreements in industry. First, by assuming that certain practices were *in themselves* against the public interest and putting the onus on firms maintaining such practices to prove otherwise, policy towards restrictive practices showed a different emphasis from policy towards mergers and monopolies; in the latter area of policy, it will be remembered, the Monopolies Commission had to establish in each case that a special practice had operated or was likely to operate against the public interest.

Secondly, given that the exact phrasing of the seven gateways in the 1956 Act was vague (e.g. how exactly are terms like 'specific', 'substantial', 'serious', and 'persistent' to be interpreted in practice?), much depended on the way in which the Restrictive Practices Court interpreted the meaning of the Act. In this regard, there is no doubt that the Court has taken a very hard line indeed. The following examples give an indication of its approach.

The Chemists' Federation took their case to the Court soon after the passing of the 1956 Act, and attempted to defend their supply of certain medicines only to licensed chemists' shops under gateway one, arguing about the possible dangers to the public if medicines found their way into the 'wrong hands' (as the Chemists' Federation saw it). The Court, however, rejected the argument. In another early test case the Court accepted the argument for the agreement in the context of one of the gateways, but still rejected the case for continuing the agreement by invoking the 'tail-piece' of the 1956 Act. This happened in the case of the Yarn Spinners Association which defended its minimum price agreement between the different producers on the grounds that it would cause serious unemployment in the cotton industry in Lancashire (i.e. gateway 5). The Court accepted the Association's argument on this point but found against the price agreement because, on balance, it felt the argument was outweighed by the possible detriments to the public interest due to the existence of excess capacity in the industry and the undesirable effect of the price agreement on exports.

Certainly, the Court did find in favour of a very few agreements, but even its decisions on these cases provoked a good deal of controversy. The Black Bolts and Nuts case rested on the argument that a price agreement was to the specific benefit of consumers since they knew the terms of sale of the goods and so would be spared the inconvenience of 'shopping around'. This argument was accepted by the Court on this occasion but rejected in other cases. The Court also allowed the Cement Makers Federation to maintain a scheme whereby individual producers had an agreement to charge a common delivery price for cement to all customers, irrespective of their location. This was a case in which prices were well out of line with marginal costs because customers living far from the manufacturers would be supplied at a price below the cost of actually supplying them, whereas nearby customers would pay a price above marginal cost. The Court accepted this cross-subsidisation because the Cement Makers Federation argued that the scheme reduced the risks faced by individual firms and hence led them to accept a relatively lower rate of profit than they would do otherwise.

Over the period 1956–72, only 46 cases were defended before the Court, and of these only 11 were allowed to maintain their restrictive practice. There is also no doubt about the effect of the 1956 Act in breaking up restrictive agreements between firms who did not even bring their cases to the Court.

During the sixteen years following the passing of the Act, over 2,800 restrictive practices provided for by the Act were in fact registered, and about 2,500 of those were voluntarily abandoned. To some extent, this success ratio by abandonment must be attributed to the attitude taken by the Court to the relatively few test cases which attempted to justify their restrictive agreement before it.

Whether or not, however, the abandonment of such agreements actually led to more competition in specific industries, or was simply replaced by practices not covered in the 1956 Act is another matter. Certainly there is some evidence to show that price reductions followed the abandonment of restrictive agreements in some trades. But there was growing concern in the early 1960s about the effects of individual resale price maintenance, and about the alleged substitution of informal or information agreements between firms for the formal ones banned by the 1956 Act. Further legislation in 1964 and 1968 dealt with these matters.

Resale Price Maintenance

In 1964, the Resale Prices Act was passed to deal specifically with individual resale price maintenance (RPM). This practice had been very popular in some industries, notably in the supply of cigarettes and confectionery. The whole issue was brought to the public's attention by the growth of supermarkets which attempted to defy RPM agreements by vigorous price-cutting of some goods (especially cigarettes and confectionery). The 1964 Act was, in spirit, remarkably like the 1956 Act in that it simply presumed RPM to be against the public interest, with the result that firms wishing to maintain RPM agreements had to defend them in front of the Restrictive Practices Court. The five relevant gateway clauses were:

(*a*) That the quality or variety of goods for sale would be substantially reduced by the removal of the agreement.

(*b*) That the number of retail outlets would be substantially reduced by the removal of the agreement.

(c) That the price of the good at present subject to RPM would be increased in general and in the long-run if the agreement was removed.

(d) That there would be a change to health by the removal of the agreement.

(e) That there would be a substantial reduction in necessary pre-sales or post-sales service for the good if the agreement was removed.

As in the 1956 Act, there was a 'tail-piece' which stated that the Court had to be satisfied that, on balance, the benefit of allowing the agreement to continue was not outweighed by any detriment to the public interest. The Court has interpreted the spirit of the 1964 Act very strictly, with the result that most RPM agreements have been voluntarily disbanded. Perhaps the most significant key case came in 1967 when the manufacturers of chocolate and sugar confectionery (who themselves had been very strict in their belief in and application of RPM agreements) came before the Court. The Court found against their case, and it is probable that firms with much less convincing arguments for maintaining agreements were frightened off by this decision.

Informal Agreements

Many firms whose restrictive practices were dropped following the 1956 Act turned to more informal methods of restricting competition. A broad umbrella title for these methods is **information agreements.** For example, it became common practice in some trades for firms to exchange information about their levels of costs, prices, profit margins, sales volume and even the dimension, design and quality of their goods. This information was often intended to act as a guide to firms about the price they ought to charge, or the market share they ought to produce, etc., and so be an informal substitute for practices prohibited by the 1956 Act. However, in 1968 a further piece of legislation was passed – the Restrictive Trade Practices Act – which extended the previous legislation to prohibit information agreements.

Perhaps the major type of practice which is still officially allowed is that of fixing **recommended prices,** whereby manufacturers simply recommend a certain price which should be charged by wholesalers or retailers for their products. Examples of 'Manufacturer's Recommended Price' can be seen nowadays in many advertisements in newspapers or magazines, especially those for cars and cigarettes.

There have been arguments that recommended prices could simply be an informal substitute for individual RPM in cases where manufacturers expect that their goods will in fact be sold everywhere at the recommended price. The practice was investigated by the Monopolies Commission in 1969, and while they expressed concern at the possible danger in some individual cases, they still felt that there was no case to be made for general prohibition. Indeed the Commission argued that there might be positive merits in the practice, to the extent that it kept consumers informed about how far they were being given value for money by retailers selling at less (or more!) than the recommended price, and by the manufacturers whenever they changed the design or the quality of their products.

There has been a remarkable continuity in the development of policy towards competition in Britain since 1948, although the treatment of monopolies on mergers on the one hand and restrictive practices on the other seems so disparate. Each major Act followed evidence of the gaps uncovered in previous legislation. Perhaps the most difficult issues which remain to be settled are in the field of monopolies and mergers, especially as the movement towards more industrial concentration takes place. The initial definition of a monopoly in terms of a one-third market share remained for twenty-five years before specific proposals were brought out to lower it to one-quarter. It will be interesting to see how long it is before the revised figure is itself changed.

Conclusion

We have seen in this chapter that there are many difficulties involved in attempting to apply the concepts developed earlier in the theory of the firm to the practical problem of policy against monopolies, mergers and restrictive practices. In setting out the guidelines provided by the theory earlier in the chapter we saw that each of these guidelines has to be carefully interpreted in practice before a case for asserting that a particular firm has abused a monopoly position can be established. In some ways, the difficulties lie in putting precise quantitative values to the theoretical concepts. For example, if we are dealing with degrees of monopoly power rather than pure monopoly, what minimum degree of monopoly power should constitute a monopoly? How high are supernormal profits? What period constitutes the long-run? How can the welfare losses due to allocative inefficiency be compared with the gains realised through economics of scale? In other ways, difficulties lie in correctly establishing cause and effect. For example, should the mere existence of supernormal profits be taken as evidence of a monopoly, or are high profits derived by other means? Do barriers to entry derive from production conditions which make for economies of scale, or are they simply created by a firm to preserve a monopoly position?

The problems, however, should not disguise the fact that without the theory there would be little agreement about the nature of the resource allocation problem posed by monopolies. At the very least, the theory does outline the main dimensions of the problem and the general features of any monopoly situation which have to be investigated. Although we have seen that the British approach towards monopoly is based on the principle of treating each case on its merits, it is fair to say that at least the same conceptual apparatus is applied to the analysis of every case, along the broad lines suggested by the theory. In all the Monopolies Commission's reports, the discussion is couched in the language of many of the concepts we have developed in the theory – market structure, market share, profits, product differentiation and advertising, barriers to entry, economies of scale, etc. If economic theory has done no more than set the framework within which policy problems can be analysed, it will have still fulfilled an important task.

Suggestions for further reading

Readers can find good standard treatments of microeconomic theory in R. Dorfman, *Prices and Markets* (Prentice-Hall, 1967), and at a more advanced level in R. H. Leftwich, *The Price System and Resource Allocation* (Holt, Rinehart and Winston, 3, 1966). R. G. Lipsey's *Introduction to Positive Economics* (Weidenfeld and Nicolson, 3, 1971) has an excellent exposition of demand and supply analysis, and indifference curve theory is developed more fully in A. W. Stonier and D. C. Hague, *A Textbook of Economic Theory* (Longmans, 3, 1964). Courses in economics are increasingly using mathematical concepts and analysis, and students will find it worthwhile consulting R. Morley, *Mathematics for Modern Economics*, in this series.

A collection of articles showing how microeconomic theory can be applied to real-life problems is contained in D. Watson (ed.), *Price Theory in Action* (Houghton Mifflin Co, Boston, 1969). A more succinct coverage can be found in the chapter, 'Industry and Commerce' by J. R. Cable in A. R. Prest (ed.) *The UK Economy: A Manual of Applied Economics*.

Empirical evidence concerning the theory of production and costs is contained in C. F. Pratten's *Economies of Scale in Manufacturing Industry* (C.U.P., 1971) and some attempts to measure production functions and cost curves (drawn from USA Industry) are among a collection of readings, *Economics of Industrial Organisation*, (ed.) D. Needham (Holt, Rinehart and Winston, London, 1970). There is a large volume of literature on the theory of the firm, especially the controversy about the profit-maximisation assumption. An excellent survey of the debate is given by F. Machlup in an article called 'Theories of the Firm: Marginalist, Behavioural, Managerial', *The American Economic Review*, March 1967.

Setting the theory of the firm in the context of structure-behaviour-performance relationships is largely due to an American economist, J. S. Bain, and his *Industrial Organisation* (John Wiley, New York, 1968) is the authoritative textbook. A shorter treatment is given in

R. Caves, *American Industry: Structure, Conduct, Performance* (Prentice-Hall, 1967). A useful introduction to the British evidence is presented in M. A. Utton, *Industrial Concentration* (Penguin Books, 1971), and a more comprehensive coverage is found in K. D. George's lucidly written *Industrial Organisation* (George Allen and Unwin, London, 1971). An introduction to the ideas of game theory is provided in M. Peston and A. Coddington, *The Elementary Ideas of Game Theory* (CAS Occasional Papers No. 6, HMSO 1967).

Official government publications on cases examined under the laws on mergers, monopolies and restrictive practices, provide interesting illustrations of the application of theory to practice. Reports by the Monopolies Commission and the Registrar of Restrictive Practices can be obtained at H.M. Stationery Offices.

Index

Index